THE
BARTLETT
2013

The Bartlett
School of Architecture
UCL

The Bartlett
School of Architecture
2013

Architecture was taught for the first time at UCL in 1841. Today The Bartlett enjoys an impressive national and international reputation not only due to its long-standing tradition, but also to its continuous wealth of activity, far-reaching networks and always-extraordinary production.

The Bartlett stands, more than ever, for a great variety of positions. Its strength lies in its diversity of approaches and agendas that reflect the multicultural and plural condition of London, and the trans-modern society we live in. From strong historical and theoretical arguments to the more pragmatic approaches of construction, the school explores advanced computational methods along with a return to more narrative and illustrative work. Contextual conversations are simultaneously being developed through traditional drawing and crafting techniques as well as innovative robotic protocols. More than anything else, we have seen an increased preoccupation with socially and environmentally sensitive design solutions.

There is a huge shared sense of positivity when looking at The Bartlett's future. 2012/13 saw a big investment in technology, with the creation of B>MADE, which is now arguably the most cutting-edge workshop facility in the UK. There is also new and additional space available for the School. The commitment of the Dean, Professor Alan Penn, enabled us to launch an expanded facility at the Royal Ear Hospital, which will have a lasting impact on the Bartlett community. The School also saw the birth of B>PRO – Bartlett Prospective, the new umbrella structure for all post-professional Masters courses, which works as a forum for prospective architecture, urbanism, design and theory at an advanced level. Lastly, we are part of a newly created multidisciplinary organisation, the UCL Centre of Excellence for Sustainable Design, promoted by the Royal Academy of Engineering.

Activities at The Bartlett have happened at an unprecedented rate this year, reflecting the sheer energy and dedication of everybody in the School. In 2012/13 alone we hosted, alongside the well-established Bartlett International Lecture Series, a new range of smaller lecture series lead by key staff, which attracted over 50 speakers to the school. The Bartlett also hosted Smartgeometry, which returned to London ten years after its foundation. The week-long event saw a record level of participation and experimentation with new work. Furthermore, five teams of Bartlett staff and students (more than any other university in the UK) were selected to be part of the Mayor's Wonder, Incredible Installations series for the London Olympics. Several installations were built around London – in Euston Square Gardens, Parliament Square, South Kensington tube station forecourt, the Cutty Sark, and Victoria Park – with great impact in the media and public realm.

Behind all this are our incredible students and staff, who have worked relentlessly to accomplish what makes The Bartlett so well known: rigorous criticality, uncompromised creativity and invention, a self-conscious expression of talent, and unlimited production.

We would like to congratulate everybody for their achievements and extend our sincere gratitude to them for having made The Bartlett, once again, a special place. We thank our consultants, our critics and examiners, all invited guest speakers, and our sponsors for their generous contributions. As ever, it has been an extraordinary privilege to work with you all.

Professor Frédéric Migayrou
Bartlett Professor of Architecture

Dr Marcos Cruz
Director of the Bartlett School of Architecture

Contents

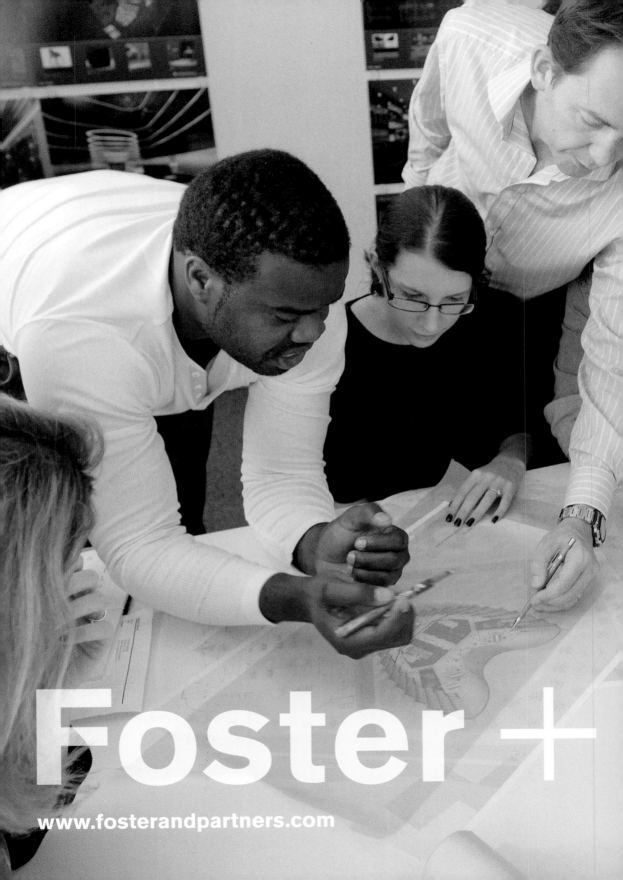

Foster +

www.fosterandpartners.com

Partners

fletcher priest architects
trust

**ALLFORD
HALL
MONAGHAN
MORRIS**

Morelands
5-23 Old Street
London EC1V 9HL
T 020 7251 5261
info@ahmm.co.uk
www.ahmm.co.uk

North London Hospice
Client: North London Hospice

Coca-Cola Beatbox, Sponsor Pavilion, London (2012)

We work for those moments you'll never want to forget.

Rogers Stirk Harbour + Partners

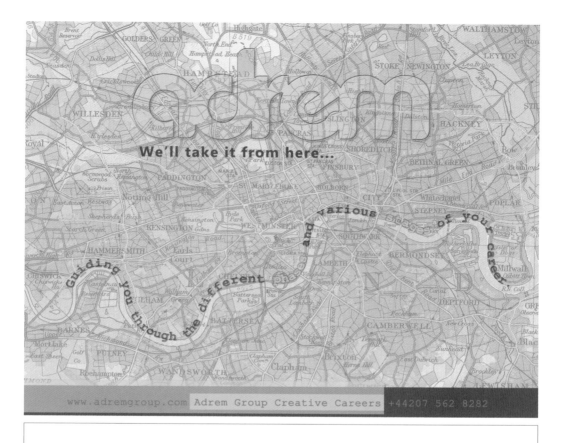

Foster + Partners

fletcher priest architects
london + kōln + riga

Rogers Stirk Harbour + Partners

The Leverhulme Trust

WilkinsonEyre. Architects

Hawkins\
Brown

VAa
Vidal y Asociados arquitectos

**Roca
London
Gallery**

BuckleyGrayYeoman

make

14

The Bartlett School of Architecture would like to thank our sponsors and partners for their generous support:

Bartlett International Lecture Series
Fletcher Priest Trust

Bursaries
Rogers Stirk Harbour + Partners
The Leverhulme Trust

Summer Show Main Title Supporter 2013
Foster + Partners

Bartlett Book 2013
AHMM

Show Opener's Prize
Wilkinson Eyre Architects

Supporters of the Summer Show
Nüssli
Rogers Stirk Harbour + Partners
Hawkins\Brown
ATP Latham
Vidal y Asociados Arquitectos
Roca
BuckleyGrayYeoman

Private Reception
Adrem
Haines Watts

Rogues & Vagabonds Alumni Dinner
Adrem

Prizes
AHMM
Next Limit
Make
Max Fordham

Partners
London Festival of Architecture
Design Council

Design

The process of design is at the core of architecture, painting and sculpture and yet today the term extends far beyond the realm of these classical disciplines. If we examine the complexity of urban life, our experience encompasses all facets of the environment: physical, experiential and climatological. The imaginative leap that is required to create a piece of design often recalls poetry, prose, music and dance, these are sometimes subliminal and at other times direct references, blended with technological and historic data required to make a piece of architecture.

The expectations of this School are therefore a reflection of Renaissance ability where the attention to scientific detail must be underpinned by an understanding of cultural context. The emphasis is not only on the production of artefacts but also of ideas that lead to all manner of speculation about the future. The drawing is now a means of expression but the advent of CADCAM, digital fabrication digitisation and computational script demand a mastery of not only the historic means of representation but also the tools of the 21st century and beyond.

From the new foundation programme to doctoral research, the Bartlett School of Architecture encourages and emphasises design experimentation that is informed by social responsibility and stimulated by the creative dialogue between writing and making. The relationship between the drawing, text, artefact and building are multidirectional. For example, the drawing may lead to building, but writing may also lead to making and building may lead to writing and drawing. It is impossible to summarise all the influences that are brought to bear in the production of the work you see in the Bartlett Book, yet it is all the result of serious and well-researched endeavour. The Book represents only the tiniest fraction of work undertaken throughout the year and it is near impossible to describe the level of commitment demonstrated by both students and staff in the production of these drawings, models and installations. The work must be seen as a celebration of imagination and activity and also a very serious contribution to the debate as to how society might live in the future.

Each year The Bartlett awards a number of prizes, some very historic and others kindly donated by contemporary practice. I am delighted to announce that this year Make are awarding three new prizes to our first year BSc students.

Professor Christine Hawley
Director of Design

Prizes

BSc Architecture Year 1

Building Design Prize, sponsored by Make
Cara Williams
Model Design Prize, sponsored by Make
Jun (Michelle) Ho
Drawing Design Prize, sponsored by Make
Thomas Cubitt

Good Honours' Standard Work
Cara Williams
Thomas Cubitt
Yangyang Liu

Herbert Batsford Prize
Jarrell Ye Lone Goh

Grocer's Company Scholarship
Max Palmer

BSc Architecture Year 2

Narinder Sagoo Drawing Prize
Emily Priest, Unit 6

BSc Architecture Year 3

RIBA Donaldson Medal
Chengqi John Wang, Unit 9

Fitzroy Robinson Drawing Prize
Vanessa Lafoy, Unit 8
Anthony Williams, Unit 2

Dean's List (first class honours in BSc)
Robin Ashurst, Unit 8
Chiara Barrett, Unit 4
Leo Boscherini, Unit 4
Jiong Jiong Chen, Unit 4
Finbarr Fallon, Unit 8
Max Friedlander, Unit 9
Martyna Marciniak, Unit 1
Vasilis Marcou Ilchuk, Unit 8
Yoonjin Kim, Unit 0
Vanessa Lafoy, Unit 8
Matthew Lyall, Unit 1
Daniel Scoulding, Unit 4
Chengqi (John) Wan, Unit 9
Anthony Williams, Unit 2
Tae-In Yoon, Unit 8

MArch Architecture Year 4

Rogers Stirk Harbour Bursary
Sandra Youkhana, Unit 11

MArch Architecture Year 5

Sir Banister Fletcher Medal
Tamsin Hanke, Unit 17
Thandi Loewenson, Unit 10

Fitzroy Robinson Drawing Prize
Farah Badaruddin, Unit 11
Tim Zihong Yue, Unit 12

Dean's List (Distinction in MArch Arch)
Steven Martin Ascensao, Unit 20
Farah Badaruddin, Unit 11
Christine Bjerke, Unit 12
Ione Braddick, Unit 16
Alice Brownfield, Unit 17
Graham Michael Burn, Unit 12
Yu-Wei (John) Chang, Unit 10
Freya Cobbin, Unit 22
Alexandra Banksie Critchley, Unit 11
Alisan Dockerty, Unit 11
Jacob Down, Unit 23
Douglas Fenton, Unit 24
Tamsin Hanke, Unit 17
Ben Hayes, Unit 17
Kaowen Ho, Unit 23
Sonila Kadillari, Unit 11
Yee Yan (Adrienne) Lau, Unit 11
Le (Lulu) Li, Unit 22
Thandi Loewenson, Unit 10
Steven McCloy, Unit 10
Joanna Pawlas, Unit 20
Alexander Reading, Unit 17
Harriet Redman, Unit 11
Samantha Rive, Unit 16
Luke Royffe, Unit 11
Tomass Svilans, Unit 23
Kieran Thomas Wardle, Unit 12
Viktor Westerdahl, Unit 10
Owain Williams, Unit 12
Clarissa Yee, Unit 22
Zihong (Tim) Yue, Unit 12

Professional Studies

From day one, architecture students are asked to question the role and function of the architect in a profession and the construction industry which are constantly in state of change through innovation in design and procurement; technological advances; economic pressures and politics.

The Bartlett's commitment to delivering high quality education in professional matters runs throughout the school's teaching and learning at undergraduate and postgraduate level.

The teaching programmes draw on a wide range of expertise. The multidisciplinary structure of the Faculty provides a community where preconceptions are continually challenged through encounters with fellow students, teachers (many of whom run their own practices) and numerous visiting experts.

Students' own individuality, their ambitions and career aspirations are nurtured within the framework of innovative Professional Studies courses, as well as through informal advice on practice and employment.

The Bartlett School of Architecture has an outstanding track record in the range of practices that graduates later join, ranging from the smaller niche specialist design practices to multidisciplinary global conglomerates.

Susan Ware
Director of Professional Studies

Prizes

BSc Architecture Year 3

Professional Studies Prize
Arthur Kay, Unit 0

Part 3

Ross Jamieson Memorial Prize
Joshua Scott – Summer 2012
George Metcalfe – Autumn 2012

Year 1: the Production of the Built Environment

BSc Architecture students work with Planning and Construction and Project Management students on the 'Production of the Built Environment' course which introduces the various professionals and organisations involved with the process of producing buildings, towns and cities. The broader social, political and economic forces are explored through project work both individually and in multidiscipline group work. A field trip in the second term enables students to apply the analytical skills interpreting the context of the built environment taught in the first term, in a European city.

Year 3: Preparing for Practice

In preparation for the year out in practice students are introduced to the practice of architecture through research-led group presentations and lectures into selected subjects. Students gain an understanding of the construction process and the possible range of experiences available during a year working in practice. The understanding of roles and responsibility of the architect in the design, procurement and construction of projects inform the students' design work. Students are introduced to architectural practice and management, current professional issues and the processes and relationships within the construction industry, including the brief, construction team, communication, sustainability, cost and economics, contracts and professional liability.

The Year Out

The year out course continues the students' connection with the Bartlett and provides career guidance, support and monitoring of practical experience through individual tutorials and themed recall lecture and seminar days.

Year 4: Design Realisation Programme

The Design Realisation course in Year 1 of the two-year MArch (ARB/RIBA Part 2) programme brings together professional practice, technology and construction through a unique configuration of individual design units, practice tutors, technical consultants and visiting lecturers. The course introduces students to core knowledge that is required in the realisation of buildings in professional architectural design practice. Students consider the influence of, and develop an attitude towards, construction, technology and the profession, which are all seen as having an integral role within the creative design process. Students are introduced to elementary matters involved in running of architectural consultancies and building projects; the progression of works from commission to completion and the broad range of strategies that influence the design and construction of buildings. Students will demonstrate through an individually authored report an advanced understanding of and significant abilities in core knowledge that is required in the realisation of buildings.

ARB/RIBA Part 3

The ARB/RIBA Part 3 course and examination is open to non-Bartlett students and is truly international, attracting candidates from over 25 different countries. The course prepares candidates for registration as an architect in the UK through a comprehensive modular taught course. The Part 3 lecture course is available for architectural practices as Continuing Professional Development.

ARB Prescribed Examination Preparation Workshops

The Bartlett in association with the RIBA North West and ARB provide a workshop programme to guide international students wishing to register as architects in the UK under the EU Qualifications Directive though the preparation of documentation and presentation of portfolios for the ARB Prescribed Examination.

History & Theory

Architectural history and theory is a staging post, a provisional place of reflection, a continual project. And it is omnipresent, for every architect, every historian, every theorist, whether knowingly or not, uses some intersection of history and theory every time they design, document, discuss or speculate.

At The Bartlett, architectural history and theory interjects at all levels, from introductions to architectural analysis, from encounters with buildings to the elaboration of critical processes, from public discussions to individually focused research projects, and from factually-based empirical studies to theorised speculations and creative writing practices.

Professor Iain Borden
Director of Architectural History & Theory

Prizes

BSc Architecture Year 3

Distinguished Work in History & Theory
Julian Siravo, Unit 7

BSc Architectural Studies Year 3

Distinguished Work in History & Theory
Amalie White, Architectural Studies

MArch Architecture Year 4

History & Theory Prize
Joel Cady, Unit 17
Thomas Pearce, Unit 23

MArch Architecture Year 5

Ambrose Poynter Prize
To Be Announced

Julian K. Siravo
BSc Architecture, Year 3, History & Theory of Architecture
The London Hackspace: Exploring Spaces of Integration and Transformation in a Hacker Community

In order to understand more about the nature of hackerspaces, I joined London Hackspace and embarked on building my own 3D printer. Open day and night, members come to London Hackspace to socialise, work, learn and build. Joining London Hackspace has given me an inkling of our future, a growing sense of our changing world, especially the ways in which and where we learn and work. It provided a glimpse toward a changed world of manufacturing where new forms of production and local consumption could have profound implications.

The London Hackspace is divided into two large spaces: a physical workshop and a computing area. The growing relationship between code elaboration and physical production becomes remarkably obvious in the spatial layout of the place. In fact, the presence of a workshop was considered essential by all the members interviewed who said "We are one of the only hackerspaces to have this exact balance and it is building a community which is polyvalent in its skills. We see each other doing cool stuff. Each of us wants to know more. Some are makers and are starting to learn about computers; others understand code and are starting to make things with their hands."

As the world around us becomes more digital, understanding and engaging with digital systems and technologies can empower not only individuals, but entire communities. Through a better understanding of the spatial and programmatic questions posed by hackerspaces, it will be possible to incorporate the openness and fluidity of the digital world and apply it to creating an alternative built environment, one which is radically different from the alienated scenario that characterises our contemporary societies.

Daniel Leon Fenster
MArch Architecture, Year 4, BENV GA02 Advanced Architectural Studies
Western Motifs and Chinese Architectural Identity

The ubiquity of Western architectural motifs in contemporary China, ranging from Spanish style high-rise villas to whole imitation Norwegian towns, is often dismissed as a 'disneyfication' of western ideas. It is seen as lacking cultural legitimacy. This article argues that, instead, it represents a distinctly Chinese method of city-making. The ease with which Chinese cities transplant symbols of alien places and times into their fabric has deep historical and cultural roots. Indeed it is perhaps the defining characteristic of the Chinese city.

From the ancient imperial building codes until today, Chinese cities have taken instant legibility as a guiding principle. The architecture forms a precisely defined code of symbols which communicate specific messages. Western motifs in today's globalised Chinese architecture stand for exactly the same – the conveyance of particular meanings in the Chinese context. It is thus, in effect, part of a long tradition and form of a visual language economy.

Much commentary on Chinese architecture revolves around a search for authenticity based on updatable local forms and refuses to see the use of foreign styles as an integral part of a language-economy rather than as momentary exoticism. But the use of 'traditional' local motifs in contemporary architecture emerges from the same practical considerations of communication as foreign ones. Any authenticity only lies in the pragmatic underlying Confucian principles which have always sanctioned such radical hybridisation.

By celebrating the appropriation of foreign motifs into such hybridisation towards the development of a legible but dynamic visual language, a city model emerges that is radically different from the urban imaginations of Western modernity.

Technology

Earlier this year, UCL was recognised as a Centre of Excellence for Sustainable Building Design by The Royal Academy of Engineering. The award is bestowed upon UCL's Faculty of Engineering and The Bartlett and I wish to thank all Architecture staff and students for their significant contribution towards this esteemed award. In particular, I wish to thank our Environmental Design Tutor Oliver Wilton for his leadership and commitment in making this happen, and we are looking forward to accelerated collaboration across the campus.

This year also sees the introduction of two new awards. Firstly, in memory of an inspiring teacher and talented architect, the AHMM Victor Kite Prize is awarded for the best work in Design Technology (Year 2), a module that evolves students' technical and architectural expertise in detail design. The introduction of this award also recognises the impressive elevation of innovative in Year 2, particularly in relation to integration between technology and computing. Secondly, we are very pleased to announce that Max Fordham have inaugurated a new prize for Excellence in Environmental Design and Sustainability in MArch Year 5. The prize is awarded for the project or thesis with the greatest level of ambition, originality, technical innovation and philosophical rigour in the field. Lastly, Next Limit are inaugurating a series of prizes for BSc Year 1 students demonstrating promise in the use of digital visualisation. Including the school's already established awards in Technology, this year's suite of awarded projects reflects a vibrant, rich and diverse culture for innovative and speculative propositions on how architecture is imagined, researched, made, inhabited, adapted, and tested.

I also wish to welcome UCL's dual Institute of Making and Materials Library as a new and highly appreciated initiative with which our students have established a strong and profitable affiliation. I am also pleased to announce that The Bartlett's suite of diverse workshops including woodwork, metalwork,

CADCAM and DMC, will next year be united as The Bartlett Manufacturing and Design Exchange, B>MADE, with new facilities in robotics and 3D scanning. This is a seminal step forward in identifying our facilities as an essential backbone to research and teaching and offers highly deserved recognition for all involved on the influence and contribution they make to our students' wealth of knowledge and experience. Whilst congratulating all graduates on another magnificent year's work, I trust they will support me in expressing heartfelt gratitude towards our workshop staff as together we embark on a new and exciting era. Finally, I sincerely thank my colleague Mark Smout for his role as Acting Director of Technology this year whilst I enjoyed some precious research leave.

Professor Bob Sheil
Professor of Architecture and Design through Production

Prizes

BSc Architecture Year 1

Next Limit Prize for Digital Visualisation
Jun (Michelle) Ho
Jarrell Ye Lone Goh

BSc Architecture Year 2

Victor Kite Prize for Design Technology, sponsored by AHMM
Max Butler, Unit 6

BSc Architecture Year 3

Environmental Design Prize
Yoonjin Kim, Unit 0

Making Buildings Prize
Matthew Lyall, Unit 1

MArch Architecture Year 4

Leverhulme Trust Bursary
Rodolfo Acevedo Rodriguez, Unit 12
Kirsty Williams, Unit 22

Design Technology Prize nominations
Alistair Browning, Unit 17
Joseph Paxton, Unit 21
Anja Leigh Kempa, Unit 10
Daniel Lane, Unit 11
Andrew Walker, Unit 14

MArch Architecture Year 5

Max Fordham Environmental Design Prize
Sonila Kadillari, Unit 11

Sir Andrew Taylor Prize
Unit 22, MAMM Pavilion

Leverhulme Trust Bursary
Samantha Rive, Unit 16

Research

Research at the Bartlett School of Architecture emerges from the understanding that architecture is an exceptionally transdisciplinary subject. We use methodologies from across the arts and humanities, social sciences, engineering and practice to produce innovative scholarship in architectural history, theory, criticism, and design. Our research extends beyond speculative and critical design – a historic strength of The Bartlett – to engagement with social, political, environmental and urbanist concerns. It results in diverse outputs, ranging from books and buildings to installations and urban proposals, which exert a considerable international influence on both architectural design and scholarship.

The School has a world-leading research position which is reflected in our achievement of the highest rating among the Architecture and Built Environment submissions to the UK 2008 Research Assessment Exercise (RAE), with the highest percentage of world-leading 4* staff outputs.

Currently our projects are clustered around six broader thematic areas of research: History and Theory of Architecture; Building Practices; Sustainable Urbanism; Craft, Technology and Computation; Histories and Practices of Ecology; and Performative and Speculative Design. Each area incorporates design-led, historical and theoretical research modes, and many researchers are active in multiple areas, overlapping traditional boundaries and pointing to new transdisciplinary questions.

Research themes we are currently working on include: the spatial, material and contextual innovation of buildings; sustainable communities and everyday urbanism; historical scholarship in the area of modernism across cultures; design research and aesthetics; colonial and postcolonial studies on architecture; critical spatial theories and practices; representation and drawing; craft, digital fabrication and material innovation; advanced computation and robotics; performativity and interactivity; landscape and environment; architecture's intersection with fine art, geography, philosophy, anthropology and film.

Situated within UCL, our research culture reflects the University's position and its Grand Challenges in Sustainable Cities, Global Health, Intercultural Interaction and Human Wellbeing. The Faculty of the Built Environment and other University departments offer a wealth of expertise and we increasingly team up with colleagues across the Faculty and UCL.

We attach great value to the ongoing interaction between research, teaching and learning. Our large international student communities in the MA, MArch and PhD programmes are a key constituency in the School's research culture and we continuously foster a variety of research exchanges between staff and students. These exchanges are increasingly enriched by the vibrant community of external specialist consultants and research associates, who share their own expertise with the School on a regular basis.

Located within the centre of London, we are privileged to have many opportunities to collaborate on research projects with the most creative partners, while we also work with a variety of national and international research centers and public engagement institutions.

The following list presents a selection of achievements by research staff during this year.

Dr Yeoryia Manolopoulou
Director of Architectural Research

Selected Awards and Honours

Izaskun Chinchilla (Izaskun Chinchilla Architects)
Refurbishment of Garcimuñoz Castle, Cuenca, Spain
Special Mention, Arcvision Prize Women and
Architecture 2013

Dr Edward Denison
*Architecture and the Landscape of Modernity in
China up to 1949*
Commendation, RIBA President's Award for
Outstanding PhD Thesis Research 2012

Professor Colin Fournier
Chief Curator, Hong Kong section, UABB Shenzen
and Hong Kong Bi-City Biennale of Urbanism and
Architecture, 2013

**Professor Murray Fraser
(PART / Palestine Regeneration Team)**
*Regeneration of the Historic Centre of Birzeit,
Palestine (part of RIWAQ's 50 Villages Project)*
Shortlisted, Aga Khan Award 2012

Professor Jonathan Hill
Weather Architecture (Routledge, 2012)
Shortlisted, RIBA President's Award for Outstanding
University-Located Research 2012

Dr Yeoryia Manolopoulou (AY Architects)
Montpelier Community Nursery, Camden
Shortlisted, RIBA Award 2013

**Professor Niall McLaughlin
(Niall McLaughlin Architects)**
*Student Accommodation, Somerville College,
Oxfordshire*
Winner, RIBA Award 2012
Block N15 façade, Olympic Village, Stratford
Winner, British Precast Concrete Federation
Creativity in Concrete Award 2012
Bishop Edward King Chapel, Oxfordshire
Shortlisted, RIBA Award 2013

Josep Miàs (Miàs Arquitectes)
Banyoles Old Town Refurbishment, Girona, Spain
Winner, Marmomacc International Stone
Architecture Award 2013
Torre Baró Apartment Building, Barcelona
Shortlisted, City of Barcelona Architecture and
Urbanism Award 2012
Plug-In Office Building, Barcelona
Shortlisted, City of Barcelona Architecture and
Urbanism Award 2012
Annexa-Joan Puigbert School, Girona, Spain
Nominated, European Union Prize for Contemporary
Architecture / Mies van der Rohe Award 2013

Professor Frédéric Migayrou
Jury member, European Union Prize for
Contemporary Architecture / Mies van der Rohe
Award 2013

Dr Peg Rawes
AHRC Research Grant for *Equalities of Wellbeing in
Philosophy and Architecture* (Co-Investigator),
2013-15

Wonder Installations – Pavilions for London 2012
Laura Allen and Mark Smout (SmoutAllen), Luke
Pearson and Sandra Youkhana (You+Pea), and
Professor Iain Borden
Universal Tea Machine
Alisa Andrasek and Jose Sanchez (biothing)
BLOOM _ Crowd Sourced Garden
Dr Marjan Colletti and Dr Marcos Cruz
(marcosandmarjan)
The Alga(e)zebo
Professor CJ Lim, John Chang, Samson Lau and
Martin Tang
Tr(ee)logy
Dr Yeoryia Manolopoulou and Anthony Boulanger
(AY Architects)
House of Flags

Programme Structure

The Bartlett School of Architecture offers a comprehensive range of programmes, including courses directed at those seeking to become professional architects, as well as other programmes with specialisms in advanced architectural design, history and theory, and urban design.

Professionally Accredited Programmes

Undergraduate

BSc Architecture (ARB/RIBA Part 1)
3 years, full time (FT) study plus 1 year in practice

Postgraduate

MArch Architecture (ARB/RIBA Part 2)
2 years FT

Certificate in Professional Practice and Management in Architecture (ARB/RIBA Part 3)
6–12 months part-time (PT) study plus 24 months in practice

Non-professionally Accredited Courses

Undergraduate

BSc Architectural & Interdisciplinary Studies (formerly BSc Architectural Studies)
3 years FT / 4 years FT with Year Abroad

Postgraduate

Postgraduate Certificate in Advanced Architectural Research
3 months FT / up to 2 years PT

Post-Professional Masters Programmes

B>PRO
MArch Graduate Architectural Design (GAD)
12 months FT
MArch Urban Design (UD)
12 months FT
MA Architectural History and Theory
12 months FT

MPhil/PhD Programmes

MPhil/PhD Architectural Design
3 years FT / 6 years PT

MPhil/PhD Architectural History & Theory
3 years FT / 6 years PT

Short Courses

Summer School
2 weeks in August

Summer Foundation
8 weeks from July to September
or
5 weeks from July to August

Programmes

BSc Architecture ARB/RIBA Part 1

BSc Architectural Studies

In Transit: A Journey in the Life of Year 1

Frosso Pimenides, Patrick Weber

The Bartlett's BSc degree programme aims to develop a creative, diverse and rigorous approach to architecture and design from the outset. Year 1 is centred on the design studio and is taught to the year as a whole. Students learn to observe, draw, model and design through a series of creative tasks, before embarking on an individual small building project sited in the context of London.

The main intention of the first year at The Bartlett is to explore 'ways of seeing' – understanding and interpreting objects, events and places, and learning to look beyond the visible into the unseen and absurd qualities of things and places. In this way, a place can also be seen as something with its own identity, which each student can personally interpret. The importance of character and personality is emphasised throughout the design process, whether it concerns analysis, site interpretation or architectural vision. A number of recording techniques are used as a way of clarifying the subject rather than as purely graphic representation. Through being aware of the possibilities and limitations of various techniques, each student learns to express, and then develop critically and appropriately through their own intuition, an idea for an architectural proposition.

Architecture is explored individually through cultivating ideas, exploring imagination and nurturing curiosity. Students explore, describe and communicate their ideas through a range of two- and three- dimensional techniques. The aim is to be serious, passionate and ruthlessly experimental – always pushing the boundaries of possible realities.

Being open and naïve in their working method, students are encouraged to take risks. Not being afraid of making mistakes forms the basis of the approach: a mistake can often form the basis of a new idea, a different way to see the world. It is the path to new possible architectures.

The life of our first year students is a continuous process of testing, questioning, rethinking and visually communicating a series of design explorations over the course of the year as part of a studio culture, a community and the city of London. It is a journey of learning skills and knowledge that give students the tools to think, experiment, make lots of mistakes, celebrate their failures and finally have fun designing.

Students started the year by exploring the condition of being in transit, having just arrived in London and at University. They questioned this notion by designing and fabricating a London 'suit' that addresses the new experiences whilst remembering their past.

After this they worked in groups on an installation project in Sir John Soane's Country House, Pitzhanger Manor in Ealing. Each of the six groups adjusted the given spaces through the installation of a site-specific interpretation of a suitcase. The process of designing was a collaborative experience, where students worked in groups to conceive, prototype, test and craft their 1:1 temporary installations. Their designs considered Soane in transit, his life as a journey through the museum, his journeys to and fro between his two houses and the journeys of his artefacts.

In the second term the whole year group explored Genoa through surveying. Dissecting a very specific set of locations through sectional drawings revealed qualities of the place.

From February onwards each student was asked to first gain an understanding of the wider urban context of Camden, as an inbetween place, a place of transit and a place in transit. Students were subsequently asked to reimagine the lodging house for present day Camden, react against its seedy past and design a place that provides generous, engaging, uplifting spaces of temporary and permanent inhabitation.

Special thanks to: Abi Abdolwahabi, Bim Burton, Nick Westby, Martin Watmough and Richard Beckett from the Bartlett Workshop, and to Danielle Hodgson, Afra van 't Land, Rachel Antonio, Patrick Laing.

Thanks to Carol Swords, Beth Walker, James Willis, and all the staff of Sir John Soane's Museum and Pitzhanger Manor.

Year 1 Staff
Tim Barwell, Margaret Bursa, Johan Hybschman, Lucy Leonard, Brian O'Reilly, Sara Shafiei, Matt Springett, Nikolas Travasaros

Architectural Media Studies Tutor: Joel Cady
BASc – Architectural Media Studies Tutor: Dimitri Argyros

Year 1
Kamola Askarova, Annecy Attlee, Florence Bassa, William Bellamy, Flavian Berar, Uday Berry, Hoi (Christy) Chan, Nicola Chan, Yee Ki (Kiki) Chan, Hsiao (Cindy) Chen, Pui Choi, Boon Yik Chung, Oliver Colman, Samuel Coulton, Douglas Croll, Thomas Cubitt, Naomi De Barr, Christophe Dembinski, Danny Dimbleby, Patrick Dobson-Perez, Kat Feltwell, Lucca Ferrarese, Grace Fletcher, Kelly Frank, Vincent Fung, Egmontas Gerasimovas, Ren-Zhi Goh, Jarrell Ye Lone Goh, Cheng Guo, Yangzi (Cherry) Guo, Alice Hardy, Francis Hardy, Katja Hasenauer, Sarah Hindle, Hilda Hiong, Jun (Michelle) Ho, Jessica Hodgson, Tae (Freddie) Hong, Patrick Horne, Cheung (Ivan) Hung, Lubna Ibrahim, Aqsa Iftikhar, Angus Iles, Niema Jafari, Niki-Marie Jansson, Rikard Kahn, Mouna Kalla-Sacranie, Lee Kelemen, Dina Khaki, Richard (Will) Kirkby, Subin Koo, Nikolas Kourtis, Clarence Ku, Kaela Kwan, Yiki Liong, Daniel Little, Wenya Liu, Yangyang Liu, Kin (Glynnis) Lui, Jonah Luswata, Alan Ma, Sonia Magdziarz, Michael Mcadam, Zi (Kevin) Meng, Douglas Miller, Matei-Alexandru Mitrache, Masahiro Nakamura, Robert Newcombe, Morenike Onajide, Max Palmer, Oliver Parkinson, Tobias Petyt, Sylwia Poltorak, Rosa Prichard, Louise Rymell, Soma Sato, Francesca Savvides, Laura Skudder, Anastasia Stan, Emilio Sullivan, Sophie Tait, Sheau (Amanda) Tam, Yu (Nicole) Teh, Minh Tran, Shi (Kiki) Tu, Laszlo Von Dohnanyi, Astrid Von Heideken, Valerie Vyvial, Zhi (Ernest) Wang, Angus Whitehead, Allegra Willder, Cara Williams, Priscilla Wong, Sammy Yeung, Yuanchu Yi

Fig. Y1.1 – Y1.3 Mrs Soane's Gloves. The installation responds to the etiquette of being greeted and admitted into Pitzhanger Manor. It is formed of two connected parts, so that when a visitor signs in using the sliding pencil at the stand by the door the gesture is translated into a unique movement by the pendulum at the reception desk. As gloves become unique to their owner over time, our installation allows each visitor to initiate a personal show that reflects the grand nature of Mr Soane, his wife and his house.

Fig. Y1.4 Visitors Card Holder. The installation seeks to capture the movement of visitors entering the grounds of Pitzhanger Manor to produce a display based upon the traditional visitors card communication system. Three delicate arms register visitors as they pass through the pedestrian gate to Pitzhanger Manor. This movement causes folding in the faceted panel on the vehicle side of the gate. The visitor experiences a detachment from the visual message, similar to the delay associated with the posting of a traditional calling card.

Fig. Y1.5 Sarcophagus. The Sarcophagus acts as the focal point of the Sir John Soane'd Museum, drawing you through the building on a journey of Soane's collection in order to reach it. However, this experience is ultimately unfulfilled, as once you reach the sarcophagus you cannot touch it. The installation addresses this tactile curiosity through a set of four fragments unpacked around Soane's bedroom at Pitzhanger Manor. These pieces enable the visitor to inhabit the room through touch, by performing the everyday actions of opening a door, a window, a drawer, and by resting their head on the bed.

Y1.4

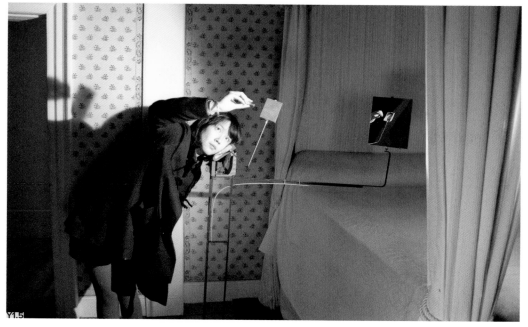

Y1.5

Fig.Y1.6 – Y1.7 Empty Pistol Case: The installation is inspired by the empty case that once displayed a 19th century pistol that was stolen from the Sir John Soane's Museum in 1969. It responded to the missing artefact by analysing the etiquette of a pistol duel and interpreting this ritual in the act of unfolding two opposing 'suitcases' within the space of the library. This unpacking follows a pre-defined choreography that is set out through a language brass inlays.

Fig. Y1.8 Model Temple of Vesta. The Temple of Vesta was centred around a sacred fire that had to be kept alight constantly. The installation responds to the idea of tending a fire, by picking up air currents created by visitors' breath and movement. A series of finely balanced sails are placed in the breakfast room so that under certain conditions, the sails rotate, each sail fitting and just clearing the next one so that the gust is transferred across the room to the hearth.

Y1.6

Y1.7

Y1.8

Fig. Y1.9 Thomas Cubitt, Camden Lock Allotments Lodging House. **Fig. Y1.10** Jarrell Ye Lone Goh, Inverness Street Writer's Lodge. **Fig. Y1.11** Zi (Kevin) Meng, The Boater's Lodging House. **Fig. Y1.12** Jun (Michelle) Ho, Sliding Lodging House, Buck Street.

Y1.9

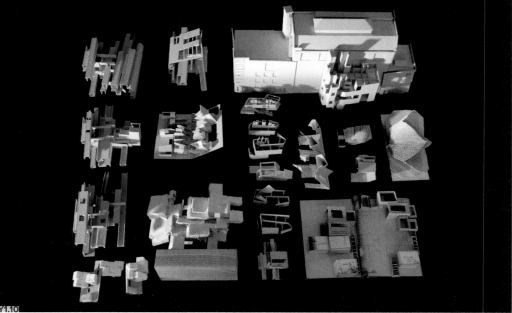

Y1.10

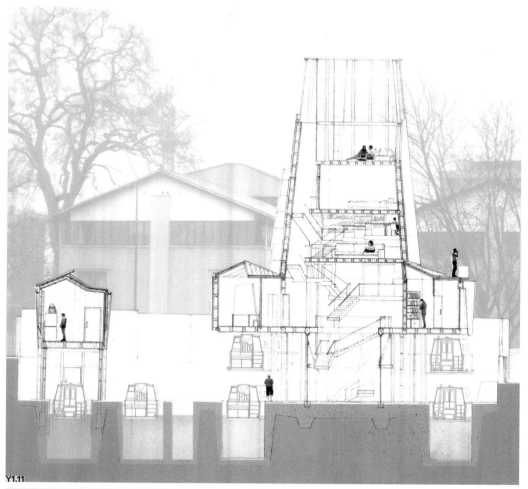

Y1.11

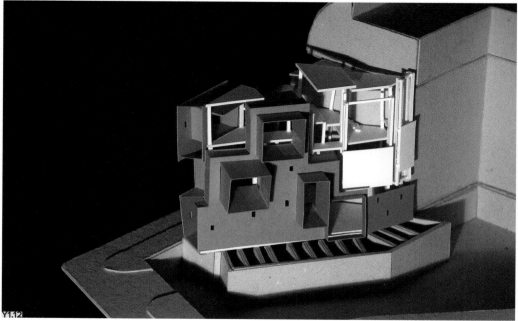

Y1.12

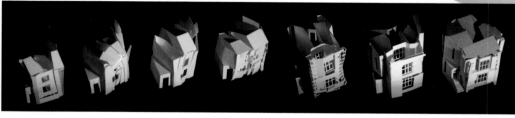

Fig. Y1.13 – Y1.16 Cara Williams, Magician's Lodging House. The lodging house is a magician's trick, rebuilding the façade of No. 50 Hawley Street, a lone terrace house found by the discovery of a photograph of the street taken in 1972. The lodgers unknowingly share the house with the magician, apart from when they catch brief glimpses of him and the secret garden through a sequence of windows. The only way to understand the magician's trick is to sit on the bench next to the lamppost facing the site: from here the lodger's inhabitation and a glimpse of the magician's secret stage is revealed.

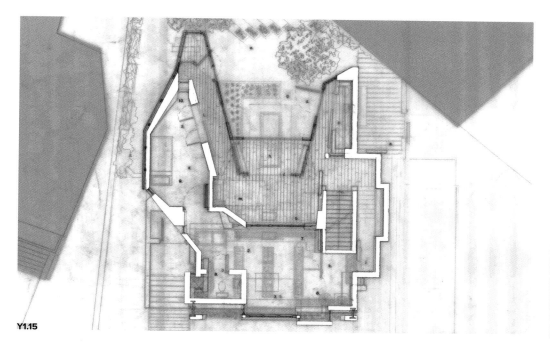

Y1.15

Y1.16

Unit 0
Exchange

Murray Fraser, Kenny Kinugasa-Tsui, Justin C.K. Lau

The Bartlett School of Architecture 2013

Unit 0's underlying aim is for students to learn how to carry out intensive research – into architectural ideas, urban conditions, cultural relations, practices of everyday life – and then use their findings to devise innovative and challenging proposals for the contemporary city. Students are asked to grasp the unique speculative space offered by academic study and combine this with a commitment to social engagement and urban improvement, as if their projects were actually going to be built. A clear understanding of the technological, environmental and developmental issues involved in architecture is also vital.

Furthermore, in order to develop their designs, students are expected to capitalise on the full range of methods of investigation and representation: sketches, models, digital fabrication, photography, drawings, computer renders and animations. In their approach, students should allow for intuitive and spontaneous design-based responses. After all, strong design ideas produced by speculative or lateral thinking can stimulate theoretical investigations just as much as the other way around.

The theme we set our students this year was the concept of 'exchange'. This term of course carries many meanings. Exchange is used as the principle for the trade of goods and services, originally on a barter system, later as a financial transaction between buyer and seller – of currency, commodities, information data spread by modern communication technologies, and such like. Yet it could simply refer to an exchange of ideas, or of bodily contacts, among a small group or even just between two people. On a wider scale, when talking of processes like globalisation, it can also refer to sweeping cultural interchange between different ethnic groups or countries around the world. Unit 0 regards architecture as a discipline which is very much rooted in the exchange of ideas and material expressions on multiple cultural levels. Today, in our fast moving digital-techno-media culture, many fragments of the 'foreign', both material and

psychological, penetrate intimately into our daily lives. Instead of viewing this as loss of cultural authenticity or as a process of homogenisation, we see global exchange in architectural production as creative and positive. When it comes to buildings, the idea of exchange can be traced in a range of ways: aesthetics, economics, construction methods, thresholds between inside/outside, feedback cycles and user adjustments. It was hence up to each Unit 0 student to research into exchange and come up with an interpretation to explore through their design work.

To start the year, we asked students to think about cultural interchange by studying various London-based collections of Chinese artefacts. At the same time they divided into groups to research specific themes in relation to the NoHo site in Mortimer Street – formerly the location of Middlesex Hospital, and undeveloped for many years following the 2008 economic crash. Students then began to design and make their own individual designs/models/installations as their initial project for the year. They then were allowed to remain with this site for their major project or else find another site of their choosing which better suited their idea of exchange. The ensuing research encompassed many fields: anthropology, history, ecology, climate, economics, sociology, technology, etc. High-end computer modelling and communication tools associated were combined with more traditional design techniques, thereby addressing distinctions between actual and virtual, digital and analogue, scientific and artistic, and instrumental and philosophical.

Several questions were posed to the Unit 0 students. How can your site become a place of exchange for the future? How might global influences shape a new identity for your chosen site, as well as for the rest of London? How might the different uses you are proposing enhance urban and cultural interaction? Design investigations were required to deal explicitly with issues of site, ground, space, form, structure, environment, production, occupation, performance and display.

Meanwhile, the Unit 0 field trip enabled us to examine Beijing as an increasingly globalised city. China is just one of the overseas locations that London interacts with, but is likely become an increasingly important one as global wealth and power continues to shift to Asian countries. How might this global change reshape London for the better? Our trip involved visiting architectural schools and well known architectural practices in Beijing, as well as looking at historical and contemporary buildings and parts of the city – not least a detailed study of some of its surviving *hutong* districts.

Thanks to our visiting critics and lecturers:
Abi Abdolwahabi, Ben Addy, Laura Allen, Abigail Ashton, Tim Barwell, Camillo Boano, Anthony Boulanger, Rhys Cannon, Joseph Conteh, Lorene Faure, Katy Ghahremani, Anneli Giencke, Jon Goodbun, Penelope Haralambidou, Linnea Isen, Tobias Klein, Guan Lee, Ifigeneia Liangi, Dessislava Lyutakova, Yeoryia Manolopoulou, Jack Newton, James Redman, Min Jeong Song, Sarah Stevens, Ben Stringer, Nicholas Szczepaniak, Joanna Ewa Szulda, Michael Tite and Barry Wark.

Technical Tutors: Aran Chadwick (Atelier One), Bill Watts (Max Fordham)

Year 2
Marcus Cole, Ysabel Kaye, Paalan Lakhani, Smiti Mittal, Cheol-Young (Nick) Park, Marie Walker-Smith

Year 3
Nicolas Chung, Malina Dabrowska, Arthur Kay, Yoonjin Kim, Lauren Marshall, Huma Mohyuddin, Julia Rutkowska, Jack Sargent, Peter Simpson, James Tang, Miljun (Celeste) Wong

Fig. 0.1 – 0.4 Yoonjin Kim, Y5, Apple River, Mortimer Street, London W1. Site context model; general aerial view; internal perspective; long section. Local residents earn tokens by saving energy in their homes, and can then exchange these for apples or cider grown by an agricultural cooperative on the large NoHo site. High-level walkways enable visitors to experience the orchard while below a river of apple juice flows from the trees where the fruit is picked to a central processing point.

0.1

0.2

0.3

0.4

Fig. 0.5 – 0.7 Huma Mohyuddin, Y3, Muslim/Christian Exchange, Mortimer Street, W1. Perspective of the mosque entrance; isometric view of the water collection system; interior perspective of the ablution room. Linked and yet also differentiated by their religious water rituals, here an ecumenical mixing of Muslim and Christian worship is facilitated by food grown on site for use in a community restaurant. **Fig. 0.8** Pete Simpson, Y3, Fitzrovia Arts Hub, Howland Street, W1. South elevation. In bringing artists back into central London and connecting them with Fitzrovia's burgeoning art scene, the building combines artists' studios with community spaces where local residents can take part in art projects or engage in lifelong learning in a range of skills and subjects. **Fig. 0.9 – 0.11** Malina Dabrowska, Y3, Furniture

Design and Manufacturing Facility, Tottenham Court Road/ Grafton Way, W1. Aerial view; permanent shuttering detail; chair design. By offering open access to the latest digital design and fabrication equipment, made freely available by phone apps and online services, customers can use this facility to create their very own prototype furniture.

0.5

0.6

0.7

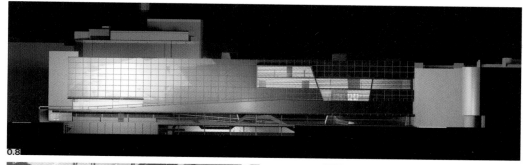

0.8

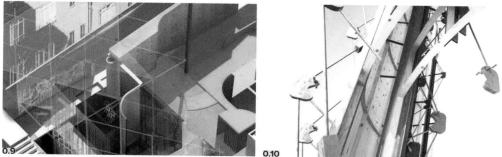

0.9

0.10

0.11

Fig. 0.12 Yoonjin Kim, Y3, The Reward System, Lower Lea Valley, E16. Sectional model of the project. Sited where the River Lea meets the Thames, as the central hub of a London-wide agricultural cooperative, members can bring produce to the weekly floating market, charge up batteries to collect free power, or debate alternative social and economic ideals. **Fig. 0.13 – 0.14** Marcus Cole, Y2, Rehabilitation through Occupation, Centre for Addiction Care, Millfield Lane, N6. Massing model and interior perspective of the communal living space. This building responds to the notion of 'negative exchange' by tackling issues surrounding drug rehabilitation treatment. Located on the borders of Hampstead Heath, the design blurs the threshold between nature and architecture to offer a sense of calm within the city. **Fig. 0.15** Marie Walker-

Smith, Y2, Dim Sum Trade Project. Perspective of a typical mobile unit. A series of customised mobile dim sum kitchens move slowly around the central parts of London to provide a network of street food outlets selling authentic Chinese food. **Fig. 0.16** Miljun Celeste Wong, Y3, Facade of Fish, Billingsgate Market/Canary Wharf, EC3. Interior perspective at basement level. This fish restaurant and aquarium complex taps its power from the discarded waste heat of the adjacent Canary Wharf office megaliths, while also linking to Billingsgate fish market. Above, in a curved tower, specialised eateries serve up Chinese delicacies such as abalone.

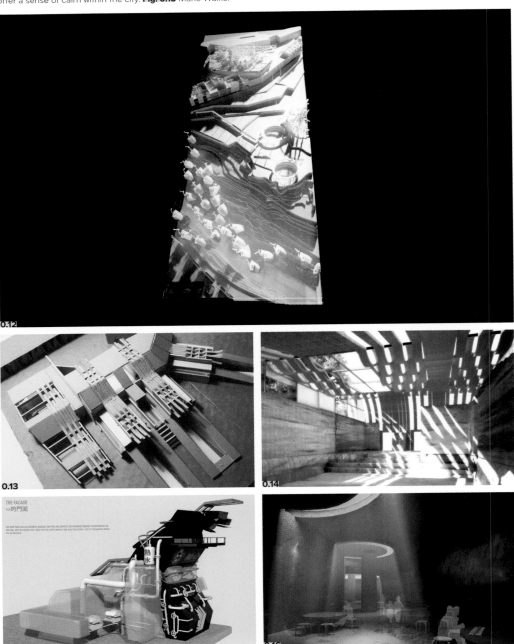

0.12

0.13

0.14

0.15

0.16

Fig. 0.17 Nicolas Chung, Y3, The Social Tea Machine. General arrangement of a tea-making machine. This collectivised and mobile tea device can be located in many different spots around London to help revive the lost tradition of tea dances as sociable events.

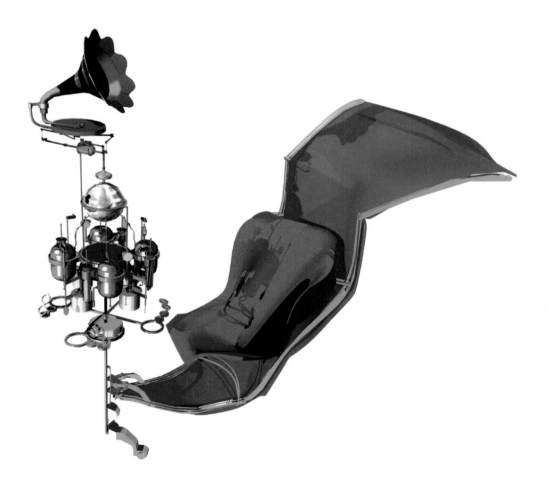

Fig. 0.18 – 0.19 Arthur Kay, Y3, Crossing Generations, Lupus Street, SW1. Massing model and exploded isometric showing all the floor levels. On the site of the demolished Pimlico Comprehensive School, the intermixing of learning and leisure activities for the very young and very old takes place on the building's stepped terraces. **Fig. 0.20 – 0.21** Jack Sargent, Y3, The Evaporated University, Mortimer Street, W1. Conceptual sketch and roof plan. Now we can no longer afford to build new universities, this scheme provides just the most essential educational functions set within a busy urban park which students engaged in 'blended learning' have to share with everyday city users. **Fig. 0.22** James Tang, Y3, a Hotel in Soho, Great Windmill Street, W1. Second floor plan. The combination of a gourmet hotel and short-term pods for tired restaurant

workers in nearby Chinatown creates a labyrinth of varied lighting and acoustic characteristics to suit different needs.

0.18

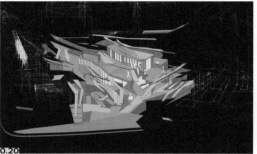

0.20

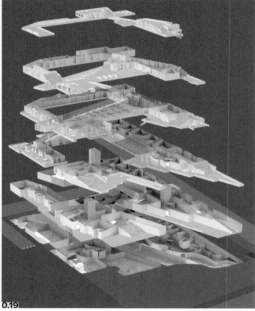

0.19

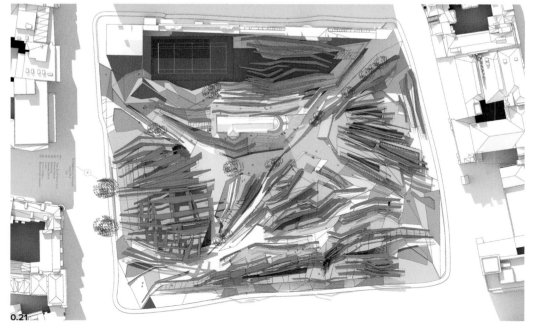

0.21

0.22

Undercurrents

Penelope Haralambidou, Michael Tite

2013. Digital technology has irreversibly percolated into everyday architectural practice. Yet architects face a series of paradoxes: the gap between drawing and making has never been smaller, but the distance between the architect's hand and the final object has widened; although computation offers a platform for inexhaustible – and often uncritical – form-making, digital drawing techniques are still based on an antiquated monocular understanding of space, forgetting the 'other' eye; and the latent potential of material innovation and craftsmanship remains hugely underexplored.

Moreover, whilst the young moguls of Silicon Roundabout seem to have harnessed technological undercurrents to stimulate meaningful social change – at the same time as turning a healthy profit – young architectural innovation can appear to be weighed down by bureaucracy, overwhelming competition from developers or big practice, and the on-going recession.

Can a productive rethinking of technology unlock architecture's current stalemate? And how can architectural education prepare the young architect facing these ground-breaking shifts in digital technology that are reshaping the profession?

This year Unit 1 is looking for a gear shift: one that sees architects crossing the entrepreneurial skills of speculative business startups with the cutting edge technical knowledge of software engineers. A redefinition of the profession that seeks to tap into digital undercurrents and which uses inventive homegrown technology as a trigger for new spatial ideas to create buildings that affect positive change. A quiet revolution perhaps.

Meanwhile, we are told that we are in the midst of an Olympic honeymoon. Britain, or more specifically London, is suddenly renowned for embracing multiculturalism and diversity, it excels in sport and is spreading legacy wealth to impoverished regions. A powerhouse of cultural achievement, nourished on the generosity of approved multinational sponsors. Mother London finds herself in uncharted waters of positivity.

But was not long ago, when the media had declared London a war zone swamped by BBM-powered youth on the rampage for widescreen TVs, Air Max Ones, and bottles of Evian... the narrative of London could be seen to be at a kind of uncomfortable tipping point.

This year Unit 1 will employ technological innovation in search of the magical and the common, the rebellious and the new in our own back yard, here in London. We will look for the forgotten places that we have read about in books and seen in films and propose a future for our city that is not controlled by big banks or corporate middle management and is also resistant to the threat of teenaged mercenaries. We will take our city back.

Seed

The first project, entitled 'Seed', is the design of a speculative pavilion for London.

The pavilion, a longstanding architectural typology commonly associated with English landscape follies, saw a rise all around London before and during the games. Within the Olympic park, pavilions became architectural manifestations of corporate sponsorship – the closest that architecture comes to a spatialised logo.

Seed questions the presumption that the pavilion is a temporary, cheaply built installation serving a corporate message. It can be sculpturally experimental or a choreographed event; preserve wildlife habitats or experiment with surprising materials such as chemicals or air; try to generate revenue or further growth; last for the long term or blossom momentarily; carry a political message; consist of a field of components; or exist in physical and digital realms simultaneously. While embracing the pavilion's decorative and playful nature – often perceived as superficial – we propose cutting-edge structures that not only dazzle but also educate, become vehicles for research and encapsulate a critical architectural position. Our Seeds tap into the undercurrents of the city and perform strategic 'revelations'.

Venice Biennale
In preparation to our second project, also based in London, and continuing our search for new architectural ideas we visited this year's Venice Biennale, a hub of talent and innovation from all over the world.

In Venice and Vicenza we visited buildings, which at the time of their conception and construction were only possible due to their authors' speculative use of ground-breaking technologies: visual and representational; material and structural; as well as promoting social innovation in accordance to the humanist revolution of the Renaissance.

Boom
The second project, entitled Boom, focused on the Lea Valley, a physically and socially fluid region, which exemplifies London in a state of becoming. The two sites of the most recent traumas – Tottenham Riots and Stratford Olympics – sit within a short seven-mile stretch of the city. Rich in industrial history and biogeographic diversity – even with the deterministic addition of the Olympic Park – this part of London is rapidly transforming, driven by strong undercurrents while its future is hanging in the balance.

Whereas Seed aims at affecting localised change in a highly speculative, fast and experimental way, Boom is the design of a small- or medium-scaled public building which seeks to 'take root' in the context in which it is located and draw on cultural, physical, economic, social and historical particularities. In Boom we aim to 'cultivate' the technological invention of Seed – the architectural prototype – towards an individual architectural

language. The Unit was joined again by Levitate Architects for the Year 3 Technical Study and by Picture Plane for architectural visualisations. We also collaborated with architectural entrepreneurs ScanLab to explore the creative potential of the 3D scanner.

Unit 1 is underpinned by a stimulating and nurturing studio environment, where we foster a strong collaborative ethos. We encourage students to be experimental, creative and independent designers, each with their own unique architectural voice.

We would like to thank our critics: Ben Addy, Alessandro Ayuso, Greg Blee, Mark E. Breeze Alastair Browning, David Buck, Matthew Butcher, John Cain, Rhys Cannon, Michele Carrara, Luke Chandresinghe, Emma Cheatle, Ming Chung, Kate Davies, Jo Dejardin, Max Dewdney, Murray Fraser, Stephen Gage, Spencer Guy, Ryan Hakimian, Christine Hawley, Jonathan Hill, Adrian Lahoud, Chee-Kit Lai, Joerg Majer, Ana Monrabal-Cook, Tim Norman, Luke Pearson, Sophia Psarra, David Roberts, Eduardo Rosa, Tim Sloan, Amy Thomas, Kenny Tsui, Nick Tyson, Cindy Walters, Victoria Watson, Andrew Whiting and Paolo Zaide.

Year 2
Laurence Blackwell-Thale, John Cruwys, David Flook, Gregorios Kythreotis, Abigail Portus, Ellie Sampson, Saskia Selwood, Elin Soderberg

Year 3
Benjamin Beach, Carl Inder, Pavel Kosyrev, Matthew Lyall, Martyna Marciniak, Isabel Ogden, Jasper Stevens, Corina Andra Tuna

Fig. 1.1 Elin Soderberg, Y2, Student Accommodation, Carpenters Estate, Stratford, fragment of long section. A series of allotment-like individual gardens, private rooms and shared spaces are elaborately interconnected using a system of soft 'knitted furniture', which are supported off harder structural surfaces. **Fig 1.2 – 1.3** Abigail Portus, Y2, Reservoir of Sound, Walthamstow Reservoirs, roof model and interior perspective of stage. The Reservoir of Sound music venue straddles the threshold between two large North London reservoirs. As water levels change between the bodies of water, two 'curtains' of perforated brick are made to slide past each other, signaling the beginning of a performance. **Fig 1.4** Carl Inder, Y3, Eel Kiosk and pirate TV transmitter, Bromley-by-Bow, Model. The project recognises the diminishing influence of pirate broadcasts on counter-cultural discourse due to the progression of digital technology. A complex tidal 'Fyke Net' construction serves to both capture Eels, which are then prepared and served in a small kiosk, and to camouflage a pirate TV transmitter. **Fig 1.5** Martyna Marciniak, Y3, Temple of Water, Shadwell Basin, Axonometric cutaway drawing. Situated on a series of terraces which step down to the Thames, a sequence of mysterious, ever-changing pools serve to disconnect bathers from the city. The journey culminates in full immersion into a warm, malleable pool that floats within the Thames itself and is composed of unique phase-change materials. The building rapturously dissolves the boundaries between the city and the river, the physical and the real.

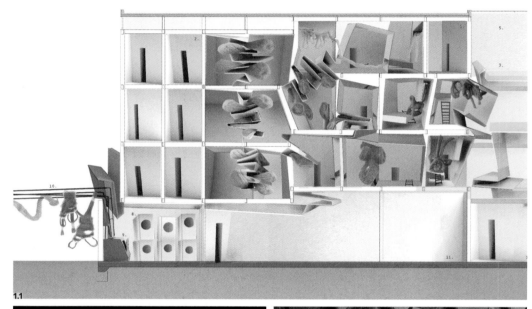

1.1

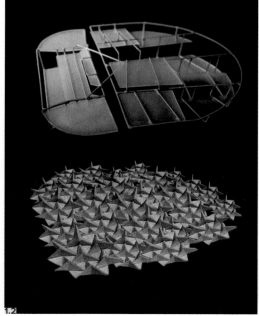

1.2

1.3

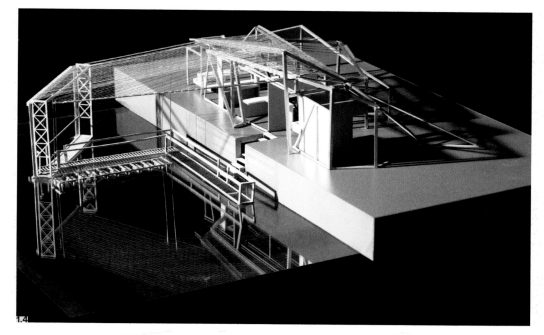

1.4

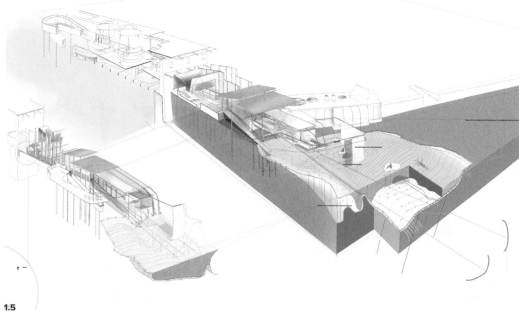

1.5

Fig 1.6 Pavel Kosyrev, Y3, Biomimetic Bus Station, Tottenham, conceptual ideogram. Challenging the apparent banalities of waiting for a bus, the building celebrates the behavioural quirks of passengers and marries them with fluctuations in local environmental conditions to create a slow moving yet highly tuned site-specific environment. **Fig 1.7 – 1.8** Ellie Sampson, Y2, Sainsbury's Community Centre, Hornsey, long section and front elevation. Anticipating the impact of a new supermarket on Hornsey Lane, the project imagines an alternative future for the site, where a section 106 agreement requires Sainsbury's to provide onsite community facilities. The project explores a series of complex juxtapositions that might result from the merger. **Fig 1.9** Isabel Ogden, Y3, Robotic Cancer Treatment Centre, Homerton, perspectival section. The facility houses cutting-edge surgical robots that reduce the physiological impact of invasive surgery. Conceived as a 'carer' and through the manipulation of different forms of light (gamma, x-ray, daylight) the building is strategically organised to speed up the process of recovery. **Fig 1.10** David Flook, Y2, ELUTech, Stratford, axonometric. The East London University Technical College marries an existing Building and Crafts College with a new research facility for UCL. Exploring themes of displacement, copying, repetition and the uncanny, ELUTech is designed in two mirrored parts, where the plan of one building is replicated in the section of the other.

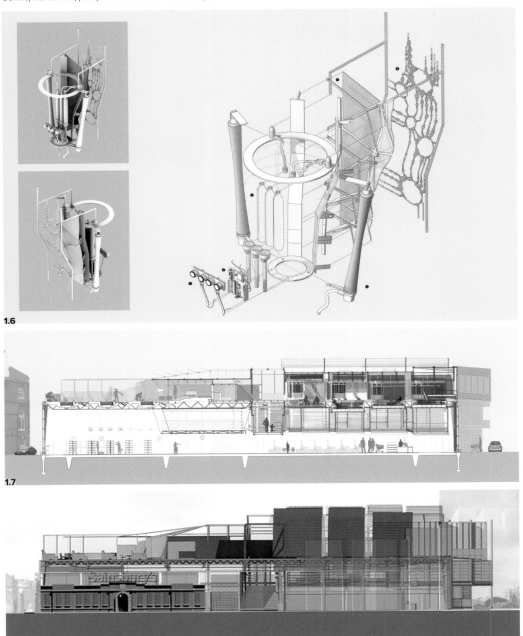

1.6

1.7

1.8

1.9

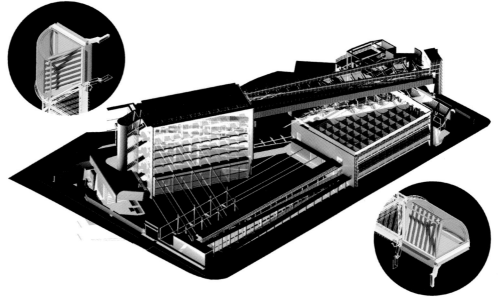

1.10

Fig 1.11 Laurence Blackwell-Thale, Y2, Pixel Pool, Tottenham, ground floor plan. The Pixel Pool is a sequence of swimming pools that give the swimmer a heightened experience of each stroke in relation to the bodies of water they move through. Set in the strange post-industrial landscape of the Lea Valley, the pools enable a new kind of wild swimming. **Fig 1.12** Corina Andra Tuna, Y3, UCL Learning Centre, Carpenters Estate, Stratford, exploded axonometric. The new Learning Centre seeks to simultaneously dismantle the brutalist post-war architecture of the Carpenters Estate and the institutional structures of UCL. A new 'porous' architecture is proposed that is 'open', linked-in with its surroundings, and allows spatially interconnectivity between local groups and the university.

1.11

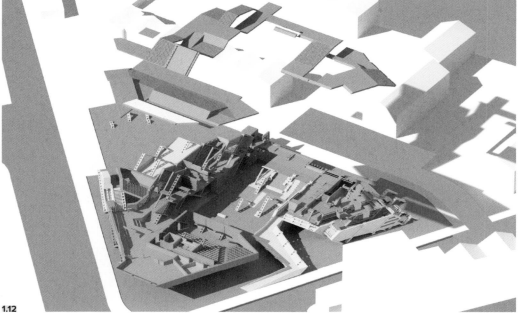

1.12

Fig 1.13 John Cruyws, Y2, 'The Law', Tottenham, cross-section. Addressing new worrying trends in public prosecution that emerged during the 2011 riots, the Magistrates Court—located on the site of the burnt-down Carpet-Right Store—acts as a new interface between the judiciary, police, press and public. **Fig 1.14** John Cruyws, Y2, Tottenham Hale Koban, Tottenham, axonometric views. Taking the police as the client—and in response to the 2011 riots—a deployable police station seeks to improve the image of the police whilst 'maintaining the peace' by stealth. **Fig 1.15** Benjamin Beach, Y3, Self-build housing, Carpenters Estate, Stratford, construction sequence of housing module. Designed in resistance to UCL's planned redevelopment of the Carpenters Estate, the project imagines an alternate future for specific, current residents where customisable self-build housing and 'sweat equity' is used as a catalyst for community empowerment.

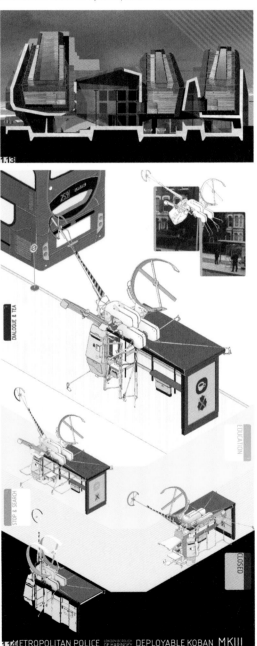

Fig 1.16 Gregorios Kythreotis, Y2, GUILD, Retail Bridge, Stratford, axonometric cutaway. Linking into the proposed 'Greenway', a new bridge is conceived as an inhabitable link between the Carpenters Estate, the proposed UCL Stratford campus and pedestrian traffic flows. The building incorporates 3D printing technologies both into the programme and fabric of the building. **Fig 1.17** Jasper Stevens, Y3, New Tottenham Town Hall, Tottenham Green, bird's eye view. A new Town Hall situated in Tottenham Green aims to make politics accessible, giving the town hall back to the citizens of Tottenham. The institution reconfigures familiar physical materials such as Portland stone and brick into the public realm, but also creates an online presence, whereby space can be remotely 'curated' in response to the specific spatial needs of the occupants.

Fig 1.18 Matthew Lyall, Y3, This is not a (Show) Home, Bromley-by-Bow. The Lower Lea Valley is part of the Thames Redevelopment Area and is due for large-scale redevelopment in the coming years. The project explored how, in these landscapes, architectural representations gain significance when used to advertise developments, pre-sell apartments and actually construct buildings. A 'holographic show-home' is proposed whereby ceiling-mounted holographic plates can be arranged to simulate studio, 2-bed and 3-bed apartments within a black-box environment. The installation itself ascends the building construction as work progresses, incorporating the view into 'the sell'. The use of holography blurs the distinction between 2D and 3D representation and serves as an enigmatic and marketable advertising device.

1.16

1.17

60

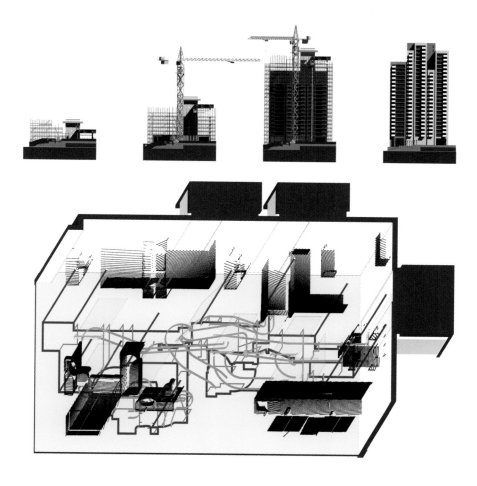

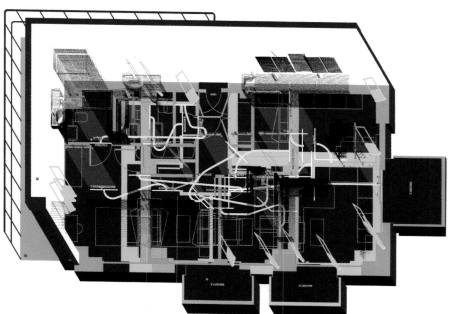

1.18

Newtopia

Damjan Iliev, Julian Krueger

Utopian places are a contradiction in terms: '*ou*' is the Greek word for 'not' and '*topos*' means 'place'. The utopian place is a place which does not exist. These non-existent places have always inspired and fuelled the imagination of philosophers, writers and architects to create models of ideal communities, technical perfection and formal purity.

By 2050 over two thirds of the world population will live in cities. How will the natural environment cope with this new growth? What does this mean for human life in the new urban millennium? How will cities have to change to accommodate this phenomenon? What new utopia will emerge in this time of crisis?

This year Unit 2 explored the ideas of utopia by learning from New York, a city which has always been a backdrop and inspiration for visionary thinking. We invited the students to contemplate on the future of a city like New York: to imagine, design and explore their own utopia for a metropolitan living.

Warm Up

The Unit responded to the Museum of Modern Art (MoMA) P.S.1 pavilion competition in Queens, New York. The brief involved proposing a site-specific, inhabitable pavilion, which extended the museum's internal programme and provides facilities for the annual 'Warm Up' music and performance festival. The challenge was how to create a temporary outdoor structure that can generate comfortable micro-climatic conditions for large public gatherings. The structure had to address environmental issues including sustainability, recycling and responsiveness to atmospheric characteristics such as light, temperature, humidity, airflow and sound.

The spatial and functional implications of the project were key requirements for both the museum and music festival and had to be explored through various tectonic analyses relating to mass, volume, form and surface.

The Term 1 project was considered a warm up experimental exercise with an underlining ecological agenda where students were expected to develop a unique architectural aesthetic through the use of various formal and conceptual tools derived from both digital and analogue methods of working.

Field Trip: New York City

In early December the unit travelled to New York, a city which seduces visitors with its pulsating and vibrant energy. We explored new architecture, climbed the classic skyscrapers, strolled along the linear gardens on the High Line, and took part in the New York City life. A visit to MoMA P.S.1 helped the students to contextualise and fine tune their Term 1 pavilion projects.

The field trip main goal was to explore and record the Brooklyn/Queens waterfront edge. Bound between the East River and Brooklyn/Queens Expressway, this is the place where the relentless city grid begins to dissolve. It was once the heartbeat of a thriving urban metropolis before its occupants relocated to cheaper and readily available lands on the periphery of the city. At present the waterfront is a large de-industrialised zone: a terrain vague full of unused ship building factories and cargo storage complexes. This urban void characterised by public vacuum and ecological disbalance is most evident in areas such as Brooklyn Navy Yard, Red Hook, Hunters Point, and Bushwick Inlet. And yet this area is one of New York's most extraordinary physical assets.

Newtopia Emerging

New York City waterfront is the longest and most diverse of any American city. Recognising its untapped potential, the city planning authorities have issued a set of urban and architectural initiatives such as Vision 2020, New York Waterfront Action Agenda, and NYC-2030. All these initiatives share a common ground to promote a sustainable symbiotic relationship between man-made structures and nature to benefit the environment and achieve higher quality of life.

The Term 2 project synthesised the requirements of the Vision 2020 plan: a legitimate interest in sustainable energy, industry and culture that can create new building ecologies and 'soft' adaptive infrastructures along the East River waterfront.

Coming back from the field trip, the students proposed a building project that established new models for living and working in the metropolis of the future. They were asked to create an imaginative urban plan, a 'vision' of their site that summarised their utopian agenda and formed the necessary substructure to develop the project in further detail.

Third year students worked on programmes for complex and technologically sound buildings which were well integrated into the urban, social and natural environment. Second year students pursued a more exploratory approach to building design, paying close attention to conceptual clarity and spatial organisation.

Unit 2 encouraged the use of various cutting-edge design techniques: 3D-modelling, Ecotect analysis, reverse engineering, Rhino scripting, plug-ins, rendering, laser-cutting, rapid-prototyping and CNC milling. These techniques allowed students to proliferate their abilities in architectural design and representation, resulting in 'newtopian' architectures for the future.

Thanks to all our guests for their wit and wisdom: Johan Berglund, Andrew Best, Dan Bucsescu at the Pratt Institute, Harry Bucknell, William Firebrace, Timo Haedrich, Steven Johnson, Ekaterini Maria Konidari, Krasimir Krastev, John Ward Regan at NYU, Luis Reis, Yael Reisner, John L. Veikos, Mersiha Veledar at Cooper Union, Barry Wark and Martin West.

Year 2
Yin Fung Jacky Chan, Yvonne Cheng, Clare Dallimore, Rufus Edmondson, Alexandra Edwards, George Proud, Hei Man (Belle) Tung, Park Hin Yeung

Year 3
Qidan Chen, Melanie Cheng, Qiuling Guan, Anthony Williams, Ka Yu (Jamie) Wong, Shou-Hang (Tim) Wu, Tung Ning (Vincent) Yeung

Fig. 2.1 Hei Man (Belle) Tung, Y2, P.S.1 Landscape Pavilion, Perspective Render. The design extends the museum courtyard area by providing auditorium seating space, bar, temporary pool and a small stage for the Warm-Up music festival. **Fig. 2.2** Alexandra Edwards, Y2, The pavilion contains an exhibition about hurricane Sandy's impact on New York City. The design derives from the New York Grid which is transformed into a three dimensional structure and forms the different spaces of the pavilion. **Fig. 2.3** Melanie Cheng, Y2, Dancing stage and film platform, Perspective Views. The elevated structure is surrounded by screens for live performance projections. It contains a bar and several dance floors. **Fig. 2.4** Clare Dallimore, Y2, P.S.1 Pavilion, Render. The shading canopy is made from photo-reactive acrylic panels which store energy during the day and emits an ambient glow during the night. **Fig. 2.5** Yvonne Cheng, Y2, Perspective View. This canopy is made from hydro-active fabric which harvests moisture from the air. The collected water is stored and released to cool the dancing crowds.

2.1

2.2

2.3

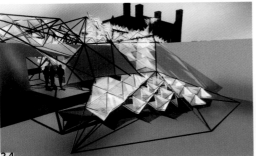

2.4

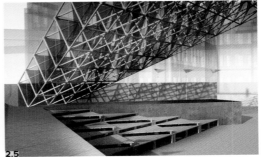

2.5

Fig. 2.6 George Proud, Y2, Interior View. The pavilion is constructed from timber logs and serves as an extension to a nearby timber merchant. The timber is arranged to aid the curing process and also allow light within its interior. **Fig. 2.7** Park Hin Yeung, Y2, PS1 Kitchens, Nighttime render. The pavilions provide small eating and cooking areas for a variety of food from around the world. The pavilions are designed to be erected quickly and reused after the festival. **Fig. 2.8** Qiuling Guan, Y3, Physical model. During the day the pavilion is used by the local skateboarding community. At night the skating ramps are transformed into seating and dancing stages. **Fig. 2.9** Shou-Hang (Tim) Wu, Y3, Isolation Space, Physical models and Longitudinal Section. The individual pods are sound insulated and provide different opportunities to relax during the music festival. The timber grid-shell structure is padded with foam panelling to enhance its acoustic performace and also protect the nearby residential community from excessive noise levels.

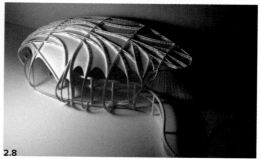

Fig. 2.10 Hei Man (Belle) Tung, Y2, New York Wetland, The building is embedded into a large marsh landscape, softening the waterfront and helping to prevent damage during storm surges. It comprises an information centre, a veterinarian clinic for birds as well as a number of hides for birdwatchers. **Fig. 2.11** Rufus Edmondson, Y2, East River Yacht Club, Williamsburg. This building is suspended over the water and provides wine bars, restaurants and small aquaculture farming facility where the once famous New York Blue-point oysters were produced. **Fig. 2.12** Shou-Hang (Tim) Wu, Y2, Algae research centre. The building consists of a research facility, library and auditorium. The outer façade skin is used to breed algae, provide alternative source of sustainable energy and reduce excessive solar gains.

2.10

2.11

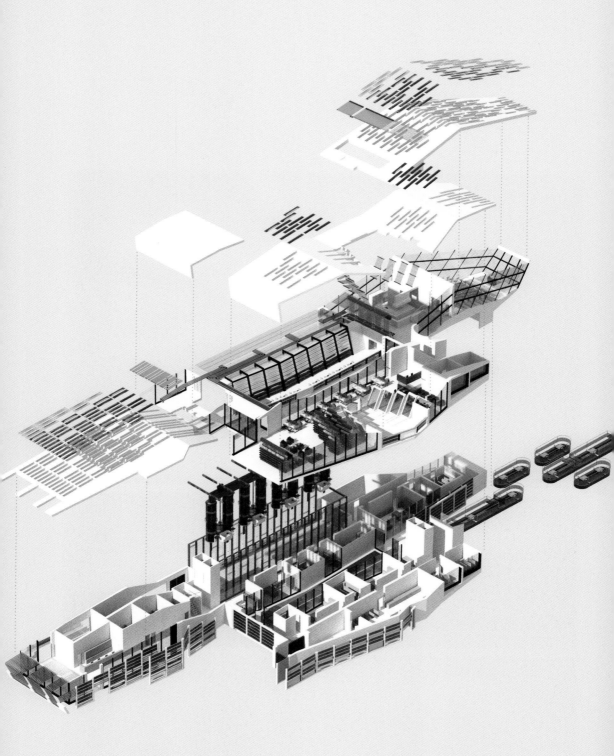

2.11

Fig. 2.13 - 2.14 Yin Fung Jacky Chan, Y2, Brooklyn Beer Spa, Axonometric and Interior view. Beer spas are popular in some parts of Europe. This will be the first American beer spa. A micro brewery is integrated within the core of this building and beer is used for the different pools of the spa. **Fig. 2.15** Qidan Chen, Y3, Ferry Terminal, Physical model. The building is part of a wider system of artificial landscapes used to purify large quantities of water, currently flowing unfiltered into the East River. **Fig. 2.16** Ka Yu (Jamie) Wong, Y3, Capsule structure, Aerial View. The building provides structure and services for small residential capsules. The individualised pods vary in size and can be easily transported to other locations around the world. **Fig. 2.17 – 2.18** Tung Ning (Vincent) Yeung, Y3, Brooklyn Navy Yard Bathhouse and Oyster Farm, Interior

View and Ground Floor Plan. Bathhouses along the two main rivers in New York had a long tradition but vanished due to water pollution. This building uses oysters which are farmed on the roof to filter the water used for the bathing pools. **Fig. 2.19** Park Hin Yeung, Y2, Brooklyn Green House and Food Market, Interior View of mushroom farming facility. The building houses a variety of greenhouses, public market and cafeteria introducing new gardening and growing technologies to the public.

2.13

2.14

2.15

2.16

2.17

2.18

2.19

Fig. 2.20 – 2.23 Anthony Williams, Y3, Salmon and Seaweed Farm and Market. Designing for a volatile future, where extreme weather events like Hurricane Sandy are becoming more frequent, the proposal is a salmon and seaweed farm and market, on the waterfront of Red Hook. Its permeable, surge-proof structure will act as a storm defence for the vulnerable community behind. Working within New York's 'Vision 2020' scheme, the project aims to fully integrate itself into its community, offering much needed jobs while supporting various local businesses with its products and by-products. The building is a community hub that brings the unique light quality of seaweed across its canopy, casting a golden glow within the market and ever-changing,slow-moving shadows over its floors.

2.20

2.21

2.22

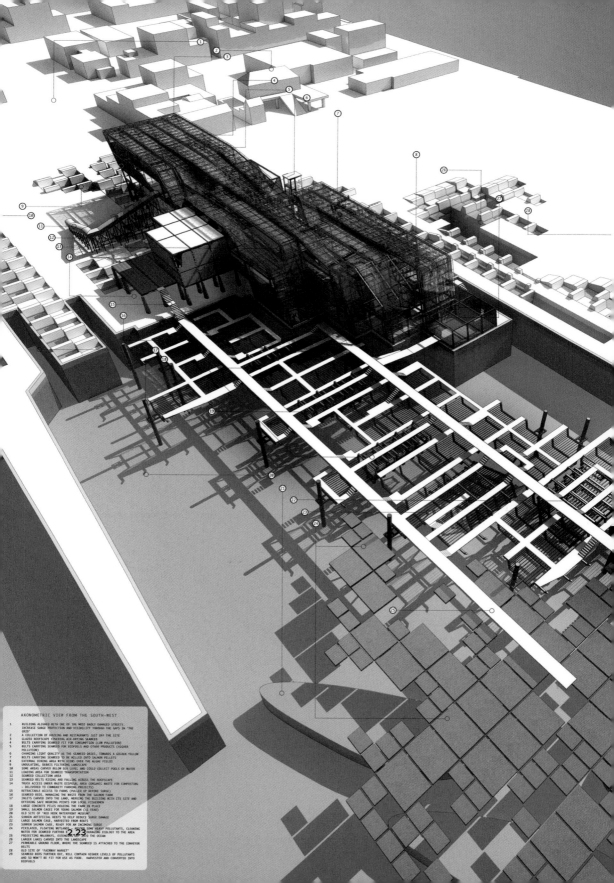

AXONOMETRIC VIEW FROM THE SOUTH-WEST

1 BUILDING ALIGNED WITH ONE OF THE MOST BADLY DAMAGED STREETS TO
   INCREASE SURGE PROTECTION AND VISIBILITY THROUGH THE GAPS IN 'THE
   GRID'
2 A COLLECTION OF HOUSING AND RESTAURANTS JUST OFF THE SITE
3 GLAZED ROOFSCAPE COVERING AIR-DRYING SEAWEED
4 BELTS CARRYING SEAWEED FIT FOR CONSUMPTION (LOW POLLUTION)
5 BELTS CARRYING SEAWEED FOR BIOFUELS AND OTHER PRODUCTS (HIGHER
   POLLUTION)
6 CHANGING LIGHT QUALITY AS THE SEAWEED DRIES, TOWARDS A GOLDEN YELLOW
7 BELTS CARRYING SEAWEED TO BE MILLED INTO SALMON PELLETS
8 EXTERNAL DINING AREA WITH VIEWS OVER THE ALGAE FIELDS
9 UNDULATING, DEBRIS FILTERING LANDSCAPE
10 SOME AREAS CARVED BELOW SEA LEVEL AND COULD COLLECT POOLS OF WATER
11 SEAWEED COLLECTION AREA
12 LOADING AREA FOR SEAWEED TRANSPORTATION
13 SEAWEED BELTS RISING AND FALLING ACROSS THE ROOFSCAPE
14 TRUCK ACCESS UNDER WASTE DISPOSAL AREA (ORGANIC WASTE FOR COMPOSTING
   - DELIVERED TO COMMUNITY FARMING PROJECTS)
15 RETRACTABLE ACCESS TO FARMS (PULLED UP BEFORE SURGE)
16 SEAWEED BEDS, MANAGING THE WASTE FROM THE SALMON FARM
17 INLETS CARVED INTO THE LAND, MERGING THE BUILDING WITH ITS SITE AND
   OFFERING SAFE MOORING POINTS FOR LOCAL FISHERMEN
18 LARGE CONCRETE PILES HOLDING THE FARM IN PLACE
19 SMALL SALMON CAGES FOR YOUNG SALMON (<6 YEAR)
20 OLD SITE OF 'RED HOOK WATERFRONT MUSEUM'
21 SUNKEN ARTIFICIAL REEFS TO HELP REDUCE SURGE DAMAGE
22 LARGE SALMON CAGE, READY FOR AN INCOMING SURGE
23 SUNKEN SALMON CAGE, HARVESTED FROM BOATS
24 PIXELLATED, FLOATING WETLANDS - ABSORB SOME HEAVY POLLUTANTS, CLEANING
   WATER FOR SEAWEED FURTHER OUT AND ENCOURAGING ECOLOGY TO THE AREA
25 PROJECTING WALKWAYS, EXTENDING OUT TO THE OCEAN
26 LARGER LANES CARVED INTO THE LANDSCAPE
27 PERMEABLE GROUND FLOOR, WHERE THE SEAWEED IS ATTACHED TO THE CONVEYOR
   BELTS
28 OLD SITE OF 'FAIRWAY MARKET'
29 SEAWEED BEDS FURTHER OUT, WILL CONTAIN HIGHER LEVELS OF POLLUTANTS
   AND SO WON'T BE FIT FOR USE AS FOOD. HARVESTED AND CONVERTED INTO
   BIOFUELS

New Horizons: Iceland and the Arctic Shift

David Garcia, Jan Kattein

Warmed by the Gulf Stream, geysers and hot springs, caught between two major tectonic plates, this land of endless volcanic activity is also home of Europe's largest glacier. At the edge of the Barents Sea the forces of nature in are omnipresent. The deafening crunch of the calving glaciers, the howling of the wind storms, eternal darkness during the winter months and volcanic eruptions that transform geography at such levels, that national maps have to be redrawn every five years.

Only a few years ago, Iceland was the economic promised land. Its fortunes turned as the economic crisis hit. Four years later the financial sector and big business are still clearing the mess. The ashes of a cataclysmic implosion often harbour the greatest social and political potential. Micro enterprises, home-workers and a buoyant creative sector are slowly but steadily filling the economic void. But in spite of the country's inherent potential the globalisation of the labour market does not leave Iceland unscathed. A steady brain drain is starting to impact on the economy.

In the context of global environmental change, free geothermal energy and breathtaking scenery are increasingly valuable assets. The Northwest passage is now a viable summer route to the east, cutting the sailing distance from Europe to China by one third and making Iceland an attractive pitstop.

How can architecture engage with a fluctuant and volatile geography? How will climate change impact on its natural environment? What innovative work patterns emerge out of Iceland's economic transformation? What new living forms come forth from a society with all-encompassing and far-reaching social ambitions? Will the country manage to turn its challenges into assets?

Mobility and adaptability are prerequisites for survival in a changing environment. Generations of farmers have lived off the land they inhabit. Some

buildings today are still built without foundations, allowing them to move and shift in line with geological realignment.

Project 1 assembles the equipment for a surveying expedition. We have tested innovative materials, explored the light and the collapsible, the resilient and the temporary, the breathable and the windtight. Advanced fabrication methods help to tackle tricky junctions. Versatility is the key to dealing with unforeseen circumstances.

Whilst on our expedition to Iceland we lived in our surveying shelters to chart our sites, during day and night, next to steam vents or ice lagoons, on black beaches, amidst geothermal banana groves, remote fishing communities and the streets of Reykjavik. This onsite approach gave us the insight into the specifics of the landscape, be it urban or rural, a pre-requisite for a responsive and contextual design response. This exposure can raise strategic questions and address real-time issues that concern the people of a nation planning for an uncertain future after economic meltdown.

Amongst many questions raised by the surveying expedition, we ask whether rich natural resources can help to devise new and innovative construction methods that are embedded in the local culture. In a country without forests will the jetsome and the floatsome of the industrialised nations establish new sustainable construction techniques? One thing is certain: Iceland has never been in a better position to establish its own very site-specific architectural language and to illustrate a successful symbiosis between man and nature.

A range of questions define the concerns of contemporary architects across the globe. Can architectural design address the community and usefully inform specific construction processes? In the context of rapid environmental and economic changes, how does architecture accommodate the changing needs of its inhabitants? How can a design explore its own performance over time? How does one design for repair and alteration?

Contemporary architecture occupies a shifting ground, a site with an alternating socioeconomic context in an unpredictable natural environment. Unit 3's research is built upon the understanding that architecture is a careful negotiation between a number of changing parameters, and often the specific overrides the generic. Innovative architectural practice celebrates a cultural identity and empowers communities to manage their own cultural and economic growth. In Unit 3 we adopt an immersive design process, which strives to bring about innovation based upon an in-depth understanding of the issues at stake, and a thorough engagement with the context at hand via inhabiting and surveying sites in depth, allowing for an architecture which is informed before being formed, and geared towards turning challenges into assets. This year's programme title, 'New Horizons', describes Iceland's emergence from economic collapse, but it also describes the emerging role of the contemporary architect as an agent for change, embedded in a specific local community and their culture, and as a catalyst between technology and nature.

Year 2
Duncan (Harry) Clover, Claire Haugh, Tomiris Kupzhassarova, Wenhao (Perry) Li, Lisa McDanell, Bethany Penman, Cassidy Reid, Samuel Tan, Ivo Tedbury, Henrietta Watkins, Timmy Whitehouse, Shirley Lee Mei Ying

Year 3
Jiatong (Karen) Hu, Him Wai Lai, Allen Wen

Fig. 3.1 Samuel Tan, Y2, Aquatic Research Shelter at the edge of the Jökulsárlón glaciar lagoon. This shelter analyses the aquatic environments of Iceland, looking at fish species, fish populations, microscopic life and its abundance. Fish traps, which are spread along each tentacle, are used to catch fish because of its passivity and unobtrusiveness, in contrast to commercial fishing methods, which have driven fish stocks into decline and reduced biodiversity. **Fig. 3.2** Lisa McDanell, Y2, Testing ice as structural material, the shelter generates layers of frost on stretched fabric. The aluminium frame incorporated a spraying system, also controllable from within the shelter, which could moisten the stretched fabric. This would then freeze overnight and act as a windbreak in its hardened state. The strength of the frozen fabric was tested by releasing each point from which it had been stretched. **Fig. 3.3** Duncan (Harry) Clover, Y2, Wearable Observatory, on the shores of Vik. Adapted for travel to remote areas of Iceland where the atmosphere can be exceptionally clear and without glare, the flexibility of a wearable tent enables one to exploit brief windows within the cloud-cover in what are at all times winter harsh weather conditions. **Fig. 3.4** Timmy Whitehouse, Y2, Kite Shelter. Deployed as a kite during the day to chart specific wind patterns in the Icelandic landscape, it harnesses the power of the wind to give the shelter structure during the night.

3.1

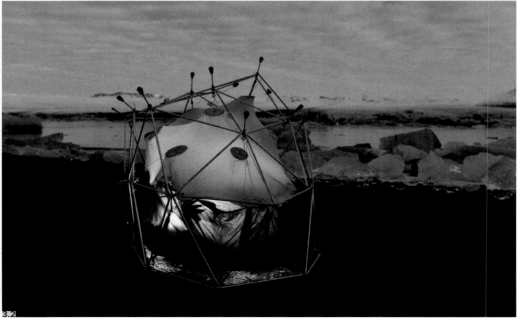

3.2

3.3

3.4

Fig. 3.5 Bethany Penman, Y2, Knitting Insulation Shelter. The objective of the shelter is to knit its own genetic code of insulation; using four different types of yarn (chunky, synthetic, UV and thin) where the problems of warmth, wind, water and light could be addressed from within my shelter. **Fig. 3.6** Cassidy Reid, Y2, Home Brew Shelter. As a critique to the ever-increasing taxation on alcohol in Iceland, the shelter taps directly into the natural birch trees in Skaftafell National Park to collect sap to produce wine as well as providing habitation. **Fig. 3.7 – 3.8** Shirley Lee Mei Ying, Y2, Internet Wifi Recorder. This shelter, which transforms into a rotating wheel, records Wifi intensity in urban and rural areas, charting the growth of domestic Internet access in Iceland.

3.5

3.6

3.7

3.8

Fig. 3.9 Tomiris Kupzhassarova, Y2, Landscape Recorder. The inside fabric layer performs as a sound recording system, threaded with wires that connect recording devices with switches and power supply. The system enables recording of the sound-scape of any location, capturing multitude of locally picked sounds that can later be replayed, acoustically recalling a distant landscape. **Fig. 3.10** Claire Haugh, Y2, Borrowed Steam Shelter. Focused on Iceland's massive geothermal resources this shelter is heated by borrowing heat from the many steam outlets that can be found in the Icelandic environment, by channelling the heat through vents and chambers in this origami inspired construction. **Fig. 3.11** Ivo Tedbury, Y2, The Micro-Allotment Shelter seeks to bring people into closer contact with the process of growing vegetables (the majority of which Iceland currently imports). At the same time it offers a possible solution to the nation's problem with cancer (Iceland has one of the highest diagnosis rates in the world). The chosen vegetable, a micro strain of broccoli, contains a high quantity of sulforaphane, an organosulfur compound that exhibits anti-cancer properties.

Fig. 3.13 Tomiris Kupzhasarova, Y4, Designed in response to the vivid music scene in Reykjavik, the building acts as series of adaptable recording studios during the year and transforms into larger performance space for Iceland Airwaves festival in October. **Fig. 3.14** Bethany Penman, Y2, Vík Wool Knitting Factory. The project is a redesign of the current structure, 'Vík Prjónsdóttir', situated in the town of Vík. It combines an existing factory and shop with a knitting retreat with a breathable fleece façade, amongst other wool related solutions. **Fig. 3.15** Jiatong (Karen) Hu, Y3, The Reclaimed Goods Warehouse & Craftsman Community is a reaction to the current recycling condition of Iceland. The centre caters for the working, living and communication aspects for designers and craftsman who manufacture recycled materials into new products for sale,

the building itself, being one of the products. **Fig. 3.16** Wenhao (Perry) Li, Y2, According to further research on Icelandic diets, consumption of sushi is rising enormously. Fish can be easily obtained in Iceland but the other major ingredient, rice, is imported. The building is a greenhouse with a restaurant which grows its own sushi rice while seawater is used to distil fresh water and create salt in return. **Fig. 3.17** Duncan (Harry) Clover, Y2, Centre for Astro-Photography: located in Iceland's central desert plains. The building was designed to architecturally manifest the performance of night photography and the way in which telescopes track the path of the stars. The building has three 'arms' in which the photographers stay the night, these independently rotate and track different constellations at night but are docked and hidden in the day.

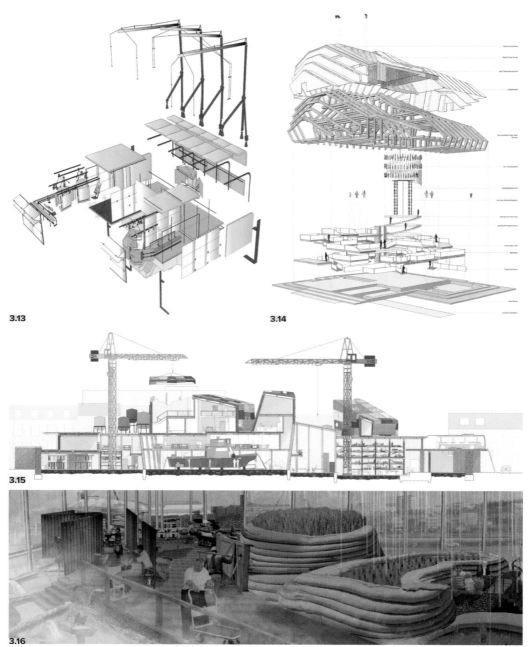

3.13

3.14

3.15

3.16

SECTION NIGHT - ARMS IN USE

HARRY CLOVER: UNIT 3
CENTER FOR ASTROPHOTOGRAPHY

SECTION THROUGH DOMED ARM - DAY TIME

SIRIUS EYE RENDER

3.17

Fig. 3.18 Claire Haugh, Y2, Responding to Iceland's volatile and constantly changing landscape, this geothermal spa's design relies on its ability to parasitically connect to the many steam vents that occur naturally around the country. The building's responses to the differing steam vents not only directly affects the architecture but also forms the basis for the atmosphere within its spaces. **Fig. 3.19** Samuel Tan, Y2, Polyculture Fish Farm, A marine research centre and fish market. The building explores the notion of commercial nature within the realms of architecture and in an environment which must encompass both the natural habitat of marine life and the controlled environment of a marine research laboratory. Whilst the aim of polyculture is to encourage a natural ecosystem, in order to achieve this, there must be a constant surveillance and interruption in the process. Compositionally, the building reflects this, yet also questions whether a 'natural' state can ever be achieved within the boundaries of commercialism and research. Ultimately, just as polyculture is a microcosm of the wider marine ecosystem, the building becomes a microcosm of man's complex relationship with nature. **Fig. 3.20** Cassidy Reid, Y2, The building proposal is a geothermal farm complex intended to strengthen local food production in Iceland. Kiwis are highly consumed in Iceland and the production of the building provides enough kiwi fruit to feed the population. The building distributes geothermally heated water through the structure helping the design to respond to the specific assets and challenges of the Icelandic landscape.

3.18

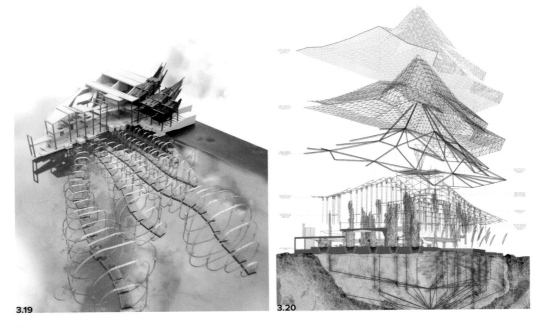

3.19

3.20

Fig. 3.21 Timmy Whitehouse, Y2, Plastic Recycling Centre, Reykjavik. In a rapidly changing Iceland, this proposal uses geothermal energy to recycle Iceland's imported plastic products and by-products. Combining the plastic sheet materials that it produces, it creates adaptable inflatable spaces, for storage, suspended viewing spaces for the public and relaxation areas for the workers. The adaptability of the inflatable spaces allows the building to respond to the changes and fluctuations in the plastics market on an international and local level. Through its performance the building is a celebration of the potentials of recycling, plastics, and geothermal energy. **Fig. 3.22** Ivo Tedbury, Y2, GM Vegetable Facility. Seeking to address Iceland's increasing incidence of cancers as the population adopts a more westernised lifestyle,

this facility on the University of Iceland campus will experiment with new health-driven vegetable strains. Fabric conveyor belts move through the building allowing the plants to be continually germinated, grown, tested and harvested, at the same time creating a synthetic meadow, lit with artificial lights from above and heated from below, where the public can picnic even in the depths of winter. **Fig. 3.23** Lisa McDanell, Y2, Ice Research Base. Sited at the tongue of Europe's largest glacier, the building extends into Jökulsárlón Ice Lagoon to investigate icebergs broken off the glacier. Research is carried out to discover life forms trapped within the ice in small pockets of unfrozen salty water. The building uses armatures and nets on which ice can form when dipped into the lake, helping scientists to understand how life survives in small crystals of ice.

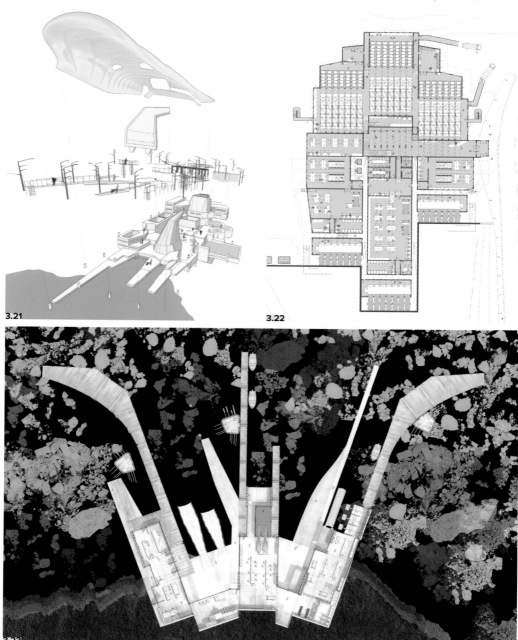

3.21

3.22

3.23

Facsimile

Ana Monrabal-Cook, Luke Pearson

'There's no more beautiful city in the world provided it's seen by night and at a distance'
Roman Polanski, *Chinatown*

'LA, the most photographed city in the world, yet the least photogenic' Thom Andersen, *LA Plays Itself*

Unit 4 this year focused on the implications of new technologies for mapping and reading space in order to propose architectures. With new digital tools, physical locations may be understood remotely, as a facsimile of the real city; does this affect how, what and where we design? We continued our exploration into architectures of public delight, antipathy or bemusement by visiting the city that can truly attest to have been founded on such principles: Los Angeles.

LA has always intertwined fact and fiction. The architecture of the city bears witness to an urban sprawl built up through capital investment and property developers who used their constructions to communicate versions of a history that is as fantastical as the productions of Hollywood itself. Buildings such as the Bradbury feature as film characters rather than subjects; they are more famous and have more distinguished filmographies than most film stars.

In decades past, before digital technologies eased direct access to information, the export of this vision of a city was primarily through creative endeavour, through writing, music and most importantly films. This allowed a city such as Los Angeles to write its own myth, rendered through architectures that suggest histories and futures that never truly existed.

New ways of remotely viewing contemporary Los Angeles allow us to see beyond the cultivated image this myth represents. We now have tools for understanding the city that take the previous notion of the 'survey' the 'map' or the 'view' and turn it on its head. These new ways of remote seeing and understanding, allow us access to a representation of the city deemed true to the source; the city becomes a facsimile.

Unit 4 poses the question: is this city – that takes pride in the image it portrays – adapting to the new and widely available surveying instruments and methods of reproduction to continue its hold on the image of the American dream? Will buildings or components be choreographed to play along with the forecasted upgrades of new technologies?

Los Angeles has been compared to the circuit board – as a vast network of information and movement. It speaks of the 'language of movement not monument' (Reyner Banham). The city is a sprawling series of fantastical infrastructures that have a direct relationship to four key systems that allow it to function.

We began by looking at: air and the relationship between the sprawl of the city and its viewing and reading from above; oil and LA as a city with underground reserves of 'black gold' and technologies for finding and extracting it; traffic and the vehicle as a forming force behind both the layout and the image of the city; and the river with potential new ways in which the 'drain' might re-manifest itself as a river and become part of the city again.

In LA we visited Case Study Houses gazing out across the constellations of street lights below. We studied the Salk Institute, its restrained use of materials and flexibility of spaces. We encountered architectures immortalised through film: Union Station, Frank Lloyd Wright's houses and the Bradbury building. We witnessed the magnitude of Mount Wilson's observatory and Hubble's legacy, and took in the acrid smell of La Brea Tar Pits. We met architects and universities to compare how LA's unique nature drives its architectural discourse.

Visiting sites studied in the first term we assessed the appropriateness of both the remote readings and subsequent proposals. Gaining first-hand experience of the scale of the city and the true context at ground level, we compared and contrasted all we thought we knew about LA to the reality we found.

Unit 4 continued to push students to question the mediums by which architecture is transmitted, with projects engaging notions such as a 'Google Picturesque' comprised of ruptured error-spaces that led to architectural aesthetics of the momentary glitch. We explored the relationship between remote viewing and ground conditions, from proposing scanned digital/physical material hybrids through to drone-operated strategies for breaking up the LA river, promoting new ecological development. Students developed strategies for tapping into abandoned oil infrastructure, produced ersatz landscapes for police training and incrementally improved regulations for emergency response buildings in a city of gridlock. We compared dromoscopic viewpoints from the car to the shifting accuracy of GPS guidance and questioned the potential changes to the urban landscape of LA with the legalisation of autonomous vehicles in California. The unit endeavoured to create architectures that contrast and speculate not only on the way we read a city, but on the nature of the reading tool itself as a potential approach for design.

We would like to thank Bryan Cantley, Neil Denari, Wes Jones and Morphosis (with special thanks to Natalia Traverso Caluana) for being so welcoming in LA.

We would also like to thank the critics this year for their invaluable feedback: Laura Allen, Abigail Ashton, Johan Bergland, Matthew Butcher, Nick Elias, Will Jefferies, Nicholas Hockley, CJ Lim, Andrew Porter, Peg Rawes, Gavin Hutchison and Rae Whittow-Williams.

Year 2
Charlotte Archer, Matthew Bovingdon-Downe, Thomas Budd, Emma Colthurst, Chloe Ellis, Christian Georcelin, Isobel Parnell, Sarah Stone, Joshua Toh Kai Heng, Daisy Urcell

Year 3
Chiara de Stavola Barrett, Leo Boscherini, Jiongjiong (Joanne) Chen, Daniel Scoulding, Saijel Anil Taank

Fig 4.1 – 4.3 Leo Boscherini, Y3, Wilshire District Fire Station. The WDFD is an 'optimal fire station' based in an area of West Hollywood suffering from the poorest emergency response time in LA. Existing design regulations were assessed in order to shave seconds off emergency response procedures through a series of incremental improvements. The roof plan shows three individual apparatus bays minimising off-site truck manoeuvres derived from the choreography of the pitstop.
Fig. 4.4 Leo Boscherini, Y3, A dynamic device to reinvigorate the roadside landscape of Miracle Mile, using the momentum of a vehicle to recreate a landscape of 'Google' architecture.
Fig 4.5 Daisy Urcell Y2, Cobalt Conference Centre is an adaptable theatre and garden powered by the movement of parking cars on the level below. Layered mesh screens and

suspended palm trees form the backdrop to adaptable meeting spaces. **Fig 4.6** Isobel Parnell, Y2, The Bay Bridge Training Centre educates the next generation of Californians to preserve the new Oakland Bay Bridge, constructed remotely in China. The building incorporates the exact joints and fixings used in the bridge to form spaces including a museum, training areas and didactic workshop. **Fig 4.7** Christian Georcelin Y2, Pembroke Business Hub. Elevation treatment of a centre for start-up businesses located off Pico Boulevard, LA, including a modulated roof system for advertising. **Fig 4.8** Emma Colthurst, Y2, The model for the 'Texture House' peels apart to create hybridised digital/physical materials that reveal this dual materiality in the difference between photographic and digitally scanned recordings of space.

4.1

4.2

4.3

4.4

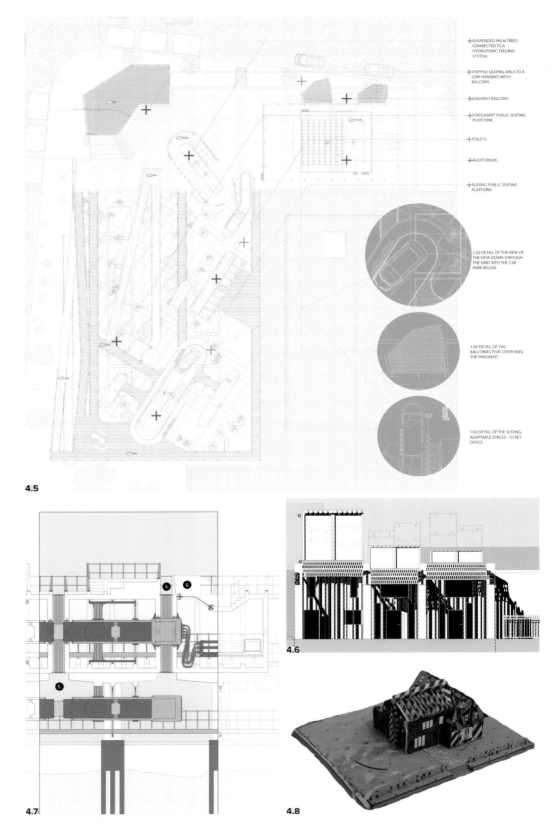

+ SUSPENDED PALM TREES CONNECTED TO A HYDROPONIC FEEDING SYSTEM.

+ STEPPED SEATING AREA TO A LOW HANGING MESH BALCONY.

+ LOUVRED BALCONY.

+ STATIONARY PUBLIC SEATING PLATFORM.

+ TOILETS.

+ AUDITORIUM.

+ SLIDING PUBLIC SEATING PLATFORM.

1:50 DETAIL OF THE VIEW OF THE VIEW DOWN THROUGH THE GRID INTO THE CAR PARK BELOW.

1:50 DETAIL OF THE BALCONIES THAT OVERHANG THE PAVEMENT.

1:50 DETAIL OF THE SLIDING, ADAPTABLE SPACES - TICKET OFFICE.

4.5

4.7

4.6

4.8

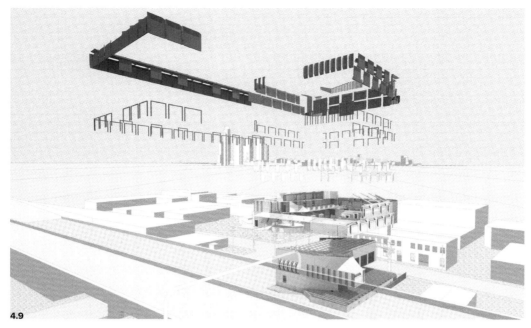

4.9

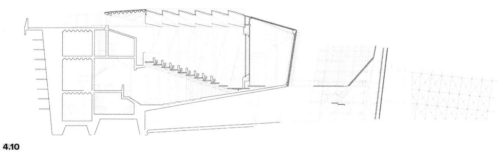

4.10

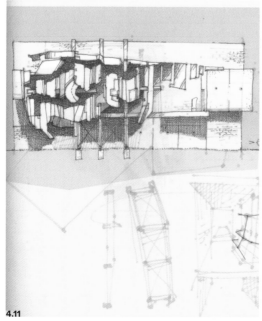

4.11

4.12

Fig 4.9 Joshua Toh, Y2, A Los Angeles atelier for a French fashion house in the centre of the LA Fashion District. The scheme builds up layers of moulded cladding panels, glass and working spaces to insulate the celebrity client from the exterior world. **Fig 4.10 – 4.11** Matthew Bovingdon-Downe, Y2, A hybrid cinema located adjacent to the cinematic backdrop of the LA river. The building offers a sequence of public spaces as ambulatory freeways forming dynamic visual connections across the various levels in the building. **Fig 4.12** Lottie Archer Y2, A Guide to the Creation of Ghost Spaces is the conclusion of a series of studies of Marilyn Monroe's house compiled from imagery available on the internet. A scaled model rendered with specific textures revealed the ghosts of the actress' life when scanned using photogrammetry software. **Fig 4.13 – 4.16**

Tom Budd, Y2, The Inglewood Oil Field Community Gardens and Market are situated on the largest urban oil field in Los Angeles. The proposal provides residents with an agricultural superstructure specifically designed to house a diverse range of naturally grown produce. Using geothermal energy acquired from pumping water into unused, capped oil wells, the building creates steam, which it then uses to power and create spaces with specific temperature and humidity related qualities. The building lies on the boundary between the suburban community and the industrial oil field. These contrasting elements are reflected in the building's design – the community gardens act as a bridge connecting people demonstrating the new ways in which it's utilisation can be beneficial to the suburban community.

4.13

4.15

4.14

4.16

Fig 4.17 – Fig 4.18 Joanne Chen, Y3, The Emergency Actions Training Centre for the LAPD sited in Downtown LA is deliberately accessible to the public to build relationships with the city's community by providing an insight into the rigour of their training techniques. The centre equips police officers with responsive situation awareness by training them through 'infinitely reconfigurable' spaces to create unfamiliar situations. The internal spaces are inspired by existing rock gardens in the original 'SITSIM' village created in 1975 with help from Universal Studios; a series of static connected facades and internal rooms designed to simulate search scenarios. The dimensions of the reconfigurable props are based on everyday items commonly used as shields or obstacles in hostage situations. The training tower becomes

a framework for applying and simulation different material environments, while presenting a fragmented totem to the institution which plays with the large scale of its surroundings.

Fig 4.19 – 4.23 Dan Scoulding, Y3, 1 North Mission. The scheme is a new transport hub for Downtown LA comprising a light rail station, office space and data centre. Through the mediation of light and heat across the massive superstructure of the scheme, a complex system of environmental conditions is maintained. The building is designed to respond to the Piggy Back Yard Conceptual Masterplan designed for the Friends of the Los Angeles river, which seeks to re-establish the waterway through breakdown of hard infrastructure and new green riverside developments. By taking the proposed 125 acre park as the instigator of a future site to come, the project

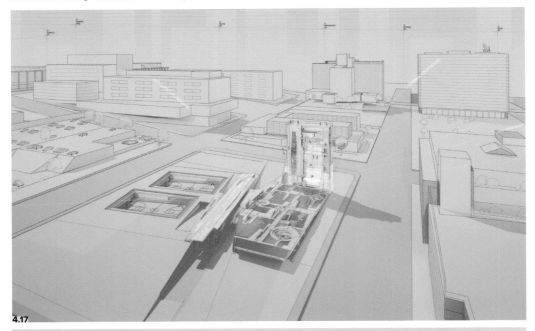

4.17

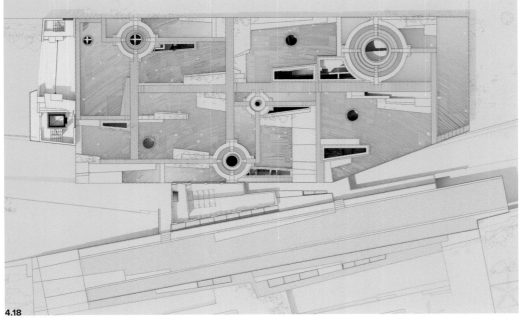

4.18

starts to explore the strategy of building a marker, where the particular requirements of space between transport hub, office space and 'lights-out' zones of non-human occupation start to mingle together. Exploiting the composition of beams and fins as environmental strategies as well as spatial conditions, the building uses the monumental scale of many of the cities public buildings, but breaks this down to a fine grained mediation of environmental conditions.

4.19

4.22

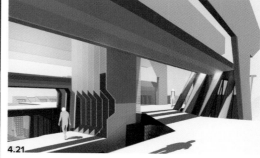

4.21

4.23

Fig. 4.24 Saijel Taank, Y3, Comicon Los Angeles. The project proposes a new convention centre for the secondary Comicon event held annually in Los Angeles. Through the mediation of natural light using a series of optical devices, a series of unitised spaces are turned into fantastical internalised worlds derived from the style, framing and spatial rules of the comic book page. Through controlled circulations, and programmatic assessment of the genres of comic exhibited, a series of bespoke exhibition spaces are woven into the larger infrastructure of the site. **Fig. 4.25 – 4.27** Chiara Barrett, Y3, The Tenets of Google Picturesque. The Google Picturesque dealt with the study of Los Angeles remotely through Google Earth and the ruptures that emerge between reality and the new forms of spatiality present within its internalised worlds.

The project catalogued and dissected the current anomalies in Google's patented algorithm The Universal Texture, using these to develop a series of design proposals that formalised the anomalies into the physical world. Through discussing ideas of resolution, distortion, inversion and datum within the structure of Google Earth space, the project proposes fragments of glitch architecture built into the existing urban fabric that would play with the constant 'optimisation' of the Universal Texture software to become an indelible legacy of current digital trends.

4.24

06
FACADE HIERARCHY

4.25

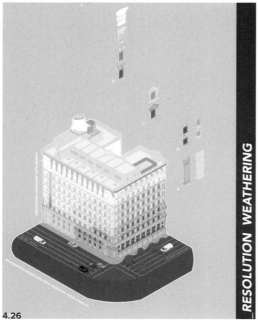

4.26

RESOLUTION WEATHERING

4.27

Fig. 4.28 – 4.29 Chiara Barrett, Y3, DARPA Headquarters Los Angeles. The project explores some of the contradictions implicit in the idea of 'controlled transparency'. DARPA is the US Department of Defense' 'blue sky thinking' arm investigating innovative technoligies across military and civilian spheres. Public access to the federal building accredits the agency with transparency, yet the public perception of the researchers within is heavily controled through an architecture of fragmentation, slippage and obfuscation. Using the techniques developed in the Tenets of Google Picturesque project, an architectural approach was derived that investigates the public face of an institution as a fragmented collage of other such hulking headquarters in the Downtown surrounds.

The building intends to embody the agency's primary aim to prevent and create strategic surprise by playing with notions of scale, proximity, resolution and materiality. A 'slipping strategy' results in the cross-fertilisation of these ideas and the manifestation of a 'Glitched' architecture specific to DARPA.

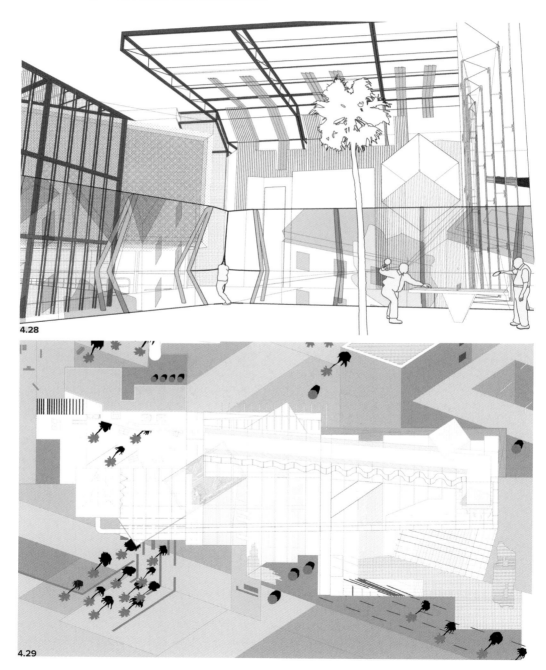

4.28

4.29

Unit 5
Supernature

Julia Backhaus, Pedro Font Alba, Bruce Irwin

The Bartlett School of Architecture 2013

As urban populations increase in density and number, and the scope and geometry of agriculture grows correspondingly, human contact with the natural world is rapidly superseded and remade. This was our starting point: An observation that in the metropolis 'nature' is visibly overwritten by human systems and can only be apprehended as a prior state, an enhanced replacement, a hybrid condition, or at times a resurgent rebellious wildness. This is the 'Supernature' we proposed to examine and within which we found space to work.

Our case study was New York City, which we visited at the end of November. New York City is often described as the paradigm of 20th century metropolis, the ultimate demonstration of human domination of nature, a Cartesian triumph of commerce and aspiration over and on top of geography and geology, flora and fauna.

In the 20th century New York City represented polar positions of modernity and obsolescence, progress and rampant and destructive capital systems. It has swung from periodic abundance and excess during the 1920s and 1980s, to fiscal and political stalemate and population flight, as in the 1930s and 1970s. These positions can be read in the artefacts of our time: from the cinema, song, and poetry of the Roaring Twenties, or the fantasies of Urban Jungle, isolation, and a mega-prison island of dystopian films of the late 70s and early 80s. And yet the very same systems of transport and distribution, property grid and money, cultural production and consumption that made New York City the main hub and principal port of North America continue, funnelling food and energy and circulating and clearing away water, waste, steam, power.

Within New York there exists scope for examinations of our topic both micro and macro, from labyrinthine water and waste and transport systems down to the subtle and the shifting foraging strategies of bees and foxes within the built environment. Potential areas of investigation would range from food production and systems of cooling, preservation and distribution, to the technological and architectural strategies for managing crises of weather and fire in vertical neighbourhoods. In a built system, the management of risk may be an unavoidable topic. The city is also a place of intense cultural production, and the representation (and thus our beliefs) of nature is correspondingly a palimpsest of celluloid and digital fragments.

City parks have a prized history in human culture and would inevitably form a part of an investigation into our idea. The urban park may represent an idea of a previous state, of 'pure' nature, or it may self-consciously conflate ecologies, combining for an enhanced super-experience, a 'better-than', idealised moment of natural history. In the near future, gene research promises enhanced tree species that might light our city streets with an arboreal glow, or suck carbon emissions more rapidly from the air, becoming more actual 'green lungs'. In a game of spatial compensation and transferral, we dot our cities with green voids, to indicate 'breathing room'. Central Park represents an idealised nature, highly constructed, though with the specific design intent of re-imaging an absent or historical natural condition. Construction photos of the installation of Central Park reveal the degree of manipulation and artistry at work in this apparent wild space within the grid.

New York offers a rich catalogue of the phenomena we are referring to as 'supernature'. A built grid surface covers almost the entire island of Manhattan, replicating (in vertical section) the ground, and taking its place functionally and apparently. In places this layering of built grounds is revealed or can be seen; in places, nature reasserts itself, and this reassertion has sometimes become the basis for new public space.

Project 1 invited research and speculation from afar in advance of our study journey. Students were asked to select an instance of Supernature within the boundaries of New York and to construct a three dimensional investigation of their findings. They were given one dimensional constraint, X = 30cm Y = 60cm, and asked to construct a supporting metal frame. The completed models were then assembled into a propositional city grid.

At the start of Project 2 we visited New York, the object of our speculations. Along the rivers and rail lines, underground, and along it we sought instances of our topic. We identified the changing waterfront as an ideal place for our proposals. Until recently New York Harbor was the site of intense industrial processing and shipping, and is now undergoing rapid transformation, from industry to fallow post-industrial abandonment, and finally to a kind of productionless rejuvenation as upmarket housing. Hurricane Sandy had recently struck the city, and we focused or investigations on some of the areas of the city directly affected by the storm, particularly the East River, Red Hook and Coney Island waterfronts. Our project proposals focused on these areas, both for their ongoing programmatic transformations and as a place of interface with larger climatic conditions. Our proposals embrace and anticipate a wide range of possibility for production and distribution, urban agriculture, cultural creation, health and housing, botany and commerce within the changing city.

We would like to acknowledge and thank our jurors through the year for their generosity of time and dedication towards our students: Laura Allen, Nuria Alvarez, Mark Breeze, Margaret Bursa, Izaskun Chinchilla, Isaac Cobo, Francisco Gonzalez de Canales, Johan Hybschmann, Carlos Jimenez, Clara Kraft, Paul Legon, Wei Fan Liang, David Roberts, Lola Ruiz, all provided very valuable insight into the work widening our vision on the subject and exciting suggestions for design opportunities. Many thanks also to Andrew Best and his colleagues at Buro Happold for technical tutoring.

Year 2
Susan (Supichaya) Chaisiriroj, Muzhi Chen, George Courtauld, Jaemin Kim, Kar Tung (Karen) Ko, Maggie Lan, Huynh Nguyen, Hoi Yiu (Carolyn) Wong, Jessica Wang, Yiren (Aviva) Wang, Anqi (Angel) Yu

Year 3
Tahora Azizy, Hannah Bowers, Katie Cunningham, Oi-Yee (Helen) Siu, Alexia Souvalioti

unit5bartlett.wordpress.com

Fig. 5.1 Jessica Wang, Y2, Banana Ripening Taxi Stand. Situated throughout the gridiron, the stands make use of existing utilities to ripen the fruits whilst offering shelter to taxis and passersby **Fig. 5.2** Hoi Yiu (Carolyn) Wong, Y2, Glowing Firefly Pavilion, Battery Park. A shelter for locals during emergency blackouts in Manhattan, the design consists of panels that replicate the skylines of New York City, and is lit by bioluminescent trees. When not in use as a shelter, firefly gardens and a bioluminescent tree nursery is offered to visitors who can take home small jars of fireflies and sipplings. **Fig. 5.3** Anqi (Angel) Yu, Y2, Snakehead Fish-o-Mat. The Chinese snakehead fish is invading local ponds and waterways, eradicating native species of fish. The Fish-o-Mat proposes a live-fish delivery system into the city's food deserts, a solution to the problems of ecology and gastronomy. **Fig. 5.4** Katie Cunningham, Y3, Mussel underwater park proposes to exploit marine invasive species with in the waters of the East River and the New York Bay for productive purposes. See also Fig 5.23. Surrogate Landscapes invited researched speculation into moments of symbiosis between human-made and natural systems, both the benign and the toxic, within specific sites in New York. The resulting proposals fitted into a miniature Manhattan Gridiron, creating an alternate New York **(Fig.5.5)**.

5.1

5.2

5.3

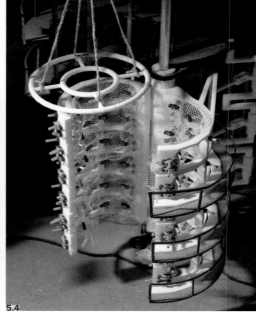

5.4

Fig. 5.6 Anqi (Angel) Yu, Y2, East River Fish Farm and Market, Brooklyn Navy Yard. An occupy-able folded canopy of ribbed fish ladders delivers live fish in channels to the market stalls from the surrounding lilypond-like fish farm. Customers enjoy Manhattan views and a sushi restaurant. **Fig. 5.7** Jessica Wang, Y2, Green Point Juicery. Artificial fruit-ripening trees form a canopy over a proposed fresh juice-making facility. The undulating roof is enclosed with staggered glass rods, fixed between the metal treetops. Visitors wander the forest floor, sipping juices. **Fig. 5.8** Huhyn Nguyen, Y2, Green Point Oil Spill Soil Reclamation Park. A Temporary elevated ground is proposed as a sky park while detoxifing the contaminated earth via phytoremediation in shallow steel planters. **Fig. 5.9** Susan (Supichaya) Chaisiriroj, Y2, Sunrise/set Pavilion in Times Square. Jetlagged travellers reset their internal clock in a skyscraper-top artificial sunrise and sunset. **Fig. 5.10** Tahora Azizy, Y3, Russian retirement Community Housing, Coney Island. Today Coney Island is famous for its Russian immigrant community, now aging and often widowed. Using light control and shadow to reproduce experiences from the users native landscape. The proposal reintroduces the natural sandscape from the beach to blanket and protects housing for the community and their pets. **Fig. 5.11 – 5.12** Yiren (Aviva) Wang, Y2, Red Hook Community Ceramics Workshop. The local community builds its own clay pit, workshop and kilns to create this art and skills training centre. Over time the facility will expand, and each expansion is an opportunity for learning new manufacturing and building skills.

5.6

5.7

5.8

5.9

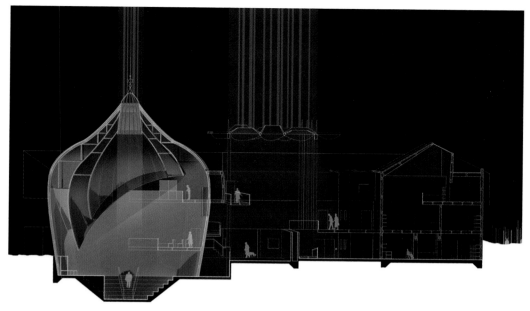

5.10

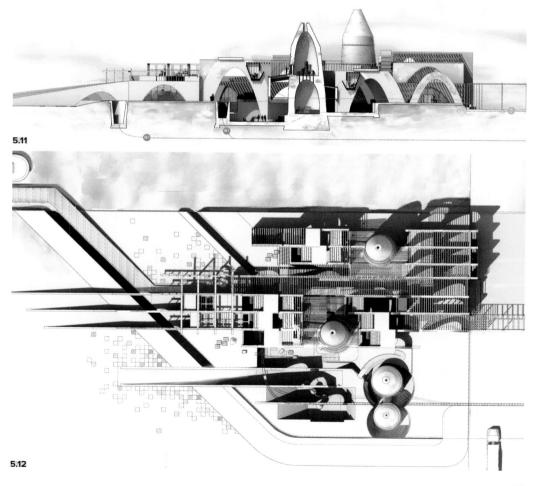

5.11

5.12

Fig. 5.13 – 5.15 Kar Tung (Karen) Ko, Y2, Coney Island USA. Sited adjacent to the storied Boardwalk, the proposal rehouses a local community centre, freakshow and trapeze training facility within paired spiralling circus canopies. Beneath the Boardwalk are support facilities and workshops, above, over, and around, are spaces and routes of aerial manoeuvre. Sunlight and shadow alternately conceal and reveal elements of structure, inhabitation and movement. **Fig. 5.16** Maggie Lan, Y2, East River Secret Cinema Studio. Shipping containers house props and sets for the production of a Secret Cinema on this former industrial waterfront site. The containers are modified to fold open for use, slipped into and out of soundstages on an industrial armature. Visitors arrive via an extended red-carpet experience, re-costume and makeup,

and are drawn into the filming itself, before finally being floated around Manhattan on a cinema barge. **Fig. 5.17** George Courtauld, Y2, Brunswick Inlet Seed Bank and Arboretum, Brooklyn. Rising sea levels pose a threat to the survival of plant species. A proposed seed market shields a research facility and seed bank pod on the shore of the East River. The pod will detach itself from its shell-market, rise, and float away as in a future flood. **Fig. 5.18 – 5.19** Hannah Bowers, Y3, Bushwick Inlet Mulberry Forrest, Brooklyn. A former industrial site is replaced with a mulberry forest and a silkworm workshop. Avenues of trees frame views to Manhattan, and branches and leaves are harvested for wormfood and composted in a bulgy skin for heat. The visitor is invited to tour the worm-homes, view weaving and dying, and enjoy the new urban forest.

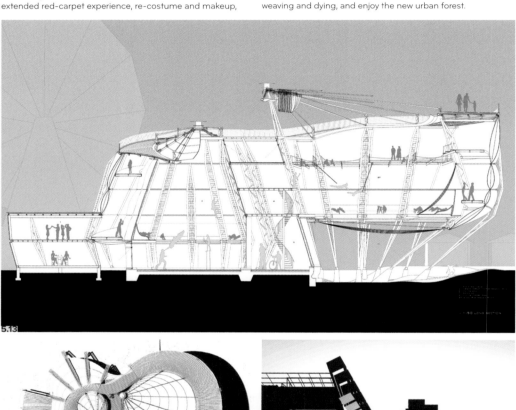

5.13

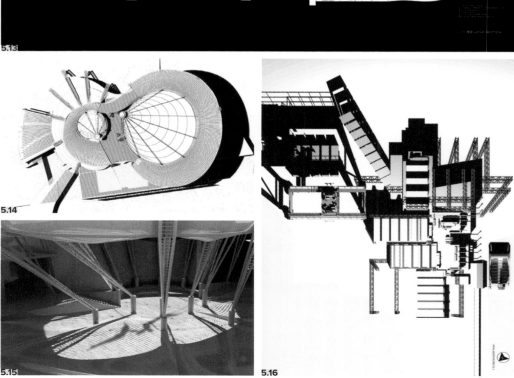

5.14

5.15

5.16

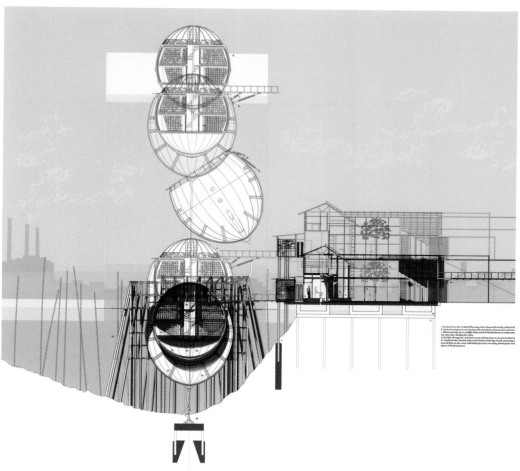

5.17

5.18

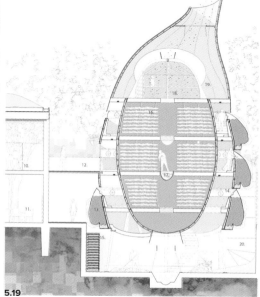

5.19

Fig. 5.20, 5.24 Alexia Souvalioti, Y3, CityHarvest Foodbank, Williamsburg. Food waste in a time of want and increasing wealth disparity is an urban travesty. This project aims to organise and spatially resolve the collection and distribution of excess food from shops, stores and restaurants. Incoming supplies arrive across the East River on box-car barges, are sorted, preserved, pickled, and repackaged for distribution via a 'supermarket', a restaurant, and via mobile food groups like Meals-on-Wheels. **Fig. 5.21 – 5.22** Oi-Yee (Helen) Siu, Y3, Mycelium Foam Formwork-Casting Facility. Mushrooms grow in concrete tubs beneath the surface of Pier K in the Brooklyn Navy Yard. The mycelium is farmed as alternative rigid foam, creating biodegradable concrete formwork. Drying towers puncture the pier surface, beckoning visitors to a mushroom restaurant. The process proposes a symbiotic relation with its industrial neighbours, using wood pulp and coffee grounds to feed the farm, and making the formwork for future industrial structures. **Fig. 5.23** Katie Cunningham, Y3, Gowanus Mussel Farm. Zebra Mussels, an invasive species brought to New York's waters on Shipping boats hulls'. Locates In Gowanus Bay, a heavily polluted site off the Upper Bay of New York Harbour, a series of mussel silos clarify water quality, creating localised zones of crystal diving conditions. The mussel shells grow over articulated structures, forming grotesque building elements in an underwater picturesque landscape . The resulting mussel-shell encrustations develop into a new architecture of underwater grotto-esquery.

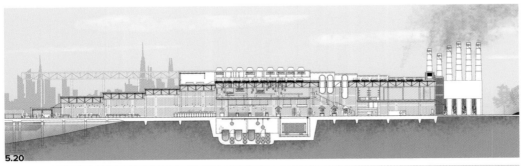

5.20

5.21

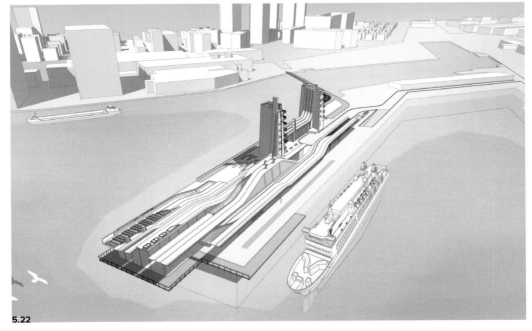

5.22

5.23

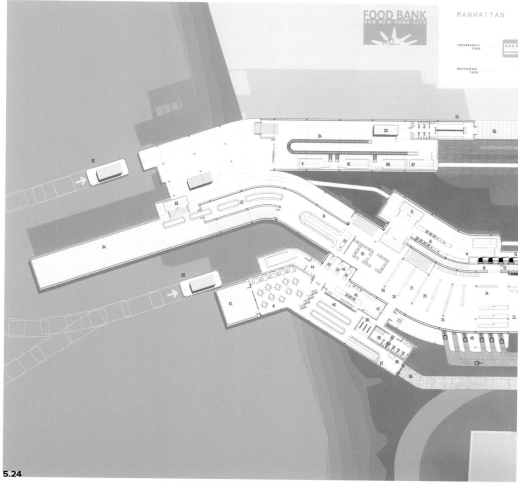

5.24

The Peckham Experiment

Christine Hawley, Paolo Zaide

In 1926, two pioneering doctors, George Scott Williamson and Innes Hope Pearse, started a radical project in South London and opened the Pioneer Health Centre. This was not a medical practice as we understand it today, but a revolutionary approach to health and wellbeing. They proposed that the medical world need not be prescriptive and responsive to specific ailments – instead, it ought to focus on why these ailments occured in the first place. With the introduction of the NHS in 1949, the emphasis was to provide facilities and resources that treated illness, the Peckham Experiment focused on the opposite – what it is that keeps people well.

This year Unit 6 set out to investigate the principles of the Peckham Experiment and their architectural consequences in the context of the 21st century. The unit took a train journey from Budapest, Vienna to Vals, Switzerland; a European cross-section that presented health as a lifestyle, not a prescription, an opportunity to observe the role that architecture plays. The themes were visible in the work of a range of architects, from the intricately detailed Post Office by Otto Wagner, the socialist living conditions of Vienna's Sargfabrik Estate, the futuristic Gasometer by Co-op Himmelblau, to Peter Zumthor's experiential Thermal Baths.

Unit 6 began the year by exploring one idea about physical or mental wellbeing. Many of these initial interests evolved into small buildings, showcasing an element of sensory and experiential wellbeing, such as fragrant gardens hidden within Regents Park, moments of refuge that reside in Canvey Island and seaweed baths excavated from a blue lagoon. Others were smaller scale insertions into daily routine, for example, napping cubicles that could be placed around London to encourage rest. Even radical public installations were created, using wallpaper, bananas and one student's wardrobe as a means of testing public trust.

The major project was sited in future Peckham and close consideration was given to the areas current,

past and future circumstances. The Unit researched different aspects of Peckham in groups, extracting a range of data and cultural information and exploring it through drawing models; collectively creating an investigative archive. By combining these findings, the Unit developed programs with either direct responses to Peckham's current condition or well-substantiated speculations about its future.

Max, Jamie, Laura and Nadia identified housing as a key area of architectural wellbeing. With a range of interlocking units and courtyard spaces, Max questioned the level of social cohesion in Peckham's existing housing typologies. Jamie responded to the isolation experienced by some in the area's sheltered housing, by designing homes for the elderly that open onto a public thoroughfare. Laura too designed housing for the elderly, where residents are encouraged to build relationships by spending time in their allotments. Nadia Wikborg's programme involved the intergration of a public laundrette, elderly housing and lemon tree gardens, with fragrances encouraging the young and old residents to intergrate.

Other students addressed the challenges of Peckham's changing and multicultural demographic. Aiko, for example, responded to the increase of young parents in Peckham, whilst Chengcheng used craft workshops to support the retired workforce of Peckham. Claire Seager and Andrew Yap explored the traditions and nutritional benefits of Peckham's diverse cuisine.

Through a range of approaches Chris Straessle, Olivia Hornby and Joyce Chen each set out to improve leisure facilities by reintroducing the theatrical arts to Peckham. Chris activated an empty park square with a highly flexible theatre that unfolds onto the landscape. Olivia designed numerous suspended spaces creating acoustic isolation from the bustle of the public below. Joyce chose to build upon the foundations of an old cinema, constructing a submerged theatre and pocketed gardens as a means of supporting Peckham's growing theatrical interest.

Catherine Penn, Yolanda Leung and Tzen Chia set out to reinvent neglected structures in key locations. Catherine and Yolanda both looked at the multistorey car park proposing programmes that support the council's initiatives to create a cultural destination, alongside a developing high street. Tzen's project transforms the nearby railway arches into bamboo-growing workshops and a public bicycle facility that creatively address the sustainable aims of Southwark.

The importance of public landscaping was explored by Joe Travers-Jones and Emily Priest. Joe designed a crematorium; translating the linear landscape into the procession of a service. Emily focused on preserving nature in the context of Peckham's ever-changing landscape, designing undulating gardens that enhance the walk up to Burgess Park from Peckham Square.

We would like to thank our technical tutor, Matthew Springett, and our critics: CJ Lim, Carlos Jimenez, Nicholas Elias and Sabine Storp.

Year 2: Max Butler, Xi Yao (Joyce) Cheng, Jamie Hignett, Olivia Hornby, Aiko Nakada, Catherine Penn, Emily Priest, Claire Seager, Chris Straessle, Joe Travers-Jones, Zisheng (Andrew) Yap

Year 3: Tzen Chia, Tom James, Heng In (Yolanda) Leung, Chengcheng Peng, Nadia Wikborg, Laura Young

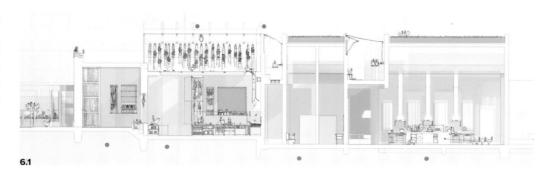

6.1

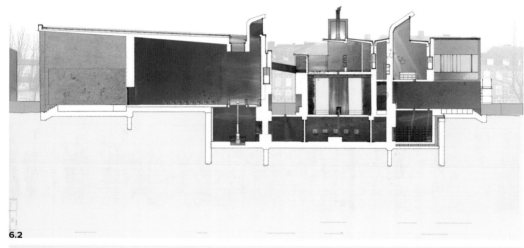

6.2

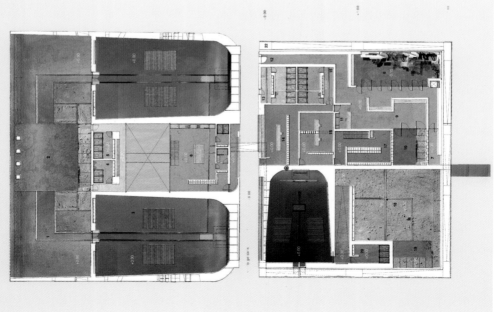

6.3

Fig. 6.1 Claire Seager, Y2, Cookery School, detail of cross-section. The building celebrates the 'coming together' that good food inspires by providing cooking spaces and a chef apprenticeship scheme for people living in Peckham. The various ethnicities of Peckham are catered for in large kitchens, arranged around courtyard dining and gardens for growing produce. **Fig. 6.2 – 6.3** Joseph Travers-Jones, Y2, Crematorium, ground plan and detail of long section. Given total privacy whilst moving through the building, each party experiences a sequence of quiet and isolated spaces, candlelit seating, and peaceful water gardens, going on to complete the funeral ceremony amongst celebratory spaces on the roofscape. The building developed from the idea of a procession; carefully chosen lighting and materiality enhance the sensory states of the service. **Fig. 6.4** Chengcheng Peng, Y3, Community Centre, external render showing overall building within context. The building offers supporting groups for expectant mothers and a short stay creche, and workshop classes to educate the local adults. Waste products from the workshop would be recycled as aggregate for concrete construction in the local area. **Fig. 6.5 – 6.6** Joyce Chen, Y2, internal view of submerged theatre and final model. By reutilising the basement foundations of the old cinema on site the building physically and socially reconstructs Peckham's performing arts culture. Constructed from the excavated earth and gabions, the auditorium is submerged into the site. Revolving mechanistic doors are an important feature, opening out onto pocketed gardens during the summer.

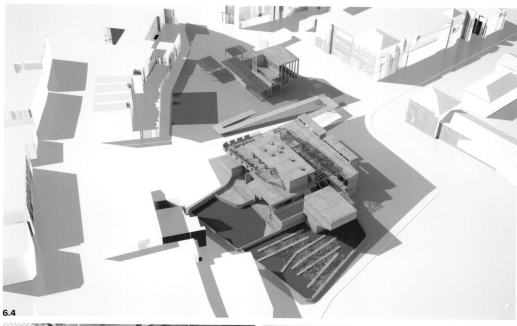

6.4

6.5

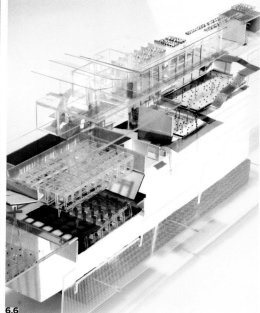

6.6

Fig. 6.7-8 Laura Young, Y3, Soil Association Research Centre & Housing for the Elderly, external view wild flower gardens and internal view looking onto allotments. On a green corridor between Burgess Park and Peckham Rye, the architecture preserves the natural qualities of Peckham's 'good soil' Prototyping new ways of cultivating environments outdoors for a wide variety of crop types, the scheme develops new elderly housing typologies based on the engagement with the outdoors, allowing occupants to establish their own ground as guardians to the gardens whilst preserving the public thoroughfare. **Fig. 6.9** Catherine Penn, Y2, The Peckham Plex Carpark, roof elevation. The project focusses on seasonal change incorporating a rooftop ice rink with dual functionality as a summer reflecting pool, and sculptural canopies channel rainwater into an outdoor 'ice bar' in winter. **Fig. 6.10** Olivia Hornby, Y2, Peckham Music Centre, short section. A community centre with auditorium, music school, cafe and musical therapy centre. To acheive acoustic isolation, the building is suspended over public open space where each acoustic space is suspended in a specific way to acheive desired musical qualities, whilst the public space below is left open to the elements. **Fig. 6.11** Max Butler, Y2, Mixed Income Housing Association, view of overall scheme, shifting from roof plan (bottom) to elevation (top). A diverse mix of interlocking residences enclose multi-level gardens and a range of communal facilities. Adjacent to streets running through the scheme sit semi-public shared gardens. Residents are encouraged to occupy and ammend these spaces.

6.7

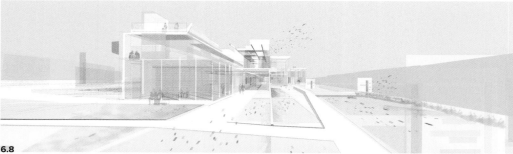

6.8

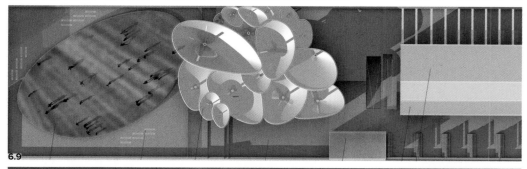

6.9

6.10

6.10

Fig. 6.12 Nadia Wikborg, Y3, Launderette & Sheltered Housing, sectional model and ground floor plan. The building brings the community of Peckham together in a landscape of fragrant lemon trees and freshly aired laundry, inviting the public to interact with the elderly residents through a lemonade cafe as well as a public garden where they can meet and exchange stories. **Fig. 6.13** Chris Straessle, Y2, A light intervention on an otherwise empty park. The main part of the building is a black box theatre, where this particular theatre design can be easily adapted to many types of performance requirements. And in response to the landscape, the building also has an open-air theatre. The theatre's double skin envelope encases pockets of inhabitation where it widens, and folds out onto the parkscape. **Fig. 6.14 – 6.15** Tzen Chia, Y3, Bamboo Bicycle Grow &

Workshop, Internal rendering of workshop and view down main corridor. The building is made up of a flexible sequence of spaces designed to suit the seasonality and cycles of everyday life in accordance to the growing rates of bamboo. Empowering the community with skills and new means of alternative transport whilst the allotment and cooking areas encourage physical and social wellness. **Fig. 6.16** Emily Priest, Y2, Preservation Gardens, Seed Bank & Research, perspectival view and sectional elevation. Suburban Peckham seems to have lost its agricultural heritage in an effort to preserve the linear park that leads up to Burgess Park, the preservation gardens become dense and sparse, and the vegetation would become experiential.

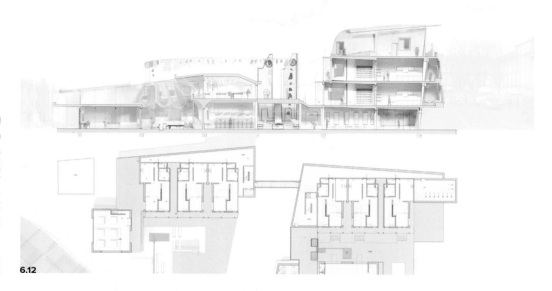

6.12

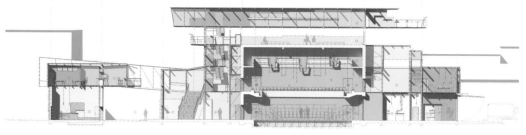

6.13

6.14

6.15

Fig. 6.16 Jamie Hignett, Y2, sheltered housing for the elderly and artists housing, axometric view with cut-away moments. A mixed typology of artists studios and sheltered housing for the elderly to reduce the isolation between these two communities. In reaction to existing unconsidered models, the scheme provides a sense of identity and autonomy to the residents. The housing for the elderly overlooks a public thoroughfare that runs through the building; elements of which can open out blurring the threshold between private and public space. The residents can inhabit the bedroom facades with their posessions to express their character.
Fig. 6.17 Aiko Nakada, Y2, Peckham Threefold, Day Care Centre & Laundrette, in response to the increase in young parents situated in Peckham this building provides a place for parents to socialise and carry out important daily tasks. The project stemmed from a delicate awareness towards the protective nature of a parent and child; the buildings structure safely encloses the child whilst providing viewing points for the parent to watch over them. **Fig. 6.18 – 6.19** Yolanda Leung, Y3, The Market Intervention. In recognition of Southwark Council's effort to improve the area of the hugely underused carpark, this project explores the notion of redeveloping the carpark into a market space with scattered mobile modules of foldable stalls and expandable kitchen pods. The reason behind the foldable modules lies in the idea of renovation, where the carpark is not completely invaded but enhanced. The exisiting gallery spaces and Frank's Cafe and Campari Bar would be retained.

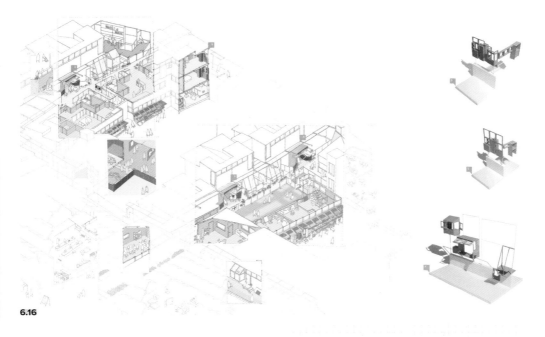

6.16

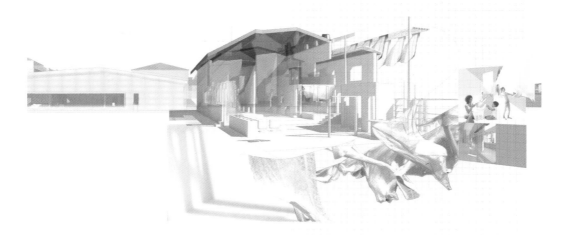

6.17

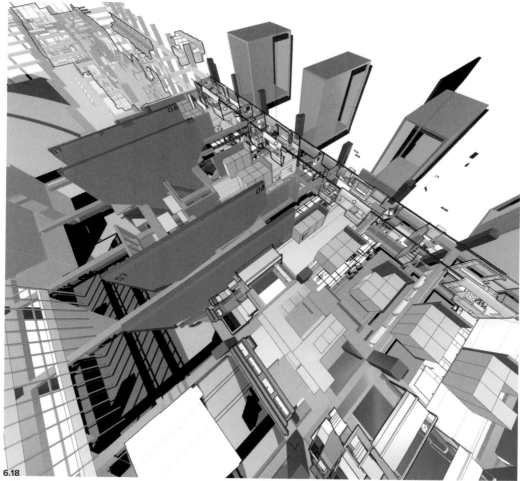

6.18

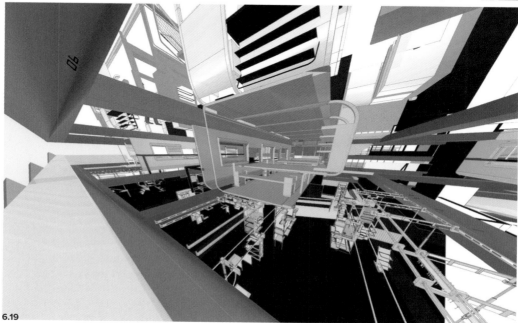

6.19

Workshop Cultures

Ming Chung, Nick Tyson

'At a point when I was stuck in my work, he asked me, "What is your guiding intuition?" I replied on the spur of the moment, "Making is thinking".'
Richard Sennett, *The Craftsman*

Unit 7 continues to investigate architecture as a material practice whereby making is intrinsic to a way of working and thinking about design. With this in mind, students are encouraged to cultivate a material discipline over the course of the year, developing material prototypes to stimulate strategic design propositions. Working from detail to strategy challenges the conventional design process and offers speculative opportunities for material invention.

Our aim is to directly connect the design studio to the places where work is made. We regard the fabrication workshop as the best environment for design ideas to be nurtured, where students can develop familiarity with both manual tools and digitally controlled machines and have contact with specialist makers. Thinking through making allows tacit decisions to be evidenced and seized upon in an open cycle of experimentation, an activity that aims to reposition materials at the centre of architectural production.

Carapace
The year began with material research and hands-on investigations for the design of a Carapace (an exoskeleton or shell) at 1:1 scale. The structure required a response to the human scale and hosted a light programme entitled 'People Meet'. Carapace was developed through detailed prototypes and hand-assembled systems that were characterised by inherent properties of the individually selected material.

An understanding of workshop culture was introduced with intensive design and make sessions, machine and software inductions and visits to unique fabrication facilities such as Grymsdyke Farm. To make visible the tacit decisions of a material-led design process, the project was documented in the form of flowcharts and instructional manuals.

The interpretation of Carapace was materially diverse and included deployable structures such as Kate Slattery's kerfed oak tensegrity framework, Tracy Xiao's woven cedar and steel gridshell and Frances Lu's cellular paper furniture. Soft systems that were generated from interlocking components or looped stitches such as Suhee Kim's non-woven body textile, Phoebe Nickols's reinforced laminated cork screens and Sonia Ho's copper and rope crochet nets. Tessellating component systems such as Julian Siravo's CNC milled, cast and 3D printed bricks and Xin Zhan's laser-cut, heat-formed acrylic trays.

Field Trip: Copenhagen
In November the Unit travelled to Copenhagen, a place with a rich tradition of design, craft and manufacture. As well as visits to seminal and contemporary Danish architecture, guided visits were made to Fritz Hansen's furniture production facilities, GXN Studio at 3XN Architects and the innovative research environment at CITA, the Center for Information Technology and Architecture. The Unit also presented projects at the School of Architecture at the Royal Danish Academy of Fine Arts.

The former Burmeister & Wain shipyard in Refshaleoen is a harbour island close to the city centre of Copenhagen and is the site location for the second design project entitled Open Guild. With the shipyard decommissioned in 1996, Refshaleoen Holding has been tasked with managing the island's future and has implemented a range of temporary strategies until redevelopment as part of the wider city plan in 2023. Regarded as a testbed for temporary uses, Refshaleoen hosts a series of creative programmes from open-air festivals to the provision of affordable work space and open source workshops. It is within this live context that Unit 7

The Bartlett School of Architecture 2013

has introduced their projects to coexist within this post-industrial landscape.

Open Guild

In pre-industrial cities, craftsmen tended to form associations based on a particular trade; confraternities of textile workers, masons, carpenters, carvers, glass workers, each of whom controlled the secrets of traditionally imparted craft skills. Open Guild suggests a re-evaluation of the traditional Guild system within the context of a contemporary material culture that includes both remote manufacture connected by open-source software and fabrication labs.

The principal field of research focused on 'Workshop Cultures' investigating hybrids of living and manufacturing, speculative models of common dwelling and the exploitation of opportunities for shared resources and energy systems. Building upon the material practices initiated in Carapace, prototypes and large-scale models were made to investigate both spatial possibilities and tectonic solutions within the context of Refshaleoen.

Inspired by the self-build assembly of a RepRap machine, Julian Siravo proposes the inhabitation of a building that makes itself, an open source factory and test rig for 3D-printed ceramic components. Phoebe Nickols' proposal for a vice-like adaptable dock for retrieved shipwrecks is informed by layered building envelopes that control environmental conditions for preservation. Kate Slattery's music hall is derived from carefully crafted studies into CNC milling and kerfed timber panels to adjust acoustic conditions. The interlocking acrylic components of Xin Zhan's light canopy facilitate optimum growing conditions by the filtering of both natural and artificial light to encourage a productive urban landscape. Frances Lu's proposal for a system of workshops and courtyard dwellings employs shipbuilding techniques to form the cellular matrix of continuous rolled steel walls.

Special thanks to our critics, guests and friends: Laura Allen, Abigail Ashton, Adam Atraktzi, Rhys Cannon, Nick Dunn, Justin Goodyer, Guan Lee, Eva Sopeoglou, Emmanuel Vercruysse, Christopher Matthews and Luis Fernandez at Atelier One Engineers, Bim Burton and Abi Abdolwahabi at the Bartlett Workshop, Jan Vejsholt and Martha McNaughton at Fritz Hansen, Kasper Guldager Jorgensen and Kim Hernforth Nielsen at 3XN, Claudia Munkeboe and Claus Gensen at Refshaleoen Holding, Paul Nicholas, Martin Tamke, Phil Ayres and Mette Ramsgard Thomsen at CITA, Victor Julebaek at the Royal Danish Academy of Fine Arts and David Briggs at Advanced Technical Panels.

Year 2
Suhee Kim, Lingzhe (Frances) Lu

Year 3
Yuen Hin (Sonia) Ho, Phoebe Nickols, Julian Siravo, Kate Slattery, Zhanshi (Tracy) Xiao, Xin Zhan

Fig. 7.1 – 7.2 Zhanshi (Tracy) Xiao, Y3, Carapace. Properties of bi-materials are explored in the design of a woven cedar and steel gridshell. The overall form is controlled by rolled steel floor templates removing the requirement for fixings at each intersection. **Fig. 7.3** Zhanshi (Tracy) Xiao, Y3, Marine City, Copenhagen. Dwelling unit model with cedar and steel grid shell, plywood perimeter beam and CNC milled cellular pontoon. The hollow cells of the pontoon are designed to flood to control buoyancy and determine a close relationship to the water. **Fig. 7.4** Yuen Hin (Sonia) Ho, Y3, Island Terminal. Copenhagen harbour model showing transportation networks that conclude in a terminus for material and cultural exchange. **Fig. 7.6** Yuen Hin (Sonia) Ho, Y3, Carapace. Crochet nets formed from single continuous looped copper thread.

Fig. 7.5, Fig. 7.7 Suhee Kim, Y2, Carapace. A replicable component made from laser-cut, non-woven fabric and synthetic leather forms an adjustable garment.

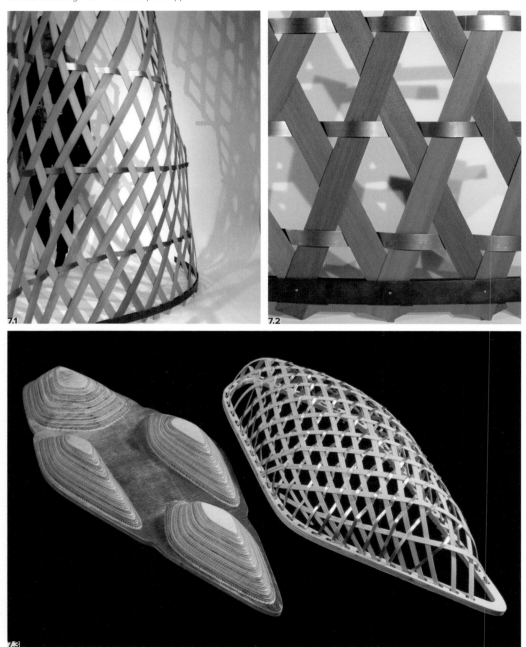

7.1

7.2

7.3

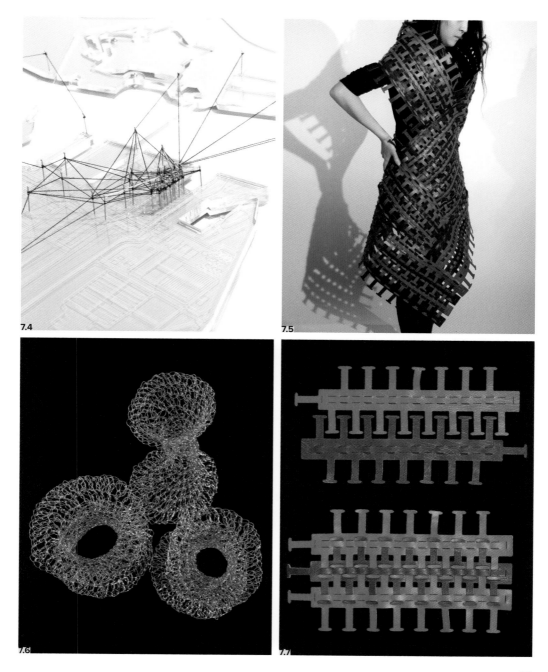

7.4

7.5

7.6

7.7

Fig. 7.8 – 7.10 Kate Slattery, Y3, Carapace. Kerfing of solid oak battens is explored to establish bending parameters and develop tensioning details in the design of tensegrity structure. Instructional diagrams set out the sequence of assembly showing deployment from a flatpack kit of parts. **Fig. 7.11, Fig. 7.13** Lingzhe (Frances) Lu, Y2, Courtyard Dwellings and Workshops, Copenhagen. Cellular units are located in relation to a matrix of continuous rolled steel walls that mediate qualities of light and connections between private and public realms. **Fig. 7.12** Lingzhe (Frances) Lu, Y2, Paper Furniture Module. Structural properties of paperboard are explored in the making of a bespoke cellular system formed from laser-cut segments.

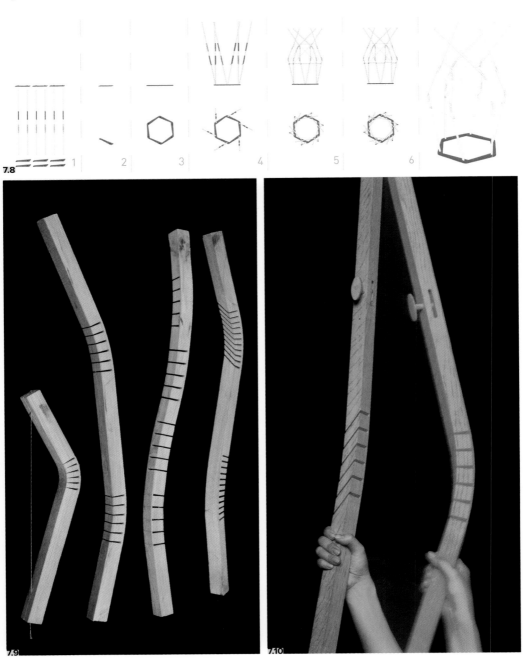

7.8 1 2 3 4 5 6

7.9 7.10

7.11

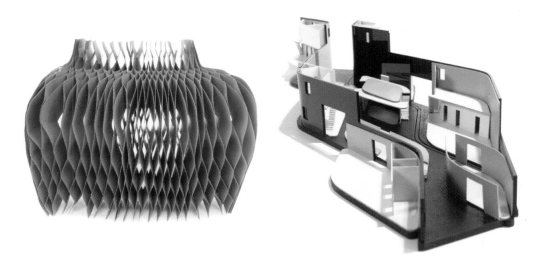

7.12

7.13

Fig. 7.14 Phoebe Nickols, Y3, Shipwreck Preservation Dock and Archive, Copenhagen. Layered building envelopes create a series of specific working platforms and controlled environmental conditions for preservation. A public interface offers a new understanding of historical artifacts through observation of the restorative process or via a more direct experience provided by the dive school. **Fig. 7.15** Phoebe Nickols, Y3, Carapace. Cork sheet is reinforced with non-woven fabric in the design of a system of interlocking laminated components that are assembled to form an acoustic screen. **Fig. 7.16 – 7.17** Xin Zhan, Y3, Proto-Agricultural Infrastructure, Copenhagen. The project proposes a restaurant, market, food labs, production buildings and landscape, to intensify growing conditions as well as host seasonal food-culture events.

The adaptable interlocking acrylic components of the canopy facilitate optimum growing conditions by the filtering of both natural and artificial light, through red and pink LED lighting establishing a temporary productive landscape. **Fig. 7.18** Xin Zhan, Y3, Light Flow. Replicable system of laser-cut, heat formed interlocking live edge acrylic trays.

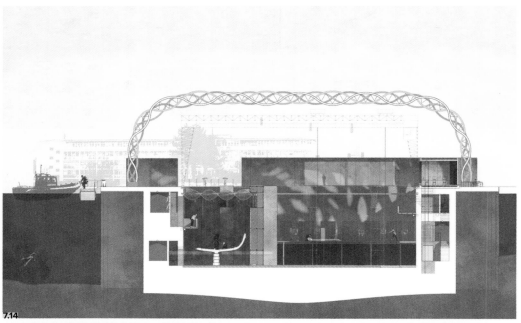

7.14

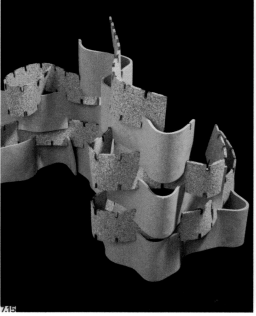

7.15

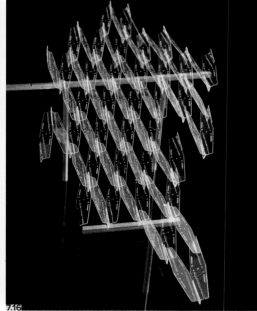

7.16

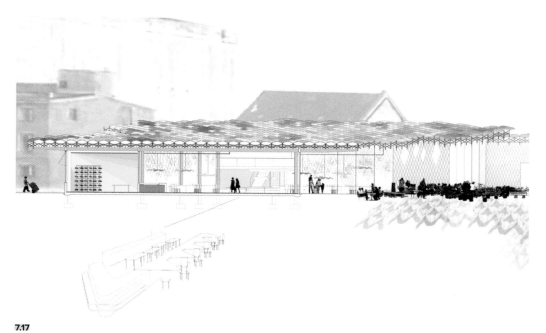

7.17

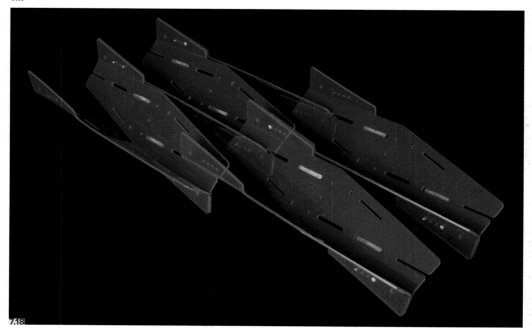

7.18

Fig. 7.19 Suhee Kim, Y2, Workshop Common Room, Copenhagen. A laser-cut Tyvek envelope encloses event space and workshop facilities and filters light in relation to seasonal activities and events. **Fig. 7.20 – 7.21** Julian Siravo, Y3, Open Source Factory and Research Lab, Copenhagen. A building system of 3D-printed ceramic components are utilised to form a series of elemental interventions within disused ship assembly shed. Workshop facilities, gantry crane with clay extruder, tunnel kiln and assembly platforms are intertwined with common spaces for social interaction and feedback. A prototypical assembly system distributed through the abandoned infrastructure promotes a self-build development of Refshaleøen Island. **Fig. 7.22 – 7.24** Julian Siravo, Y3, CNC Milled Moulds, Concrete Casts and 3-D Component Prints.

Prototypes for a tessellating brick that form a stacking topographic system.

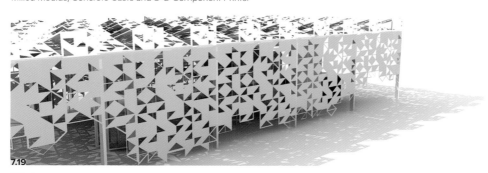

7.19

7.20

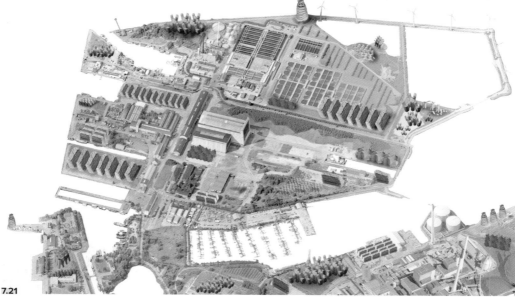

7.21

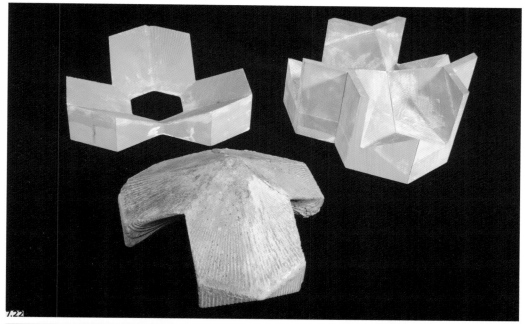

7.22

7.23

7.24

Unit 8
No Agenda

Rhys Cannon, Ben Addy

Unit 8 took the decision to abandon a thematic agenda for the year.

Clearly to have 'no agenda' is paradoxical – stating this establishes an agenda of sorts – however we framed the year this way because we were interested in the ideas, predilections, and ambitions of each individual. We continued to promote the Unit's past interests and preoccupations such as technological implementation; spatial and experiential invention and innovative representation techniques. To this end the Unit's first term work was structured around a detailed functional brief for a library, while the second and third term's work was located in a precisely defined and quantified location that would be visited on the field trip.

We travelled to Finland, visiting Helsinki, the 2012 World Design Capital, and explored some its archipelago of 330 islands before travelling through the heavily forested interior to the Finnish Lakeland and then onto the Arctic Circle. The projects were structured around the twin notions of Projection and Intervention. Projection, in the first term, comprised a detailed competition brief for a library, located either in the Aalto-designed university campus or centrally alongside the train station, parliament and cultural buildings.

A range of responses to the notion of a 21st century library arose from the students' interpretation of the brief and specifically the interaction with Finnish culture. Ness's deconstructed campus library sought to provide a series of intimate reading spaces located on the periphery of the university lake while Timmy's furnished the university with a new timber research faculty – the embedded information and expertise gathered from the study of native timber products akin to the reference volumes of a good library.

Josh celebrated the book as an artefact and represented the physical and structural qualities of volumes within the fabric, details and layout of his proposal. Further exploring the book as 'object', Jackey suggested arrays of book storage and shelving to create acoustically attenuated reading spaces. Zion challenged the organisational systems of conventional libraries and proposed new classifications which manifest in a multicoloured and mutable plan form.

The combined efforts of the Robins explored ideas of periodicals, pulp novels and book swapping, disposable reading matter provided by libraries embedded within the concourse of the rail station, engaging with a transient or commuter readership.

The Intervention project in the second term adopted the principal Helsinki harbour (recently subject to a large masterplan competition for the relocation of the various ferry terminals and release of valuable development land) as the location for all of the projects, with each student's research into the site forming the basis for their programmatic and architectural ambitions.

Reconciling the economic importance of Helsinki's centrally located ferry terminals with the value of an uninterrupted sea view for new development, Vivian Wong proposed a sunken ferry terminal in the middle of the South Harbour inlet – maintaining the horizon while corralling five different modes of transport in an interchange that is barely visible from the land edge.

Simon similarly focused on the visual sweep of the harbour, using the dock edge and sea front as a backdrop to a ballet school's performance space; layering performance, building, backdrop and audience in an ephemeral but elementally composed building. By contrast Ophelia's museum of Baltic shipwrecks developed a massive and concrete form, designed from the inside out as a collection of tectonic elements brought together on the dockside.

Jack's seasonal reading library in the first term was orchestrated to exploit the annual extremes of light and dark at the northern latitude, while his second term project developed these ideas in the context of the daily cycle of activity in an international ferry terminal. Robin Ashurst's maritime transport interchange and city market was designed around twin seasonal heat stores – subtly affecting internal temperature to profoundly affect the building operation and energy use.

Straddling a new pedestrian thoroughfare, Finbar's marine research facility combines public amenity with engineering research – dramatically revealing material effects to passersby. Robin Gu's sauna, on the island of Valkosaari, comprises a collection of built elements that in turn exploit specific aspects of the immediate context to characterise a sequence of deceptively simple spaces. Benedict's boutique water-hotel similarly draws on the surrounding environment for its internal spatial strategy.

In both projects Konrad has sought to provide expression for Finnish folk culture – first in a building dedicated to the Finnish national epic, the Kalevala, and then in a large scale music school. Robin Fu's fish market in the second term is a counterpoint to the existing historic covered market on the west side of the harbor, wrapping fish smoking and preserving facilities through the body of the building as partitions to separate market stalls and restaurants.

In the second project Timmy examined the pervasive subculture of the gaming industry in Finland, proposing an adapted park that could be turned over to large scale 'e-sports' events. Ness harnessed the spirit of the archipelago and Finnish vernacular architecture while providing much needed cultural and political representation for the people of the archipelago in the capital city.

Vasilis' dramatic underground archive in the first term was the result of a pragmatic study into book storage and circulation; his community housing

scheme in the second term was similarly the result of detailed functional research, but this time overlaid with a sensitive and lively approach to communal living and public amenity.

Year 2
Ruochong (Robin) Fu, Xiang (Robin) Gu, Konrad Holtsmark, Jack Sardeson, Benedict Tay, Simon Wimble

Year 3
Robin Ashurst, Ophelia Blackman, Tik Chun (Zion) Chan, Finbarr Anton Fallon, Man Lung (Jackey) Ip, Vanessa Lafoy, Vasilis Marcou-Ilchuk, Joshua Stevenson-Brown, Wai Yin (Vivian) Wong, Tae-In (Timmy) Yoon

Fig.8.1 Simon Wimble, Y2, Finnish National Ballet, Helsinki. The walls of the school create an ambiguous envelope, blurring the edges between the context of the South Harbour and the performance space. **Fig.8.2** Xiang (Robin) Gu, Y2, Sauna complex, Valkosaari, Helsinki. Exploded diagrams of sauna rooms. **Fig.8.3** Jack Sardeson, Y2, Ferry Terminal, Helsinki. Early sketch models of ferry terminal opening sections. **Fig.8.4** Tai-In (Timmy) Yoon, Y3, E-Sports Arena, Esplanadin Puisto, Helsinki. Composite plan of landscaped park / arena.

8.1

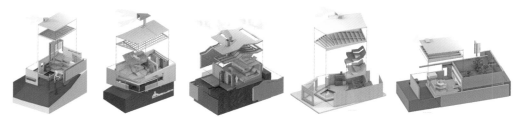

8.2

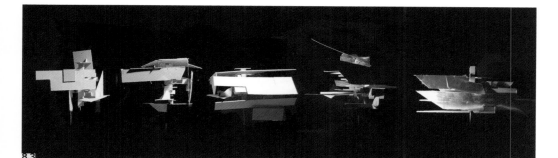

8.3

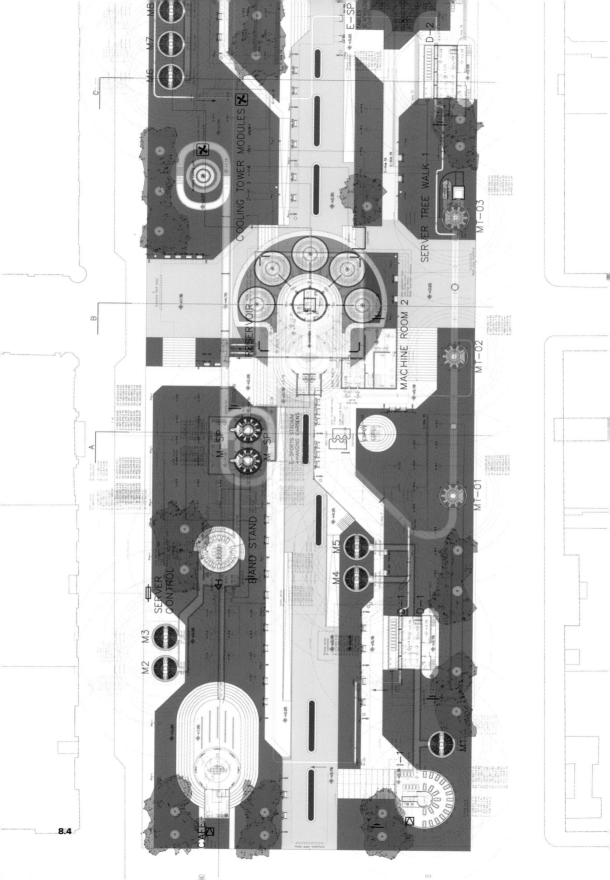

8.4

Fig.8.5 Robin Ashurst, Y3, South Harbour Transport Interchange, Helsinki. Short section through thermal stores, covered markets and upper concourse. **Fig.8.6** Vasilis Marcou-Ilchuk, Y3, Communal Housing, Helsinki, Plan view of bakery. **Fig.8.7** Ophelia Blackman, Y3, Museum of Baltic Shipwrecks, Helsinki, Model of Exterior. **Fig.8.8** Robin Ashurst, Y3, South Harbour Transport Interchange, Helsinki. Perspex ticker board rainscreen facade.

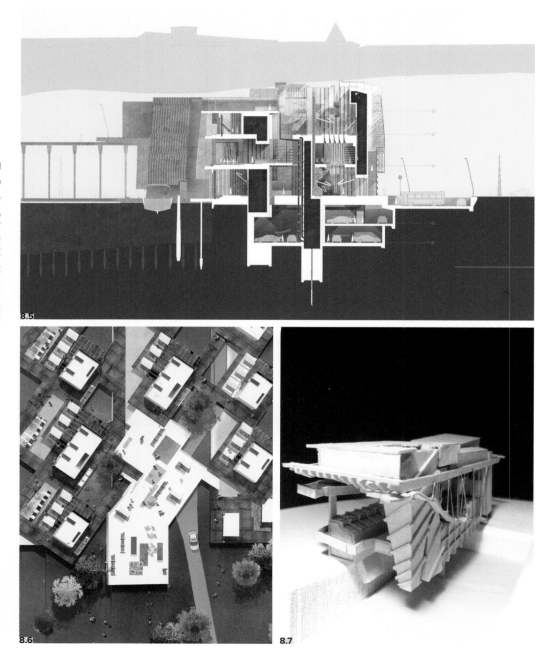

8.5

8.6

8.7

FACADE DETAIL - TRANSPORT INTERCHANGE TICKER BOARD

Light filtered through the transport interchange glass ticker board facade.

8.8

Fig.8.9 Benedict Tay, Y2, City Centre Park Library, Helsinki. Collage view from café to library landscape. **Fig.8.10** Wai Yin (Vivian) Wong, Y3, New Helsinki Cruise Terminal, Helsinki. Short section through concourses and metro lines. **Fig.8.11** Ruoching (Robin) Fu, Y2, Central Station Magazine Library, Helsinki. White card model showing main entrance, library/platform, reading rooms and magazine columns. **Fig.8.12** Josh Stevenson-Brown, Y2, Municipal Library, Helsinki. Building grid and zoning aligned to principles of book layout.

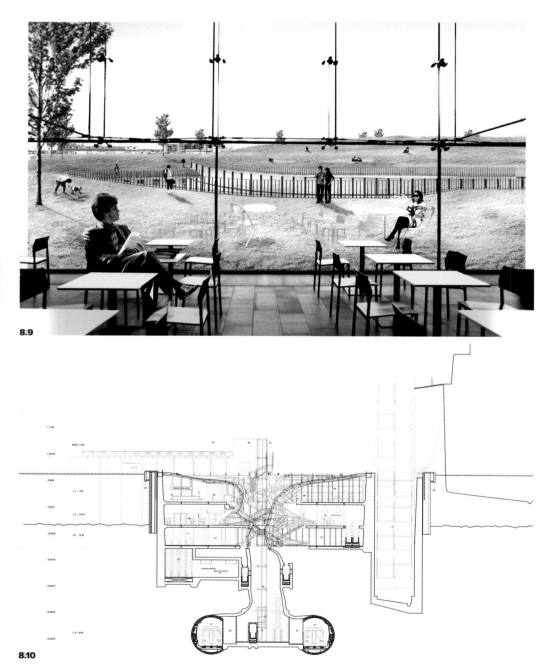

8.9

8.10

8.11

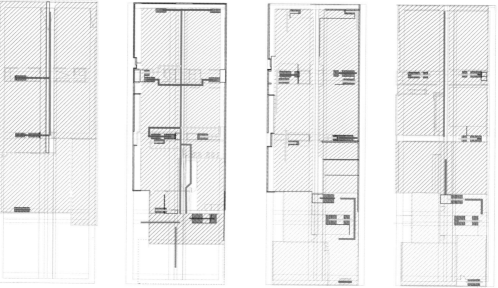

8.12

Fig.8.13 Vanessa Lafoy, Y3, Archipelago, Helsinki, South elevation. Fig.8.14 Konrad Holtsmark, Y2, Musical Heritage Centre, Helsinki, 1st floor plan. Fig.8.15 Finbarr Anton Fallon, Y3, Marine Research Institute, Helsinki. Exposing the experimental: public thoroughfare through institute. Fig.8.16 Vanessa Lafoy, Y3, Archipelago, Helsinki. Detail plan through clubhouse and postal service sorting office.

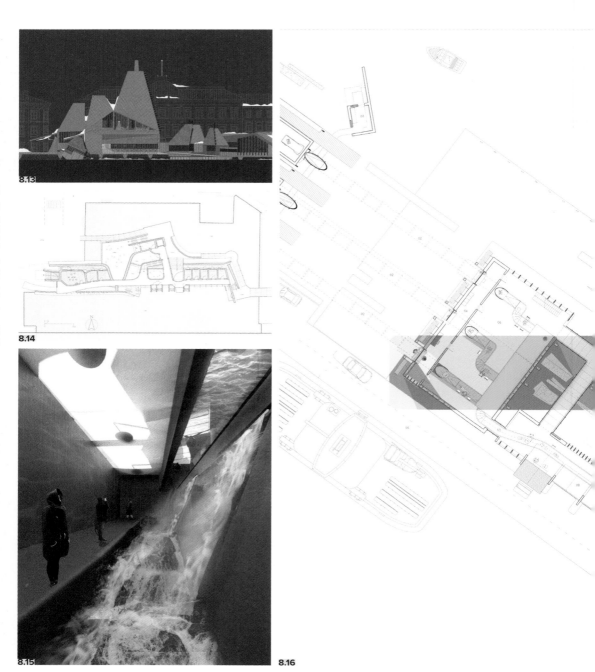

8.13

8.14

8.15

8.16

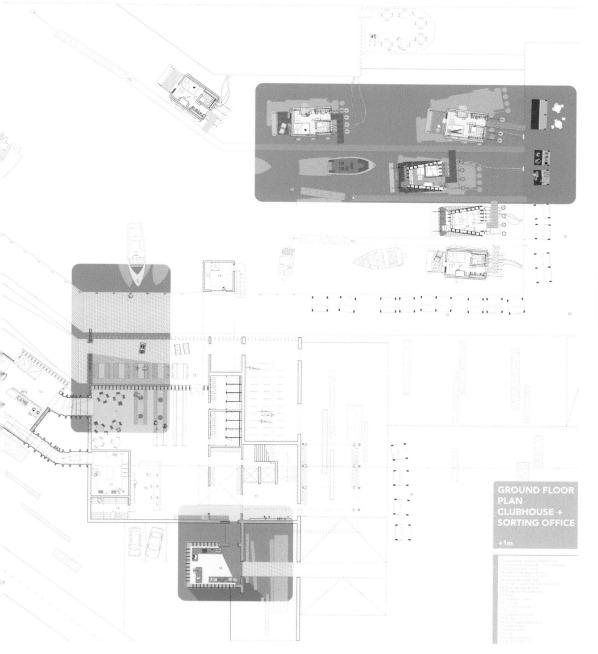

GROUND FLOOR
PLAN
CLUBHOUSE +
SORTING OFFICE

+1m

Brief City São Paulo – London

Max Dewdney, Chee-Kit Lai

The Bartlett School of Architecture 2013

'...yes it was over, it was part of London's past, it had joined all the other exhibitions, all the crashing military parades, the glittering state occasions, all the ceremony and display that come and go and help to make the public life of this city. Most of it had been pulled down now...' Extract from *Brief City*, BBC documentary, 1951

Events such as the Olympics are a form of brief city and create opportunities for cities to reinvent themselves for the world but they also bring with them questions about legacy, sustainability, economic and environmental cost. This year Unit 9 investigated the architecture of the brief city, from the 1951 Festival of Britain via 'pop-up' and the Olympics to the World Cup 2014. The architecture of the brief city explores the celebratory and ad-hoc, involving energy and innovation, but, also considers the consequences of the transitory nature of the brief city for the environmental, organisational, spatial and social aspects of urban life. The brief city encourages short-term inventiveness as a testing ground for the permanency of future projects, both social and architectural.

The brief city inhabits places that are disused and overlooked and builds into unpopular or negative spaces, bringing with it the vital energy of a society expanding into the unknown, discovering itself and redefining the individual and their relationship to the collective.

This year we focused our research between two cities in the process of redefining themselves to the world, albeit in very contrasting ways; London in the midst of defining its own post-Olympic legacy, in contrast to pre-World Cup São Paulo, once a infamous city for poverty and crime, now a global economic and cultural powerhouse.

Unit 9 was interested in the lifecycle, performance and digital mediation of the brief city through hybrid forms of architecture that combine low and high technologies. The brief city needs to be adaptable to users' needs, through function and performance, viewpoints and constructions. In pursuing their architecture, students were encouraged to make proposals that revealed interdependent relationships between permanence and temporality, reality and the hyper-real, material and immaterial, the analogue and the digital, ownership and occupation, questioning the symbiosis required for such distinct opposites. The spectacles of the Olympics and World Cup transform cities during the celebratory and temporary events. The architecture of a brief city requires the design of spatial and temporal structures peripheral to the main events and asks how can these be reclaimed or reprogrammed for the afterlife of events.

Four Dimensional City

'If temporary use is seen merely as the prototype for a long-term utilisation, then the plea for the temporary runs the risk of inadvertently demanding a right of asylum from the temporary.' 'The Temporary City' in *Four Dimensional City* by Peter Bishop and Lesley Williams

The Royal Docks is situated between City Airport and the Excel Centre, adjacent to the London Thames Barrier. It forms an axis as a portal to the newly formed city of the east and Olympic sites, and a gateway into the heart of London. Opened in 1855, it was historically built on the Plaistow Marshes and designed specifically to accommodate large steam ships, innovative in its use of hydraulic power and strategically connected to the national railway network, the remnants of which are still visible. It was the shipping centre of London until its decline and eventual closure as a working dock in the 1980s, due to wartime damage and competing technological advancements in shipping.

Post-Olympics, the area was topical as the site was earmarked for change into a new 'urban quarter' with a focus on the knowledge and green technology industries, aiming to increase cross-river and local connectivity to become a logistics hub to link into the newly forming east and to the centre of London beyond.

Infrastructure of Civility
'São Paulo is vibrant, it has a very strong physical presence... Though the private sphere remains inaccessible, everything you think and do is perceivable in the streets. In other cities, the public spaces tend to separate very clearly from daily life.'
Olafur Eliasson

São Paulo, the third largest city in the world, is a giant metropolis with a rich confluence of cultures from around the world. Like London, it is ad-hoc in nature, a dense city with a layered and complex history that incorporates Brazil's traditional and vernacular, colonial, pre-modern and modern history and is now at the heart of the country's creative drive and outward expression to the world.

São Paulo contains a potent mixture of the temporary and the permanent. The temporary encompasses the favelas and carnivals, markets, short-term housing, spectacles and events from the Grand Prix, film festivals, experimental theatre and dance, to the International Contemporary São Paulo Art Biennale. São Paulo is also home to more permanent architectural masterpieces by Oscar Niemeyer, Lina Bo Bardi and Paulo Mendes da Rocha amongst many others. Unit 9 collaborated with Escola da Cidade in locating sites for the main architectural project of the year, sited in São Paulo.

Year 2
Arti Braude, Max Friedlander, Georgina Halabi, Hao Han, Carina Tran, Chenqui (John) Wan, Nicholas Warner, Camilla Wright, Yoana Yordanova

Year 3
Alexandria Anderson, Daryl Brown, Lichao Liu, Ian Ng, Rosemary Shaw, Carolyn Tam, Panagiotis Tzannetakis

Fig. 9.1 Max Friedlander, Y2, Social Service of Commerce (SESC). SESC is a private Brazilian institution, which operates not for profit. Run by trade, goods, services and tourism business the schemes is dedicated primarily to the social welfare of employees and their families, but open to the general community. The proposal provides a SESC for central São Paulo including a theatre, cafe and social space internally and an interactive public landscape externally that adapts according to the weather and public input. The facade system is performative and changes depending on internal occupation and the external weather conditions. (Internal perspective view). **Fig. 9.2** Yoana Yordanova, Y2, SEPASB Water Managment Plant and Culture Centre. The proposal aims to promote water recycling, integrate communities and revitalise the riverside,

through the filtration of the river water and introduction of an artificial ecosystem, which creates an urban oasis landscape along the riverside. The site is on the edge of the main river, where three underground sub-rivers meet. The built-over rivers in São Paulo cause many problems due to the lack of soil exposure and high rainfall, which results in many areas being flooded. **Fig. 9.3** Hao Han, Y2, Mal Deldoro Bus Terminal and Market Exchange. The scheme is for a public bus terminal and exchange market. The programme is a response to the social fragmentation and poor transport system in the northwestern part of São Paulo. It is designed around local bus destinations, demographics and time cycles throughout the day.

9.1

9.2

9.3

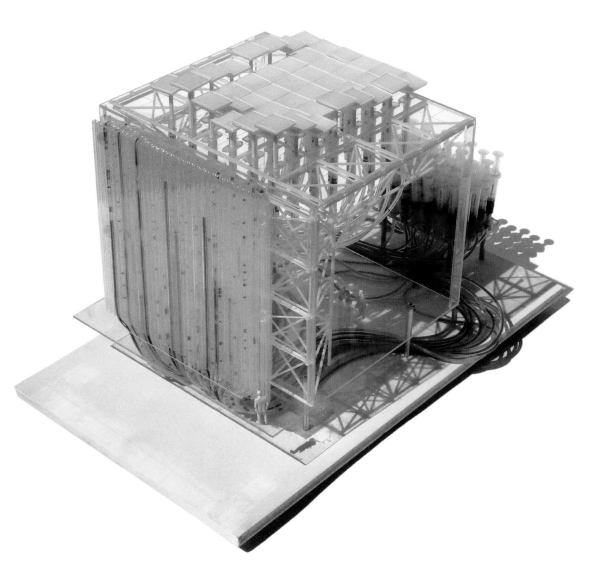

Fig. 9.4 Max Friedlander, Y2, Social Service of Commerce (SESC).1:50 Arduino working model of the intelligent facade and roof system.

9.4

Fig. 9.5 Daryl Brown, Y3, Capoeira Social Hub. Located on a fringe condition between residential and an emerging business district the building faces an existing highway and artificial river culvert. The building design augments the public space into a series of interior and exterior public and semi public spaces though interconnected circulation. Facilities include rehearsal, performance and educational spaces. **Fig. 9.6** Ian Ng, Y3, Sand Harvesting Device. The project is for the design of a mechanism that filters sand to create a prototype modular defence system for the shorelines of the River Thames, London. **Fig 9.7** Camillia Wright, Y2, Cooperative HQ. The project is sited in Newham, East London. The programme adopts the six key principles of the co-operative movement and provides a central hub for displaced communities effected by the 2012 Olympic developments. **Fig.9.8** Alexandria Anderson, Y3, Plastic Surgery Clinic, São Paulo. The project addresses the increasing demand for plastic surgery and the strive for body perfection in Brazil. The proposal contains short, medium and long stay facilities and revolves around the concept of 'beauty and the beast'. The clinical interiors are augmented with a series of devices that control users' perception of space from light to dark, with apertures and mirrors which contrast with the surrounding road, rail and artificial river that makes up the urban infrastructure.

9.5

9.6

9.7

9.8

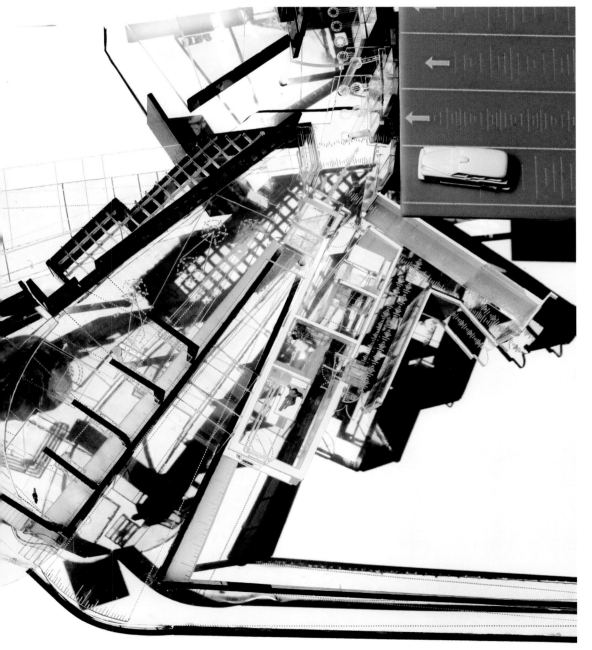

Fig. 9.9 – 9.10 Chengqi (John) Wan, Y4, Palimpsest Landscape and Printing Forum. The project addresses the site's history of failed urban landscape projects within the site in central São Paulo. The programme includes the headquarters of OCAS, the Civil Organisation for Social Action, São Paulo's 'Big Issue'. Included within OCAS is a printing press, training centre, recreational centre, and homeless accommodation set within a richly planted, programmed public landscape that is formally defined by the vertical layering of the site's rich history. **Fig. 9.11** Arti Braude, Y3, Silvicultural Centre, São Paulo. The project proposes the establishment of a Silvicultural Centre for the Brazilian Pine. It aims to encourage the proliferation of silvicultural stands on a larger scale through education, while acting also as a nursery to repopulate the city's parks.

Simultaneously, the building functions as a physical commentary on the efficient use of native timber in construction. **Fig. 9.12** Yoana Yordanova, Y2, Recycled Public Square and Bike Station. The project creates a new public square for local residents and visitors for the collection and exchange of plastic bottles. As well as a series of follies the design adapts used water bottles from nearby offices to create a floating cycle scheme. The contraption has been designed to clip onto a Barclays (Boris) bike to be used within the dock.

9.9

9.11

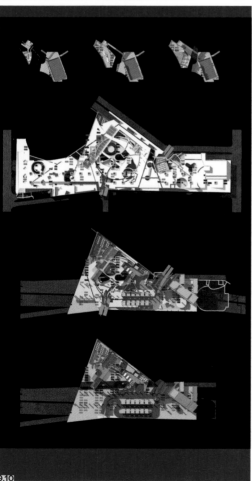

9.10

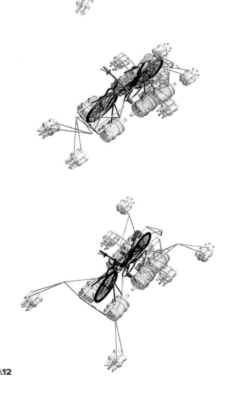

9.12

Fig. 9.13 Max Freidlander, Y2, Flag Machine. Designed for the Royal Victoria Docks, East London, the project works as a 1:1 device that uses Arduino technology to control and mix an array of colour inks which ossilate between the colours of the UK and Brazilian flags. Light is projected out to create an area for performance and celebration. Fig. 9.14 – 9.15 Yoana Yordanova, Y2, SEPASB Water Managment Plant and Culture Centre. Fig. 9.16 Ian Ng, Y3, Institute of Materials. Utilising surplus waste materials the building acts as a prototype for the use of recycled and hybrid materials in construction, specifically paper. The building includes facilities for recycling waste paper, workshop spaces, social spaces and a library. Fig. 9.17 Chengqi (John) Wan, Y2, Palimpsest Landscape and Printing Forum.

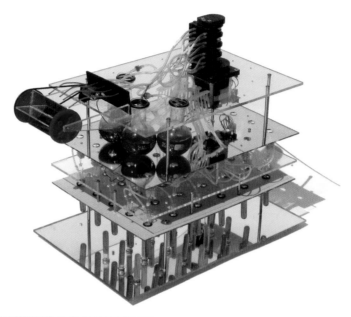

9.13

9.14

9.15

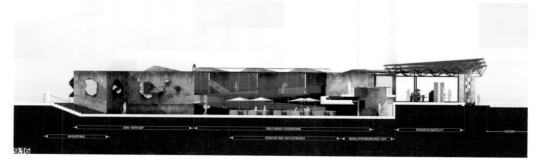

9.16

9.17

BSc Architectural Studies

Barbara Penner

The Bartlett's BSc (Hons) in Architectural Studies is a unique course that allows students to follow modules within the School in conjunction with modules in other departments of UCL. The programme has been running since 2002-3 and now has over 90 graduates and a well-established track record. Graduates have gone on to postgraduate studies and professional careers in a wide variety of fields including: journalism, landscape design, lighting design, documentary film, conservation, photography, sculpture, printmaking, arts education and management, event management, planning, law, marketing and the media, property valuation, construction management, the charity sector, and heritage institutions. They have pursued further studies at places from the Royal College of Art to ETH in Zurich as well as in various UCL Masters programmes.

The great strength of the Architectural Studies programme is its multidisciplinarity: students are able to tailor their own course of study to suit their particular interests and future postgraduate and career plans. It suits highly motivated, independent students who are interested in architecture and urban studies and who wish to take advantage of electives on offer elsewhere in UCL. Popular choices are History of Art, Management, Languages, Economics, History, Philosophy, Mathematics, Anthropology, Law, Archaeology, and Geography.

There are two specially tailored course modules for Architectural Studies students within the School, The Dissertation and Project X, extracts of which are reproduced on the following pages.

Architectural & Interdisciplinary Studies
From 2013-4, the BSc (Hons) Architectural Studies course is being renamed the BSc (Hons) Architectural & Interdisciplinary Studies. It will be available as a three year degree option and as a four year (with year abroad) degree option. As before, the programme is available as a transfer option for second and third year BSc Architecture students within The Bartlett.

Year 2
Nadira Amrani, Amanda Campbell, Stephen Henderson, Casper Horton-Kitchlew, Alishe Khan, Fong Yi Khoo, Laura Skeggs, Ou Qianwen

Year 3
Kate Edwards, Rebecca Li, Patrick O'Callaghan, Amalie White, Alexander Zyryaev

BSc Architectural Studies Dissertation

The Dissertation in Architectural Studies enables students to undertake an independent research project of 10,000 words. The emphasis is on conducting original research and producing an in-depth written report, supported by appropriate visual and textual documentation. This course is taught through individual or small group tutorials, supplemented by occasional seminars and group meetings. The aims of the Dissertation are to enable students to conduct primary research, to think critically about issues with architectural implications, and to develop and showcase practical writing and presentation skills.

Year 2
Stephen Henderson, Alishe Khan, Fong Yi Khoo

Year 3
Rebecca Li, Patrick O'Callaghan, Amalie White, Alexander Zyryaev

Amalie White, Year 3
The Bartlett, Architectural Pedagogy and Wates House – An Historical Study

The subject of this dissertation is the design of Wates House, opened in 1975 and now on the cusp of a major refurbishment. To produce this work, Amalie used interviews with Bartlett staff, journal archives, and the original designs for the building.

The year 1960 marked a significant turning point for the Bartlett when Lord Richard Llewelyn-Davies was appointed Chair of Architecture. During his time as Chair, he not only changed the Bartlett architecture course, but also created a whole new Faculty in which the discipline was to be taught. He made an amalgamation between Town Planning and Architecture, along with other research groups to form a new Faculty for UCL, The Bartlett Faculty School of Environmental Studies in 1969 (the Faculty was renamed the School of the Built Environment in 1992). This project then developed into organising the commission (1971) and construction (1973-1975) of a new building for the Bartlett: Wates House. Wates House was to physically reflect the newly established ideas in architectural pedagogy as established by the 1958 Oxford Conference. Understanding this contextual background is what makes Wates House such an important building to study. It is a living artefact of one of the most pivotal historical shifts in architectural education in Britain. [...]

The architecture firm commissioned for the design of Wates House in 1971 was Architects' Co-Partnership Incorporated (ACP). The firm was founded in 1939 and had since expanded to working in both the public and private sector in the UK and across the world. During the 1960s they had designed buildings for educational institutions such as the universities of Oxford and Cambridge and by the 1970s had gained a range of awards from the Royal Institute of British Architects, the Civic Trust and the Ministry of Housing and local government. Their profile suggested therefore their suitability for the job of designing a Faculty for UCL.

It is worth highlighting that the client for the new Bartlett building was UCL, not the Bartlett Faculty itself. UCL, an institution comprising a vast range of departments, located in the centre of London, with many listed buildings in its surroundings, meant that it was, and remains, a difficult task for it to expand and construct new spaces. Therefore, when the opportunity arose for UCL to buy a plot of land in Bloomsbury, formerly the site of Endsleigh Hotel, the agenda was not entirely focused on fulfilling the specific needs for the Bartlett Faculty alone, but on creating a new stock of spaces for the university generally. Moreover, not only did the client set the brief it also financed it, which in the economic climate of Britain during the 1970s did not allow for an extravagant design. The budget was boosted by a donation from Neil Wates's Wates Foundation (Wates was a friend of Llewelyn-Davies), giving £450,000 (with an average inflation of 6.2% a year this amount would be worth £5,386,500 in 2012). The donation was specifically given for the efforts of housing the School of Environmental Studies; hence the Wates name was given to the new building. Through this donation, the Wates Foundation set a condition that the building was to be completed within three years of the architects' receipt of the brief. In addition, the Wates Foundation had its own construction company, which UCL then employed to build Wates House. Therefore, Wates' donation was a smart investment for the foundation.

Limitations in time and budget were not the only concerns affecting the design of the Bartlett Faculty. The site itself was restricting, due to the narrowness of Endsleigh Gardens and the requirement for surrounding buildings to access daylight, which limited the height of the new building. The site, therefore, predetermined a rectangular block to occupy the space, as much of Georgian London had done, and it was likely for this reason that ACP never explored any other alternative form.

The most interesting aspect of the entire design process is the relationships between the Bartlett staff and students, and the client and the architects. An extended Wates House Committee (WHC) was set up, combining professors, junior staff and students from the Bartlett to outline the user requirements and specifications. The new building was to include workshops, demonstration rooms, laboratories for lighting, acoustics, thermal studies, wind tunnel, and a photographic room, a library for 20,000 volumes and 60 readers, seminar rooms, a college flat, and work space for some 180 undergraduates, 200 postgraduates and between 80 and 90 full-time academic, technical and administrative staff. We can see from the list of laboratories and workshops that Wates House was to facilitate Llewelyn-Davies's vision for a scientific and practical pedagogic approach to architectural education and research. This was going to mark the biggest difference in architectural education that the Bartlett had yet to experience – practical work was finally to be encouraged away from the drawing board. Although, there had been attempts to create a practical curriculum for Bartlett students, such as the Carpenters' Company classes at the beginning of the twentieth century, as well holding classes with Engineers and life drawing with the Slade School, Wates House was to provide a bespoke testing ground for environmental studies. Research laboratories and outdoor workspace was to facilitate a specialised scientific approach for architectural research that was to be progressive and innovative rather than encourage students to regurgitate historical ideas.

However, in the context of London at the time there was an alternative means for pushing architectural innovation, as demonstrated by the emerging avant-garde architectural group, Archigram, whose conceptual drawings and montages broke the boundaries of what people thought architecture and technology was capable of achieving for society. Their work was circulated amongst architectural students through their magazine Zoom, receiving a cult following. But, according to Simon Sadler:

'Some students, for example those at London University's Bartlett School swayed by lecturer John Christopher Jones's "Design Methods," disregarded Zoom as lacking substance. Jones's lofty, professional approach could hardly be more different from Zoom: Design Methods "teaches design as a series of logical decisions and not 'inspired flashes'", wrote Jones in a 1969 comparison of his own Bartlett School with the AA and Regent Street Polytechnic nearby.'[1]

Thus, the Bartlett during Llewelyn-Davies' time was becoming a practical environment for architectural education, as opposed to one encouraging philosophical and utopian ideas, as was being demonstrated by Archigram's approach. However, that is not to say the Bartlett was not concerned with design; in fact a report by Abercrombie and Hunt shows that through the 1960s design was intensified and given greater emphasis within the course.[2] In 1960, a focus on structures dominated the students' workload, but was reduced as the decade progressed, with design taking a stronger lead.

In terms of the aesthetical design of the new Bartlett Faculty building, planner Michael Edwards recalls that Llewelyn-Davies did not want the building to fossilise a moment in time nor embed a particular method of education in a structure, as he was aware education continually evolves. Instead, he believed that it would be better to have a building that was not precious, that could be reconfigured, in which walls could be knocked down and 'no one would have to worry about protecting marble floors'. [...]

Although Wates House was envisioned by Llewelyn-Davies to be flexible and free of boundaries there were other ideas about pedagogy that influenced the philosophy of the school building and its spatial configuration. In fact, the Bartlett had for some time demonstrated a serious interest and concern for monitoring architectural pedagogy and its development. It had commissioned a British psychologist, Jane Abercrombie, who had a strong interest in educational methods at UCL, to produce the aforementioned report on the Bartlett's development from 1960-1970. The report explains the

changes made in course structure and departmental structure, all supported with statistical data. As indicated by this report and others by Abercrombie (including one on medical students at UCL), she was an advocate for small group learning as the most productive means for individual development. With her presence in the department during the 1960s (she also taught psychology to the architecture students), it is very likely that she influenced the choice of the cellular structure design that was deployed in Wates House. This helps to explain why there was no suggestion in the brief for having a large gathering space or for creating a building with large, expansive, open studios.

According to a report from 1974 in Building Design a college spokesman (who could have been Llewelyn-Davies himself) stated that Wates House was to be a 'sort of warehouse', which would 'churn staff and students together'. It is unsurprising that the Bartlett should want all of its students and staff, working in the same field, the built environment, to work side by side and under the same roof, as the aim was to break the boundary between disciplines and create a cohesive intellectual hub. As Abercrombie and Hunt noted, the new faculty 'differed from others in University College in that is represented a School without departmental boundaries. It also included members drawn from ten other departments in University College'. However, the Bartlett was not the first School of Architecture designed to 'churn' different disciplines and members of the department together in order to encourage a level of intellectual exchange and social interaction. Paul Rudolf's design for the Yale School of Art and Architecture, built in 1963, was designed specifically to bring architects, planners, painters, sculptors and graphic artists under one roof. 'Each discipline has its own precise area, but when possible they are brought together (i.e. jury space, student lounge)'. Furthermore,

'[Rudolf] believed that students from all years would benefit from working together in the same environment and could learn from listening to the live criticism examinations of other students' work. It was for these educational reasons that he conceived the central teaching spaces for both the architects and designers in this form.'[3]

Thus, Rudolf's school building behaved like a warehouse in that it contained expansive open space. In contrast, the Bartlett's site for Wates House did not permit an equivalent grandiose vessel as at Yale. The nature of the site along with a philosophy to encourage small-group teaching prohibited Wates House from actually becoming a 'real' warehouse. However, at least the concept of a warehouse as an industrious environment was established at Wates House as all studio floors were left as bare concrete, providing a blank canvas to map the scars of 'messy' production such as spray-painting and plaster modelmaking. [...]

1   Simon Sadler, Archigram: Architecture without Architecture. Cambridge, MA: MIT Press, 2005, p.158
2   M. L. J. Abercrombie and S.M. Hunt, 1960-1970: Ten Years of Development in a School of Architecture. University College London, 1977

3   T. Monk, 'The Art and Architecture Building, Yale University, Connecticut' in The Art and Architecture of Paul Rudolph. West Sussex: Wiley Academy, 1999, p.42

Project X

Elizabeth Dow, Chee-Kit Lai

Project X aims to help students build a creative and reflective practice of their own. It enables them to undertake a mode of working that particularly interests them and an independent practice-based project in which they can research and pursue a subject of their preference. Students are asked to think of architecture in interdisciplinary ways, explore alternative approaches to design and situate their work within a broader cultural context. The work is developed in conjunction with a short written piece. A series of key questions confront students at different stages of the year concerning the nature of their practice, the contribution of their work to the broader field of architecture, the originality of their project, and the selection of appropriate media for the ideas pursued.

We started the year by asking the students to find an 'unloved and forgotten' architecture. Once found, they proceeded to document this piece of architecture in a manner that both complimented its qualities but also, more importantly, let us all learn to love the unloved and forgotten.

We travelled to Venice for the 2012 Architecture Biennale, which also further inspired and influenced the students' individual projects and research paths.

We were very pleased to have Professor Jane Rendell lead two workshops this year. The first encouraged the students to work together to develop, reinterpret and hybridise their initial projects and make a piece of group work. In the second, Jane asked them to develop and reconsider their design work through writing, drawing upon the themes of her 'Site-Writing' work.

Each student has followed a research path that initially stemmed from the first project, but developed in a unique and personal direction. The resulting projects are speculative and diverse, as is the use of media, ranging from casting, set design and projection to community consultation, documentary, domestic chemistry, caramelising and weaving.

Project X would very much like to thank Professor Jane Rendell and Dr Barbara Penner for their support throughout the year, as well as the critics: Christine Bjerke, Graham Burn, Grace Catenaccio, Emma Cheatle, Christophe Gerard, Kevin Green, Geraldine Holland, Rebecca Lane, Frosso Pimenides, Peg Rawes, Gabriel Warshafsky, Owain Williams and Alessandro Zambelli.

Year 2
Nadira Amrani, Amanda Campbell, Casper Horton-Kitchlew, Alishe Khan, Fong Yi Khoo, Laura Skeggs

Year 3
Kate Edwards, Rebecca Li, Patrick O'Callaghan, Amalie White, Alexander Zyryaev

Fig. X.1 Alexander Zyryaev, Y3, Questions of Representation.
Exploring methods of representation through constructing
and photographing still-life original installations and partial
facsimiles. Initially addressing gender construction present
in Disney merchandise and leading on to an inquiry into the
nature of identity and authenticity. Image: The Venus of
Willendorf is one of the earliest representations of the human
body created by mankind. The sculpture's exaggerated
features of fertility reveal the values of its harsh period.
Employing the same method of representation as a means
to reveal the power of the image and express the value of
commodities in our society today.

X.1

Fig. X.2 Rebecca Li, Y3, Community at Work. A live community project intended to engage the residents of an inner-city residential block, encouraging them to determine a programme for an abandoned rooftop space. Once engaged, the project then helps them to construct a new space to enjoy and care for together. The project draws upon the constraints and conflicts faced in practice when embracing a community into the design and planning process. **Fig. X.3** Kate Edwards, Y3, Caramel Entrapment. The sugary allure of caramel pitted against the historical association of sugar and slavery. A tableau scene is both metaphoric and literal; it entices the viewer with a pure white iced cake and table top landscape, only interrupted by delicate caramel sculptures, iconic architectural forms of the sugar industry, both past and

present. This clean and neat landscape soon transgresses into a sticky inescapable mess. The drooping caramel, the cake crumb sprawl, only begins to hint at a possible disintegration of both an industry and a commercial reputation.

X.2

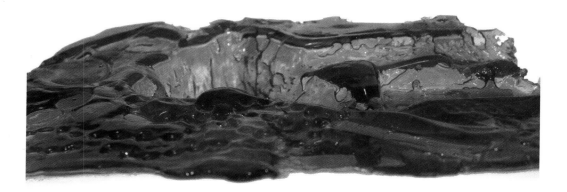

X.3

Fig. X.4 Amanda Campbell, Y2, Laura Skeggs, Y2, and Alexander Zyryaev, Y3, Basic Space. A still from a film of three bodies squeezed into tight spaces, some public, some less so. Demonstrating a new understanding and admiration for these buildings and appreciation of such non-specific available semi-public spaces. The choice of black clothing symbolised the block movement, recognising the action as an occupation.
Fig. X.5 Laura Skeggs, Y2, Breaking In - Breaking Out. The idea of 'Breaking In - Breaking Out' is explored throughout the project, from breaking into inaccessible spaces; using light, camera, vision, speculation and imagination, breaking down an understanding of physical boundaries. This theme was continued into an exploration of maps. Utilising the hybrid graphic language of map and dress patterns to consider a new understanding of how a place's history and the boundaries and thresholds of that place, might be considered, and subsequently re-considered and re-created through pattern and making.
Fig. X.6 Amanda Campbell, Y2, Take Up Space. A celebration of small sites and abandoned spaces. Challenging the conventions and limitations of habitable spaces by using the human body as a measure and scale to propose a new modular for today. **Fig. X.7** Alishe Khan, Y2, Woven Reality. A series of photographic weavings using the conventional language and craft of weaving to articulate and create hybrid vistas of Edinburgh and Venice. The invented spaces present nuanced dichotomies of factual/fictional, real/unreal and actual/fabricated space. This is a new world that might now be inhabited through imagination and subsequent narrative.

X.4

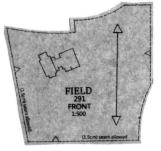

X.5

148

Fig. X.8, X.10 Kate Edwards, Y3, Memory Ornament. Cast caramel structures exploring how an initially benign, yet possibly addictive, substance might contain and evoke memories and connections to a past. Caramel can be altered and changed by burning out and re-attaching pieces hinting at a means to re-write this past. **Fig. X.9** Alishe Kahn, Y2, Woven Reality. **Fig. X.11** Fong Yi Khoo, Y2, A Guide to East London. Investigating a means of exploring and moving through the city. Initially experimenting with the surrealist Derive, extended to a technique using poetic interpretation. Understand the poem, you know where to go. Misunderstand the poem, your journey may take in new dimensions and surprising intrigue. The theme of interpretation is taken further through the creation of a graphic novel, as a guide to Whitechapel.

It uses key signifiers and poetry to make one engage with the setting in a totally new way. Among the shifting pages, the past and present are one, combining elements of the Gothic and film noir.

X.8

X.9

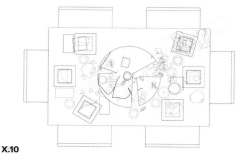

X.10

X.11

Fig. X.12 – X.13 Casper Horton-Kitchlew, Y2, Crystal Explorations. An investigation that initially explored the hidden rejected spaces of waste pipes and revealing the beauty of their mineral deposits. This inspired a 'souvenir' experiment that imported Venice canal water, condensed down from 1000ml to 100ml concentrate to meet airline security regulations, to the UK allowing for the subsequent re-hydration and the harvesting of salt crystals. The investigation of crystals continued at both macro and micro scale.

X.12

X.14

X.13

Fig. X.14 – X.16 Amalie White, Y3, Agency under Surveillance. Designs on George Orwell's 1984, applying the political and digital climates of 2013: A speculative theatre production constructing an illusion of reality and space created through projection, onto fabric screens and UCL's Senate House, and through reflection, using mirrors to set up altered perspectives. Stage becomes seating, seating becoming stage and the audience accordingly moves throughout the performance. They are both the viewer and the viewed. A device reinforced through time-lapse film techniques, allowing there to be moments when the audience see projections of themselves within the performance, filmed seconds earlier and played back. The production explores themes of surveillance, whilst performing a narrative of Orwell's dystopia.

Nadira Amrani, Y2, Disused-Space. A series of documentaries interviewing architects, managers and occupants; considering the various means of bringing 'use' to disused and underused spaces within the current financial and social climate. The reactivation of these spaces can generate new concepts occupancy and creative industry. Project work consists of audio recordings, film and documentary, some of which can be seen at architecturalstudiesbartlett.tumblr.com

X.15

X.16

BSc Architecture Unit 4 field trip – A visit to Wes Jones at Jones, Partners: Architecture in Los Angeles

BSc Architecture, Year 1 studio

Öfært
Impassable

BSc Architecture, Year 1 studio

BSc Architecture Unit 9 field trip to São Paulo –
Lina Bo Bardi's SESC building

BSC Architecture, Unit 4 field trip
– Y3 student Leo Boscherini
examining a drawing by Bryan
Cantley at his studios at California
State University, Fullerton

The Imaginarium of Urban Ecologies

CJ Lim, Bernd Felsinger

'Cities are particularly vulnerable in that they are immobile. As such, the historic sense of place, and rootedness of residents are critical attributes of cites. These strengths of place can, however, become liabilities if the local ecosystems are unable to adapt to the climate-induced changes. Climate change poses serious threats to life, and entire urban systems.' The World Bank, *Cities and Climate Change*, 2010

Increases in global temperature have caused sea levels to rise at an accelerating pace, changing patterns and quantities of precipitation as well as the probable expansion of subtropical deserts. According to the United Nations Intergovernmental Panel on Climate Change (IPCC), the greatest threat of climate change is the profound manner in which it could impact upon every aspect of our lives, from health to ecological security. By understanding the urgency of climate change as a 'security' issue, we need to recognise the importance of revolutionising and innovating our cities and its programmes; adapting to climate change is not just a matter of managing risk. No longer should the issue of climate change be considered solely in the realms of scientific policy, but is an issue that is multidisciplinary – the professions of the built environment including architects, planners, geographers and ecologists have a crucial role to contribute. Like many scientific policies, the strongest design visions and planning policies will simultaneously address problems in multiple domains and function, and to become constructs for the practice of everyday life for all ecological forms in the urban environment. The sustainability and transformation of cities can address climate security challenges, reduce greenhouse gas emissions, alleviate water insecurity, and provide economic and social benefits, but could simultaneously help establish an ecological symbiosis between nature and built form. Innovative responses and solutions should present new paradigms for urban living, while some believe that for humans to survive, we need a re-equilibrated ecosystem where we commit to coexisting with nature.

Beekeepers in the US have been reporting losses of their hives; while the British Beekeepers Association has warned that the honey bee could disappear from Britain by 2018. It seems that the bees are in crisis as a result of new and intensive farming practices. Monoculture agriculture, organised irrigation, the heavy use of pesticides, chemical fertilizers, and plant growth regulators, alongside climate change has increased the mortality rate of bee colonies at an alarming speed. The disappearance of bees threatens global agriculture that relies on pollination by bees to produce our food supply. The city and the hive, two complex systems, are under risk.

The pigeon towers of Isfahan represent one of the most remarkable examples of eccentricity in Persian architecture and an unusual exemplar of mutual interest between humans and nature. The now derelict large-scale towers adorn a landscape that is somewhat redolent of naval forts stranded hundreds of miles inland. The useful but unromantic purpose of the towers was to collect pigeon manure, a substance that had been found to be beneficial to the orchards and gardens in the surrounding plains during the 16th century. Agriculture in the fertile but nitrogen-lacking Isfahan plains was largely supported in this manner, fuelling large melon crop production in the region.

The floating, walking and flying propositions of Buckminster Fuller, Archigram, the Metabolists *et al* have all but floated, walked or flown away in recent times. Despite the marked shift, we encourage visionary propositions of architecture and the city, and the realisation of fictional speculations for a re-equilibrated real world ecosystem. We believe in speculative propositions to question the way we experience and engage with our urban environment. It is vital to fundamentally re-think how cities work in a symbiotic relationship between man and nature.

The Bartlett School of Architecture 2013

Project 1, 'What if…', speculates on alternative realities to re-evaluate the city from nature's point of view and investigate the possibilities of how nature can be a sustainable resource for the city. Project 2, 'The City', is informed by earlier individual studies to establish core interests and should form the basis of the final complex narrative and programme.

Unit 10 would like to thank Simon Dickens for his teaching of the Design Realisation module, and Pascal Bronner for his workshop 'The Drawing Imaginarium'.

Year 4

Nick Elias, Frank Fan, Ryan Hakimian, ZhiYu Huang, Anja Kempa, WooJong Kim, Jason Lamb, Samson Lau, Haaris Ramzan

Year 5

Yu Wei (John) Chang, Thandi Loewenson, Steven McCloy, Viktor Westerdahl

10.1

10.2

10.3

Fig. 10.1 – 10.2 (previous spread) Steven McCloy, Y5, EU: The Gardens of Fantastica, Paris. An allegorical city masterplan for Paris reimagining post WWII Europe as a catalyst for food & energy security, the influence is spread as the headquarters periodically move across Europe. The boulevards, city walls, landmarks, catacombs and parks of Paris are transformed and showcased with surreal energy and food infrastructure, tended to by Members of European Parliament. **Fig. 10.3** Viktor Westerdahl, Y5, The Liquid Light of Diego Garcia. A bee ecology on the remote island Diego Garcia captures the full potential of solar energy as, 'Liquid Light'. To harness this energy, without disrupting the islands fragile ecology, people settle in floating villages. These are assembled from a collection of light components, designed to minimise the

impact on the island's material metabolism. **Fig. 10.4** Yu Wei (John) Chang, Y5, The United States of Mormon Republicans, Salt Lake USA. With a population of 70,000, the Mormon community of American and the Republican Party members funds the city. The strategy is to demonstrate the impossible - sustainable living, food and energy production on the barren and environmentally harsh Great Salt Lake, and eventually leading the Republican Party to victory in the presidential election.

10.5

Fig. 10.5 Samson Lau, Y4, The Royal Borough of Summer Countryside, London. The new Royal Borough reimagines the city as a temporary event. Situated over a series of train stations, the temporary architectural icons unfold every year during the summer parliamentary recess, with country produce brought into London. Milkmaids, trapeze artists collecting eggs and children picking strawberries choreograph the making of 'Eton Mess' – all mixed in with a dash of the summer sun!
Fig. 10.6 Nick Elias, Y4, Newham: The Utility City, London. Constructed communities are rehabilitated within a new Utility City that processes London's waste through communal efforts. Active residential hives lie within a lace of green infrastructure, which is knitted into the existing Newham, where the residents work for their own upkeep and create ownership of their

architecture via meticulous maintenance. **Fig. 10.7 – 10.8** Thandi Loewenson, Y5, Melencolia, City of Sadness: A study of the anthropocene city after the end times. Melencolia is a psychotopography, existing in the mind of a failed explorer and fragmented into three 'states' of id, ego and superego. The Melencolia of the plumber, the postman and the councillor – metaphoric protagonists for each 'state' – reveals urban design proposals for the physical and psychological dimensions of the human-induced ecological crisis of the 'anthropocene' age..

10.6

10.7

10.8

Proving Ground

Laura Allen, Mark Smout, Kyle Buchanan

The Bartlett School of Architecture 2013

'A critical understanding of our own inability to control the world, it turns out, is essential to shaping it.' Elizabeth Diller in *Space Suit: Fashioning Apollo* by Nicholas De Monchaux

Unit 11 continues to explore land use and the corresponding architectures, technologies, infrastructures and ecologies inherent in the anthropogenic landscape. Last year we sought out the indivisibility of architecture and the infrastructural, social and natural landscapes of New York. This year we turned our focus to technological innovations, space spin-offs, adapted technologies and hybrid processes that result in the production of landscapes that can subsequently be defined as techno-nature. To do this, we explored the liminal and engineered landscapes of southern Florida as well as the systematic landscape of Cape Canaveral and its hinterlands of military and space industries.

In Florida, collisions between humanity, the natural environment and technology can be brutal. The cataclysmic hurricanes and fiercely powerful electric storms; attempts to shift the entire watershed of the peninsula; and the screaming acidic emissions of Saturn V's 34 Mega-Newton rockets are all examples of the capricious and diverse nature of its environments.

Surface to Air

In 1961 the first manned sub-orbital flight rose from the slowly shifting sands of the barrier islands that hug Florida's Atlantic coast. The liminal site, which started life as a node in the Atlantic Coast Defense System, was chosen for missile testing and manned flight due to a coincidence of geographical, climatic and geophysical factors. Its isolated location provided a huge over-water flight area removed from populated landmasses and shipping lanes.

Liquid Land

Florida's landscape is defined by water. The state can boast 700 artesian springs, 30,000 lakes, ponds and sinks, 1,200 rivers, streams and creeks and

4,500 islands which ring its extensive coastal edge. The Florida Everglades, a National Park and UNESCO World Heritage Site, is a vast near flat semi-tropical wetland of shallow water and soaked plains that flow slowly south to Florida Bay. In a remarkably rapid period of human intervention, a succession of unfortunate meteorological events, short-sighted political whims and unabashed hubris, the hydrological balance and lush ecologies of the Everglades and surrounding wetland wilderness were transformed from a 'River of Grass' to a fabricated, computer-controlled pumping ground supplying fresh water for the industrial, agricultural and domestic demands of the growing urban area sprawl.

Techno-Nature

Settlements, property lines and suburban sprawl are terraformed from dynamic tidal and 'liquid' land. This has been facilitated by large-scale canalisation and drainage projects intended to create a dry landscape, engineered for utility to protect inhabitants from the intolerable consequences of the natural cycles of changeable weather. The wetland topography has succumbed to technology and artifice, concealed in the flows of nature.

The Floridian environment clearly demonstrate how actions, reactions, consequences, catastrophes, coincidences, policies, and whims, can alter the environment from wilderness, to cultivated landscape via a kind of fabricated and systematic ecology, in an inextricably linked but unstable equilibrium.

The Unit 11 studio is established as a laboratory for research, invention and spatial imagination, pursued through an iterative, inquisitive and imaginative process where modelling is key. We aim to challenge normative architectural conditions through modelling by methods such as replicas, prototypes, science frameworks, operating protocols, and specimens. We examine technological strategies, geographical environments and science facts as well as science fictions, via a series of workshops and quick projects.

Our Florida workshop and site visits where in collaboration with Columbia University's Studio-X Co-directors, Geoff Manaugh author of *BLDGBLOG*, Nicola Twilley of *Edible Geography* and Professor Nat Chard author of *Drawing Uncertainty*.

Many thanks to our Unit 11 practice consultants, John Lyall at Lyall Bills & Young, Stephen Foster at Milk Structural Engineering and Dan Cash at Max Fordham and to our critics this year: Aaron Betsky, David Bickle, Daisy Ginsburg, Chris Hatherhill, Will Hunter, Johan Hybschmann, Sarah Ichioka, Alex Kaiser, Holly Lewis, Olly Wainwright, Peg Rawes, Vicky Richardson, Ben Ridley, Ingrid Schroder and Tim Waterman.

Year 4
William Armstrong, Jennifer Dyne, Daniel Felgendreher, Mara-Sophia Kanthak, Rachel King, Danny Lane, David McGowan, Sandra Youkhana

Year 5
Farah Badaruddin, Alexandra Banksie Critchley, Alisan Dockerty, Rebecca Fode, Sonila Kadillari, Yee Yan (Adrienne) Lau, Tom Partridge, Harriet Redman, Luke Royffe

Fig. 11.1 Alisan Dockerty, Y5, The Riparian Resort. The ecologically engineered resort aims to reintroduce the diversity of the historic Kissimmee River whilst providing a community for 'snowbirds', a migratory population of retirees. The resort enables the coexistence of these parallel phenomena in order to relinquish the over consuming nature of tourism, reinventing the Florida dream and developing a new type of river restoration. **Fig. 11.2** William Armstrong, Y4, The Citrus Battery. The project explores the artificial nature of the citrus industry that actively advertises itself as producing a natural product by transforming oranges into simple biochemical batteries that produce long lasting low voltage power. **Fig. 11.3** Rachel King, Y4, The Mini Golf Speciator. The project establishes a climatically adjusted local environment masquerading as a

mini golf hole. Utilising vapour from a local source, the intervention acts as a green buffer to heal the urban hardscape of Miami. **Fig. 11.4** Luke Royffe, Y5, Balancing Catastrophe - East Coast Arks. The future Floridian landscape will be transformed by the increasing frequency of catastrophic events. This will expose the inadequacy of Florida's closed forms of defensive infrastructure and defective housing typologies. The project, Catastrophology, proposes to densify Miami's housing typologies and reconfigure existing protective infrastructures. A new East Coast Reactive Levee will create a permeable threshold between Miami and the Everglades National Park. Integrated into the reactive levee, self sustaining Arks form a network of inhabited biomes that embrace the natural event of catastrophe.

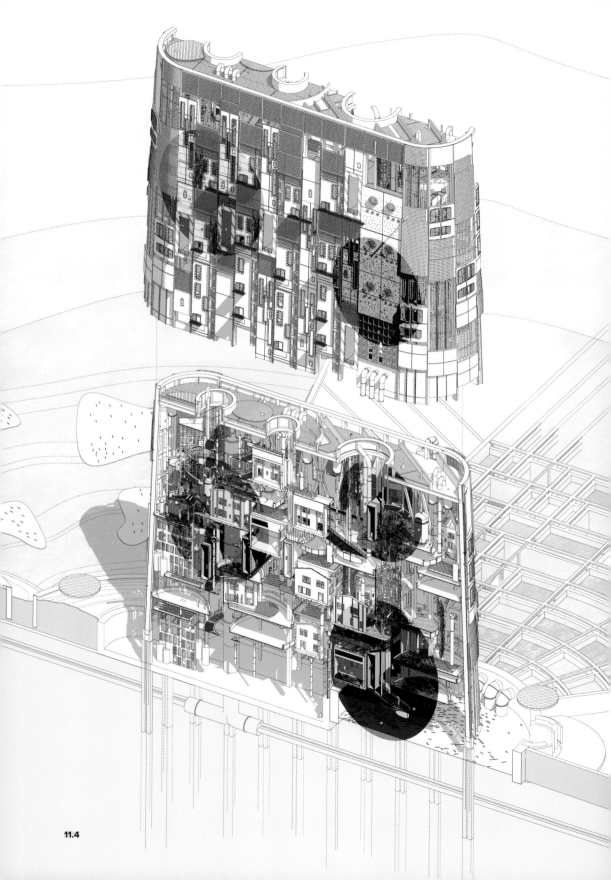

11.4

11.5

11.6

11.7

11.8

Fig. 11.5 Tom Partridge, Y5, Weirding Miami Beach. The Realigned Management plan speculates on the future of Miami Beach in a 'weirding' world, where rising sea levels and extreme weather require the reintegration of the coastal landscape into the urban street grid. The whole island acts to attenuate storms, from a new artificial beach where sand is treated as a valuable commodity to the Surgulator: an emergency energy storage device to reboot the city after a storm. **Fig. 11.6** Daniel Felgendreher, Y4, The de-watering blanket explores different strategies to enhance the consolidation of industrial waste clay present in post-phosphate mining landscapes in central Florida. The tested de-watering mechanisms were envisioned to become part of a building's structure proposing an architecture that adapts to

the altered, unstable ground conditions left behind by the mining system. **Fig. 11.7** Danny Lane, Y4, South Beach Bakery, Miami. The damp cardboard jacket behaves as an inhabitable building fabric which generates the climatic conditions demanded by the processes of the bakery. This project celebrates Florida's love of air-conditioning but challenges the routine method of how it is achieved. **Fig. 11.8** Mara-Sophia Kanthak, Y4, The Everglades Replenishment Project. A water refilling station for Recreational Vehicles on one of the tree islands in the subtropical wetlands. The water purification process is exhibited on an elevated coaster structure, combining Floridian fun park culture with a contribution to the endangered Everglades ecosystem.

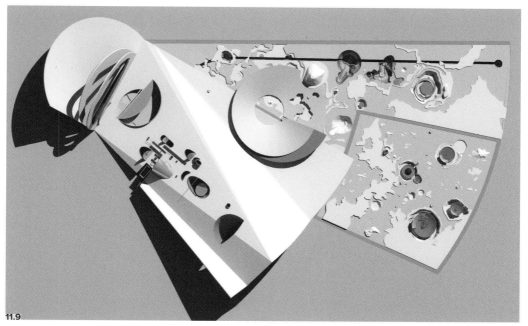

11.9

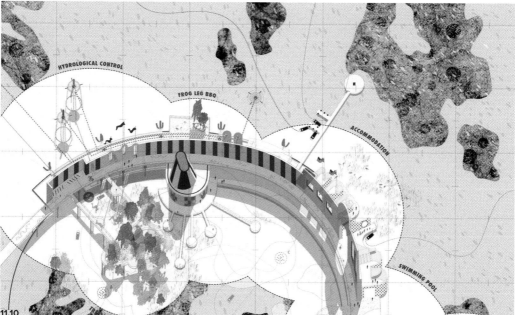

HYDROLOGICAL CONTROL

FROG LEG BBQ

ACCOMMODATION

SWIMMING POOL

11.10

Fig. 11.9 Sonila Kadillari, Y5, Pre-Ecopoiesis Mars Yard (PEMY). PEMY explores the topography and light simulations of Mars within the terrestrial setting of Florida. It functions as the main site for autonomous Mars Rover test drives, temperature resistance and colour calibration as well as providing public exposure to scientific testing. **Fig. 11.10** Rebecca Fode, Y5, The Everglades Artifice, Plan of the Pig Frog Conservation Pond. The Everglades Artifice proposes the transformation of a currently destructive limestone mining industry within Miami-Dade's Lake Belt into a productive process. It investigates how existing mining processes and infrastructures can be harnessed in order to construct a secondary artificial wetland landscape, preserving the Everglades ecosystem as a tourist attraction, ensuring an independent long-term use for the mined site. The resulting landscape typology is a hybrid of technological systems and a familiar natural environment.

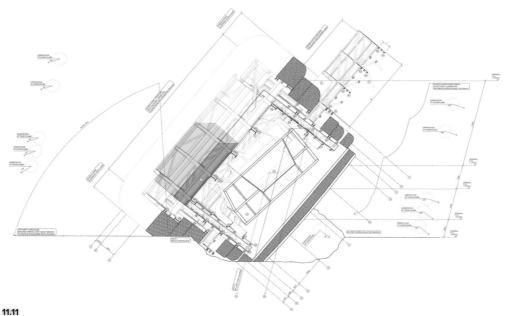

11.11

11.12

Fig. 11.11 Alexandra Banksie Critchley, Y5, Living on Unstable Ground, Florida's Sinking City, Crushed Long Section. The unstable geology of West-Central Florida frequently gives rise to a phenomenon known as sinkholes. Entire buildings can be swallowed by the ground, putting lives at risk. The proposed domestic architecture has been designed to survive their occurrence by means of a frictional dissipative steel structure, a sacrificial crumple zone and a tuned liquid damper. **Fig. 11.12** Harriet Redman, Y5, Citrus Survival Centre, Plan of the Pathogen Testing Lab. Florida's citrus industry is in a state of emergency, Citrus Canker and Greening diseases were first found in 1995 and have since spread statewide. Eradication is no longer possible. The Citrus Survival Centre employs varying levels of quarantine to create intentionally infected and sterile growing environments, to protect a sole surviving tree. Trees within one citrus species are genetically identical, by saving a single tree it is possible to regenerate a lost landscape: the citrus grove.

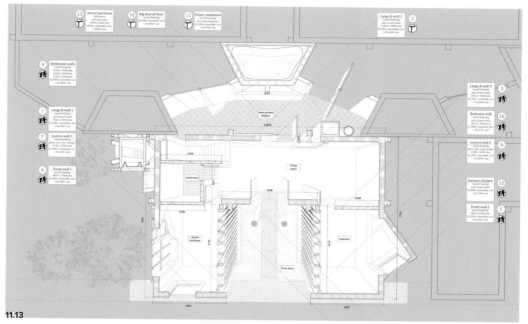

11.13

11.14

Fig. 11.13 Yee Yan (Adrienne) Lau, Y5, Reshaping Suburbia.
Taking advantage of the fact that many foreclosed homes
are sold at prices below their construction costs, their materials
are recycled and re-configured into new model homes that
co-house both locals and temporary residents. Subversive
marketing is the key to popularise this new type of domestic
architecture, which introduces healthy density and communal
living into the traditionally conservative and isolated suburbia.
Fig. 11.14 Jennifer Dyne, Y4, Symbiotic Inhalation Lichen
Laboratory: Could Cryptothecia Striata, an elusive lichen found
deep in the Floridian landscape, solve NASA's radiation crisis?

11.16

Fig. 11.15 Farah Badaruddin, Y5, From Cloud to Ground: Harnessing Lightning at Cape Canaveral. This project investigates the grave repercussions of NASA space exploration program, where it contributed to a significant amount of pollution to the surrounding Florida's landscape. The project theorised on the notion of harnessing lightning for soil remediation purposes and the fabrication of fulgurites as byproducts of lightning. This adaptive reuse is hoped to rejuvenate the surrounding landscape of Cape Canaveral and Merritt Island into a space tourism hub and Space Lightning Thrills Park. **Fig. 11.16** Sandra Youkhana, Y4, Imagineering Miami: Star Island Peak Points. Situated in the mouth of the Biscayne Bay, the island stands as a biproduct of dredging processes in Miami Beach. Plots are distinguished by their

relationships to each resident. A new terrain is created through the manipulation of site spoil with mounds acting as anchor points for temporary extensions of the island positioned along the outer edge, extending public use of the waterfront.

Unit 12
Factual Fictions

Jonathan Hill, Matthew Butcher, Elizabeth Dow

'English novels of the seventeenth and early eighteenth centuries were perceived by many of the middle and upper classes as immoral and illicit not only for their criminal content but for their very enterprise of fictionalising, inventing, forging reality, and lying. Novelists not only made up their stories, they also denied that their invented stories were fictions.' Lennard J. Davis, 1983

Histories and novels both need to be convincing but in different ways. Although no history is completely objective, to have any validity it must appear truthful to the past. A novel may be believable but not true. But recognising the overlaps between two literary genres, Malcolm Bradbury notably described his novel , 1975, as 'a total invention with delusory approximations to historical reality, just as is history itself'. Objective as well as subjective, a design is a reinterpretation of the past that is meaningful to the present, transforming both, like a history. Equally, a design is equivalent to a novel, convincing the user to suspend disbelief. Part novelist, part historian, the architect creates 'factual fictions'.

Sites of History
'The existing monuments form an ideal order among themselves, which is modified by the introduction of the new (the really new) work of art among them.' T.S. Eliot, 1917

The history of architecture can be conceived in terms of the need for individuals, or societies, to contradict, reinvent and distort – as well as affirm – a philosophical and aesthetic orthodoxy. These shifts may be necessary for the discipline to respond to changing social and cultural needs, or stem from a human desire for reinvention, which in turn affects social and cultural patterns. Students of Unit 12 were asked to challenge and expand a particular orthodoxy, to understand a particular aesthetic and philosophical position, and to create a personally driven shift in that stance.

Specification and Craft
'On a wet day it may look drab and forbidding, and they might scuttle away from it. On a sunny day it's magical, but then buildings are like that, they should be.' Denys Lasdun, 1979

For an (architectural) factual fiction to be believable there needs to be a real understanding of craft, materials and detail, which should not only have a convincing provenance and be subject to rigorous testing but also be grounded in an appreciation of the political, cultural and meteorological climates in which they can thrive.

Industries and Infrastructures for an Independent London
'But, it is manifest, that those who repair to, no sooner enter into it, but they find a universal alteration to their Bodies, which are either dryed up or enflamed, the humours being exasperated and made apt to putrifie, their sensories and perspiration so exceedingly stopped, with the loss of Appetite, and a kind of general stupefaction, succeeded with such and, as do never, or very rarely quit them, without some further Symptomes of dangerous Inconveniency so long as they abide in the place; which yet are immediately restored to their former habit; so soon as they are retired to their Homes and they enjoy fresh again.'
John Evelyn, 1661

Even in the 17th century, London was ten times the size of the second largest English city. Today, it is culturally, socially and economically distinct from the UK and has more in common with New York and Shanghai than Aberdeen and Manchester. Proposing that London should have the degree of autonomy given to Catalonia in Spain or Scotland in the UK, we asked students to design industries and infrastructures for an independent London. In Unit 12 our discussions are dialogical. Some students supported London's proposed independence, while a few suggested that it should become more dependent, and others focussed on the independence of other regions.

Unit 12 would very much like to thank Domi Oliver and Carl Vann, Design Realisation Tutors, and Ben Godber, Structural Consultant, as well as the critics: Alessandro Ayuso, Nick Beech, Shumi Bose, Carolyn Butterworth, Barbara Campbell-Lange, Nat Chard, Emma Cheatle, Tom Coward, Alison Crawshaw, Oliver Domesien, Bill Hodgson, Will Hunter, Jan Kattein, David Kohn, Adrian Lahoud, George Lovett, Hugh McEwen, Ollie Palmer, Mariana Pestana, Sophia Psarra, Natasha Sandmeier, Ruth Silver, Eva Sopeoglou, Catrina Stewart, Tom Weaver, Finn Williams and Danielle Willkens.

Year 4

Emma Clinton, Jason Coe, Daniel Leon Fenster, Alastair King, Samuel Rackham, Rodolfo Rodriguez, Louis Sullivan, Daniel Wilkinson, Xuhong Zheng

Year 5

Christine Bjerke, Graham Burn, Feras El Attar, Charlotte Knight, Anders Strand Lühr, Amy Sullivan-Bodiam, Fiona Tan, Cassandra Tsolakis, Kieran Thomas Wardle, Owain Williams, Zihong (Tim) Yue

Fig. 12.1 Cassandra Tsolakis, Y5, An alternative school of architecture in London based on decoding the underlying universal orders which structure our experience. The school argues for freedom and insight into design by encouraging fragmentation as a principle technique. **Fig. 12.2** Samuel Rackham, Y5, The Royal Meteorological Society: Exploring notions of romanticism through the marriage of art and science, the society creates meteorological phenomena within an ornamental framework, capturing the beauty of weather through architectural form. **Fig. 12.3** Louis Sullivan, Y4, The Cockaigne Academy of Sugar Production. A modern interpretation of the medieval mythic utopia of Cockaigne. An edible architecture constructed entirely of caramel and realising dependency on sugar through the built environment.

Fig. 12.4 Daniel Wilkinson, Y5, Communism I gave you my heart, you cooked it medium well. The leftovers from failed Communism are ground into aggregate for an ideological slurry. This happens in London, a result of the CPC's financial assistance to the UK.

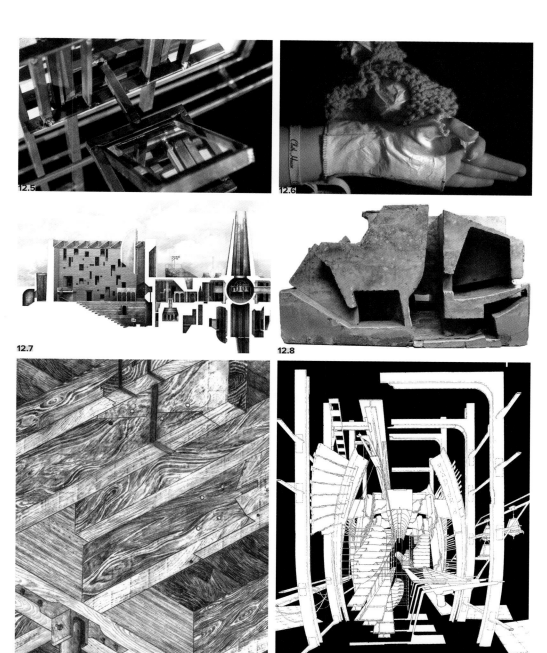

Fig. 12.5 Xuhong Zheng, Y4, Orchestration of light, shadows and politics at the New City Hall. A set of new civic halls across the city for an independent London, proposing an architecture that exploits the temporality of natural light to determine how politics and activities occur within different spaces. **Fig. 12.6** Emma Clinton, Y4, The Cloth House. The project is interested in the relationship between body and garment as an allegory for the built environment. The 'completed' building – or garment – is manipulated, adapted and transplanted by the dweller. **Fig. 12.7** Rodolfo Rodriguez, Y4, The station will accommodate the flow of passengers going to and coming from London to work, as well supply destinations with the necessary fuel to service the station building. The programme of the infrastructure is based around the meteorological calendar and the cycle of the seasons. **Fig. 12.8** Jason Coe, Y4, A Bell Foundry for New Jerusalem: A Participatory Democracy for London is realised through the implementation of an aural communication network of bells and a new civic architecture for London. **Fig. 12.9** Alastair King, Y4, Tower Hill Community: a building for a community of construction workers, critiquing the banal architecture of modern London with an architecture informed by 'A Pattern Language'. **Fig. 12.10** Daniel Leon Fenster, Y4, As disparate cultures collide, picturesque ornament is rescued from the wreckage of bland multiculturalism. Wren's heavenly domes are borrowed by Chinese companies and inverted to become a descent into glorious debauchery and frivolity.

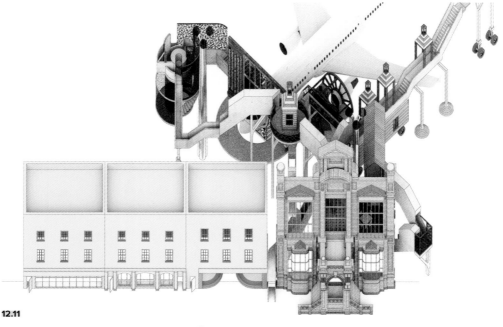

12.11

12.12

Fig. 12.11 Feras El Attar, Y5, The Aerotropolis of Sheerness.
An airport-cum-city model that encourages integration
between aviation and the city, using an architectural language
that reflects and enhances the spatial/bodily disposition
experienced in the realm of air travel. **Fig. 12.12** Fiona Tan, Y5,
A Manual Towards a New London satirises the curious habits
of Londoners as seen through Singaporean eyes. The building
celebrates and enforces the arbitrary etiquettes that govern life
in London. **Fig. 12.13** Owain Williams, Y5, The Gasification
Authority is a government energy department charged with
licensing industrial operations in UK coal mines. With reserves
set to expire within 40 years, the building considers its
imminent redundancy and the establishment of a devolved
government for the Rhondda Valley directly in its place.

12.13

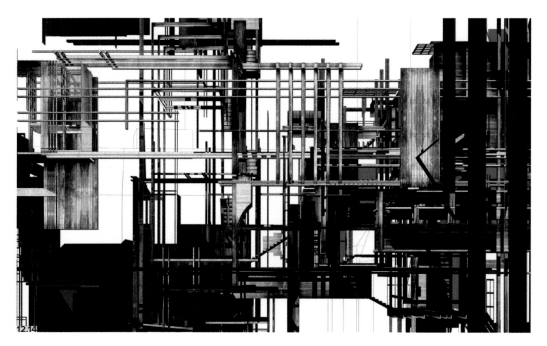

Fig. 12.14 Charlotte Knight, Y5, The City of London proposes the relocation of Gresham College as a singular institution located within Austin Friars Square to strengthen the disseminating of knowledge to encourage a cultural exchange within the city. **Fig. 12.15** Zihong (Tim) Yue, Y5, Confucian Aspirations and Self Cultivation – An Architectural Self-Portrait. The project is a series of architectural drawings portraying the consciousness and unconsciousness of a Confucian mind, which also embodies the core struggles and aspirations of the Chinese nation. The programme starts with self-cultivation, and then expands to that of family, then to community and ultimately landscape. The project puts together a picture of peace and harmony that has been lodged in the Chinese mind throughout history

12.16

12.17

Fig. 12.16 Christine Bjerke, Y5, The FX Beauties Club explores feminine economies with the focus on the historical and contemporary 'floating world' between the woman and money, power and mirrors. **Fig. 12.17** Graham Burn, Y5, Flatpack school redux: an MDF Russian Orthodox school, church and community centre in Harringay. The Orthodox Church is at the centre of Russian life: religion, education and community have come together as the spine of the population throughout history, and are deployed here in an emerging worker community. Constructed entirely from MDF, inherently fragile and responsive when exposed to weather and use, the building acts as a barometer for shifting policies and politics on a local, national and international level by being in a constant state of construction, repair and decoration to counter erosive effects of occupation and prepare for future use. **Fig. 12.18** Kieran Thomas Wardle, Y5, The Palace of Eastminster. An agoric building to temporarily house Parliament on the banks of the Thames in Essex. The Palace of Eastminster reconfigures Parliament around the notion of the public square, forcing elements of encounter and protest into the heart of the legislative programme.

12.18

Unit 14
Interface Architecture

James O'Leary, Paul Bavister

Contemporary architecture is a space of information exchange. Increasingly, architectural environments are communicative spaces where historical and contemporary architectural layers happily coexist; where spaces are crammed with competing signs that generate rich and dynamic semiotics; where the architectural object and the user fuse into a kind of composite that is locked in a continuous exchange of information. This begs a number of questions: How do we design immersive architectural spaces for this new paradigm? Of what would its materiality consist? How would we envision the parameters for such spaces? How do we make these spaces 'live'? Underlying these questions are two primary concerns: firstly, the changing nature of the material and technological layering of architectural space, and secondly, the evolving interrelationship between architecture and the user experience.

Unit 14 explores contemporary architecture as a space of communication, where architectural environments become legible spaces that can be read and interpreted by its users. Unit 14 develops tools and processes to allow students to understand and control this complex architectural matrix. We are interested in the relationships between technology, media and architecture as systems that construct spaces of meaning within a political and social realm. Here, 'soft' technological systems, as well as the 'hard' material stuff of architecture are the focus of design.

In order to explore and exploit this design potential, the Unit travelled to Mesoamerica in order to witness the *Dia de los Muertos* (The Day of the Dead) where death is celebrated as a catalyst for rebirth. We visited Mexico City, the largest metropolitan area in the western hemisphere and the ultimate city in transition, before visiting the ruined cities of the pre-Columbian societies of the Maya. Our journey fused the vibrant street life of downtown Mexico City with the ancient ruins of the Pyramids of the Sun and Moon in Teotihuacan. We began to understand Mexico as a complex terrain of overlain, inter-related

systems – some native, some imposed. The culture has evolved into a masterpiece of syncretic practice, where seemingly contradictory beliefs and practices are merged together into an inclusive unified whole. We found this profoundly inspirational. Perceptions and recordings of these conditions, whether political, conceptual or material, were crucial in gaining a critical understanding of the context of the work. We immersed ourselves in the complex semiotics of this space in the transitional time of the Mayan Fifth Sun. We were told the world would end. We never believed this for a second, but had a giant party just in case!

Message: Architecture as Semiotic Domain
At the beginning of the year the Unit worked together in a group project to establish parameters of operation, in the physical realm and the visual. The first project was a simple installation that acted as an interface to the students' interests: architectural, philosophical and personal. This week-long project established ideas and aesthetic themes that could be drawn upon throughout the course of the year.

Material: Site as Palimpsest
Thematic development then split with the fourth years developing a more complex 'interface architecture' dealing with interaction and behavioural memes that had to be sited in the city, acting as an interface between occupant and site. The interface would become an integrated object, responding to localised conditions and behavioural patterns. The finished piece was then installed and tested onsite, with the students evaluating and recording the experience. The fifth years were free to continue and develop their own themes and ideas in the context of the Unit's agenda.

Field Trip: Mexico
The fourth year building project continued ideas of semiotics and interface through a building program of the students choosing, sited in Mexico City. This led to a variety of building typologies and programs

responding to the individual ideas developed by
each student.

Between Message and Material:
a Composite Space
The final part of the year was spent developing
a 1:1 detail of the building or a thematic model or
installation that had a resonance with themes of
semiotics and interface architecture that were tied
back to the building project. Students were free
to develop ideas and themes that could be carried
on to Year 5. This led to the construction of 1:1
architectural fragments and details, responsive
prototypes, and performance prosthesis.

Unit 14 would like to thank: Alessandro Ayuso,
Dr Ana Araujo, Jason Bruges, Michelle Bush,
Sam Causer, Professor Nat Chard, Susie Clapham,
Dr Marjan Colletti, Kate Davies, Geraldine Denning,
Illugi Eysteinsson, Darren Farrell, Jason Flanagan,
Professor Stephen Gage, Ruairi Glynn, Andrew
Hamilton, Bill Hodgson, Dr Kristen Kreider,
Tim Lucas, Sam McElhinney, Will McLean, Dirk
Krowlikowski, Chris Leung, Ollie Palmer, Price &
Myers, Caroline Rabourdin, Professor Bob Sheil,
Andy Toohey, Andy Whiting, Graeme Williamson,
Dan Wright, Emmanuel Vercruysse, and all the
wonderful staff in the Bartlett workshops.

Year 4
Kyveli Anastasiadi, Aleksandra Cicha, Petr Esposito,
Yuan Ning, Sang Yong Seok, Hwan Cho Seong, Jia
Yuan Shen, Michael Slade, Kok Kian Tew, Atilla Ali
Tasan

Year 5
Suyang Xu, Hong-Jin (Chace) Leow

unit-14.net
kreider-oleary.net
audialsense.com

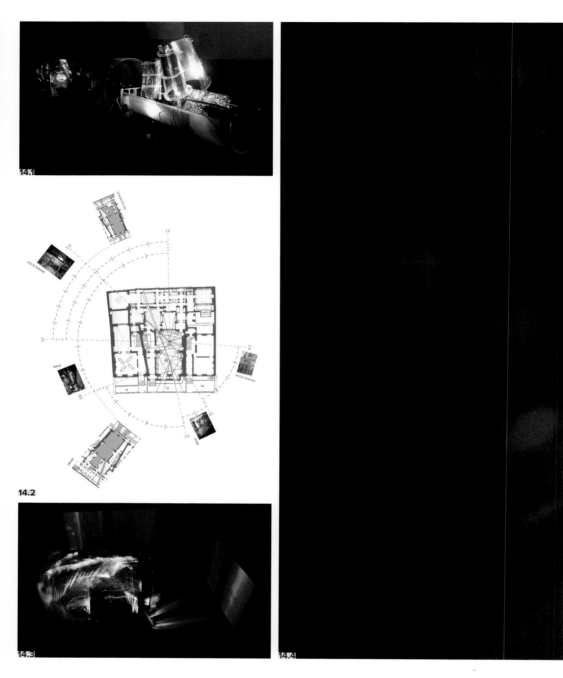

14.1

14.2

14.3

14.4

Fig. 14.1 – 14.4 Suyang Xu , Y5, Light Narratives. The project aims to investigate how narrative can be constructed in architectural spaces through manipulation and control of light and text. Light is used to communicate with occupants and navigate them through spaces with controlled sequences to experience successive events, both physical and emotional. Focussing on the rhythm of natural and artificial lighting in Sir John Soane's architecture, the project uses analysis of the quality and quantity of light in relation to surface and space to develop a series of architectural devices to engender a controlled spatial experience. Based on real events in Soane's life, the correlation between effect, light sources, light modulators and light envelopes is examined through physical experiments, forming a series of light experiences installed in Soane's Pitzhanger Manor in May 2013. **Fig. 14.1** Suyang Xu , Y5, Prototype light modulator Type 02. The bifurcating light from this architectural intervention depicted the fracturing relationship between Soane and his sons, who were reluctant to pursue careers in architecture. **Fig. 14.2** Suyang Xu , Y5, Studies and analysis of the Sir John Soane's Museum. These studies were the basis of the performance criteria for the prototypes that followed. **Fig. 14.3** Suyang Xu , Y5, Time-based representation of light modulator on site. As an occupant interacts with the modulator, the output changes, retelling the narrative. **Fig. 14.4** Suyang Xu , Y5, Light modulator Type 01. The light from this architectural intervention reflects the early career success of Soane.

Fig. 14.5 – 14.8 Chace Leow, Y5, Meta-Sensory Architecture. This project explores the possibilities of layering and merging intangible aspects of human experience over separate sites in Mexico and London, defining cultural boundaries and historical aspects specific to each society. This has been developed through the use architectural devices that propagate specific olfactory zones to engender a psychological response in the occupant. Following on from ideas generated in Mexico, Chace then looked at merging sites separated not by geography, but by time, to create site specific immersive experiences defined by historical events particular the that site. The installation shown here, an 'Extension to the Monument', recreates the sound and smell of moments of the great Fire of London, juxtaposed over the contemporaneous experience of the City of London in 2013. Fig. 14.5 Chace Leow, Y5, Detail of interaction of final 4m high installation showing architectural devices that propagate specific olfactory outputs through the use of low-frequency sound. Fig. 14.6 Chace Leow, Y5, Constructing an intangible personal architecture through the propagation of smell. Fig. 14.7 Chace Leow, Y5, The spatial extents described by the rotation of initial test armatures that generate new personal space through olfactory cues that change subtly over time. Fig. 14.8 Chace Leow, Y5, A sequence of video stills taken from a HD Video documenting a performance of the armature in Zocalo Square in Mexico City with the local 'Grupo Ollin Cuauhtemotzin' performing a smoke cleansing ritual: 'The Celebration of Limpiador'.

Fig. 14.9 Mike Slade, Y4, Marigold Oil Production Centre. Mike's project takes the Cempazuchitl Flower (African Marigold), a symbolic and integral element in the rituals of the Mexican Day of the Dead Festival, as the starting point for the designs of an essential oil production centre in the heart of Mexico City's largest flower market. **Fig. 14.10** Kyveli Anastasiadi, Y4,. Sinking Sound Museum, Tlateloco. A museum designed to slowly sink into the Mexico City soil for over 60 years, in a continual archeological dig. Sound is used to amplify the sense of the building moving, which is explored here through performance. **Fig. 14.11** Hwan Cho Seong, Y4, Museum of One Minute. An archive of the Tlateloco massacre of 1971 in Mexico City. A charged space, enabling visitors to listen to first hand audio and video accounts of the student

uprising, and subsequent government action. The surfaces of the archive act as an interface to an evolving generative compositional acoustic environment, the surface of which responds to gesture as an input. **Fig. 14.12** Petr Esposito, Y4, #iamstudent132. The project seeks to comment on the state of news and media outlets in Mexico through the student protest group #yosoy132. The device plays spliced media content which is presented in different forms through lenticular lenses. The media changes relative to your point of view. **Fig. 14.13** Jia Yuan Shen, Y4, A homeless shelter in Mexico City. The installation shown here, is based on notions of shadow theater, constructing in abstract figures the stories of the occupants of the centre.

14.13

14.14

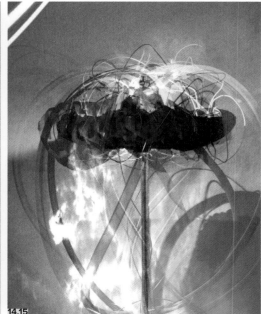

14.15

14.16

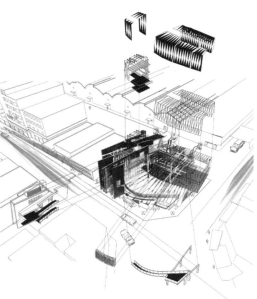

14.17

Fig. 14.14 Aleksandra Cicha, Y4, A prosthesis that seeks to capture the movement of the wearer, modulating the space that contains the action. Aleksandra's work this year has dealt with ideas of the familiar and the uncanny. **Fig. 14.15** Atilla Ali Tasan, Y4, Old Street Sensory Interface: A prototype for a large scale interface sited in the centre of Old Street roundabout. The structure shrouds itself in fog, transmitting and receiving information. It is a field of semiotic and sensory messages, gathering and distributing data from the site. **Fig. 14.16** Sang Yong Seok, Y4, Wind Collector in Teotihuacan. An Aeolian interface to a façade in a collection of artists studios in Teotihuacan, Mexico. The device collects environmental data via wind, and turns this into an 'information feed' through sound. **Fig. 14.17** Kok Kian Tew, Y4, Axonometric of a Culinary

Art Academy that allows individual cultural elements to be rearticulated and reconstituted through the sharing and controlled distribution of secret recipes through a series of carefully calibrated spaces. **Fig. 14.18** Yuan Ning, Y4, Edinburgh Drama School – An open-air theatre sited in the heart of Edinburgh. The theater seeks to synthesize ideas of site and proscenium, where the theater allows views not only of staged productions, but also frames the living city as an act of theatre itself. The image shown here, is a fragment of the skin of the building developed as a 1:1 installation, a fabric canopy responding to occupancy and environmental change, leading to new forms and behavioural patterns.

Fuzzy Bodies

Kristina Schinegger, Stefan Rutzinger, Stefan Ritter

Architecture as a field of cultural production is relative and fuzzy throughout; there are no true or false values to be detected. Design proposals are based on assumptions that are true to a certain extent and false in some aspects. Although architecture is constantly confronted with the imprecise and ambiguous it tries to evade indefiniteness by establishing fixed categories and exact boundaries. Fuzziness is no clear-cut issue, but a matter of degree and approximation.

In classical logic, reasoning arguments can only have binary values. It builds up on exact classification; sentences like 'it's a bit rainy' or 'it's quite sunny' are highly problematic to a system which is reliant on crisp expression. Identifying this as a problem for mathematics, Lofti A. Zadeh developed fuzzy logic in 1965. It allows truth values to range between 1 and 0 and enables the precise handling of approximate expressions and data sets. Fuzzy concepts are used to describe complex phenomena, which are ever-changing or evolving. Despite a wide application in other fields – such as artificial intelligence, pattern recognition, or various kinds of electronics – the term has not been coined in architecture so far. Several tendencies with similar intentions focussed instead on the blur, hybrid, collage, cross-programming and morphing.

The focus of this year was to investigate three-dimensional, programmatic and aesthetic potentials of fuzziness for architecture. We were looking for new organisational typologies, spatial expressions and atmospheric effects that would replace clear definitions and exact categorisation with range and ambiguity.

The field trip took us to Marrakesh and Fez, the sites of the individual projects. Observations in the dense and sensational Medina with its culturally, programmatically and spatially intertwined urban fabric challenged the students to rethink the binary relations of figure and ground, private and public, object and field, body and space. Fuzziness also asks for alternative methods of representation and increased resolution. Therefore the Unit employed a design methodology of continuously switching between scales, as well as switching between digital and analogue modelling techniques to inform and enrich the student's proposals.

The theme triggered a variety of individual approaches by students. One recurring interest, however, was to extract the sensational density and spatial richness of the Medina and translate them within the urban fabric of modern Marrakesh. The research in typologies such as the courtyard house, the Medersa or the Hammam led to hybrid reinterpretation of their innate rules, spatial qualities or climatic and social effects. Other students became interested in ornamentation and its relation to material performances and the sensuality of the body. Some of these themes will also continue through to the next year and form the core of investigation into the coming terms: somaesthetic; atmospheric and bodily effects of architecture; complex geometries and their underlying principles; expressive qualities of form and space; digital ornaments and material performances; kinematics and the performative qualities of change.

With the goal to materialise the fuzzy and the vague, another focus of the Unit is the research of novel materials and fabrication methods and the formulation of innovative implementation strategies. This year the students were generously supported and consulted by Francis Archer from Arup engineering. In triggering discussions our students experienced how structural performances can be a generative and informative motor to develop their design idea further and strengthen it.

Unit 15 puts great emphasis on the synchronisation of analogue and digital production and the fluid transition between them. Unlike generations of architects before them, students have become digital natives acquiring new cultural skills and tools. We consider it as a major task to foster critical evaluation of virtual experimentation and digital methodologies. Architects are facing increasingly complex questions of environmental and urban issues. The use of digital tools such as simulation and analysing software in feedback with physical models and prototypes helps students to master these complex problems in an authentic and exploratory manner.

Many thanks to our critics: Simona Auteri, Richard Beckett, Roberto Bottazzi, Marjan Colletti, Marcos Cruz, Katarina Dionysopoulou, Oliver Domeisen, James O'Leary, Vincenzo Reale, Jeroen Roosen, Kadri Tamre.

Year 4 consultants: Francis Archer of Arup Engineering, and Michael Pangalis and Andy Hutton of Max Fordham Associates.

Year 4

Jiyoon Bae, Ko Wai Cheung, Joel Cullum, Andrea Giordano, Tsun Ming Ho, Stephen Johnson, Jihum Kim, Kris Mitchell, Hyder Mohsin, Amanda Moore, Hisham Muazzam, John Wu, Rintaro Yoshida

Year 5

Ka Lai (Kylie) Chan

15.1

15.2

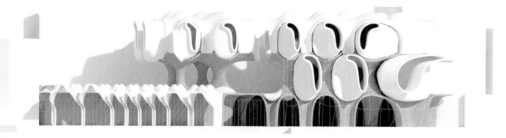

15.3

Fig. 15.1 Andrea Giordano, Y4, Reflective Digital Texture. A texture articulated by a series of extrude commands over a grid of quads resulting in a field of ambiguous forms at a range of varying scales. **Fig. 15.2** Andrea Giordano, Y4, Polymorph Texture. A texture articulated by a series of extrude commands over a grid of quads. **Fig. 15.3** Andrea Giordano, Y4, Argan Oil Hammam and Capsule Hotel , Fez, Morocco: based on a fuzzy field condition, the building proposal is a single surface reinforced concrete shell composing columns and domes of varying dimensions and featuring a traditional hammam, an argan oil health spa, and a hotel composed of bottle-rack stacked capsules. The hammam's domed ceiling produces an articulated landscape above for public gardens, pools, and an argan marketplace. **Fig. 15.4** Andrea Giordano, Y4, Digital Texture Made Physical. A texture articulated by a series of extrude commands over a grid of quads rendered physical with 3D printing. **Fig. 15.5** Andrea Giordano, Y4, Argan Oil Hammam and Capsule Hotel Scale 1:20 Sectional Model. Fibreglass reinforced plaster casted elements in CNC polystyrene molds, vacuum formed walkway and 3D printed furniture elements sprayed with iridescent paint. **Fig. 15.6** Andrea Giordano, Y4, Argan Oil Hammam and Capsule Hotel, Fez, Morocco, axonometric diagram.

15.4

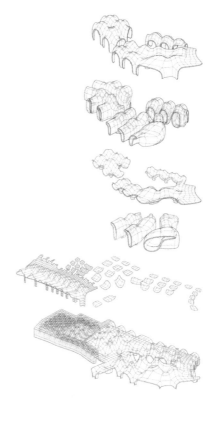

15.5

15.6

15.7

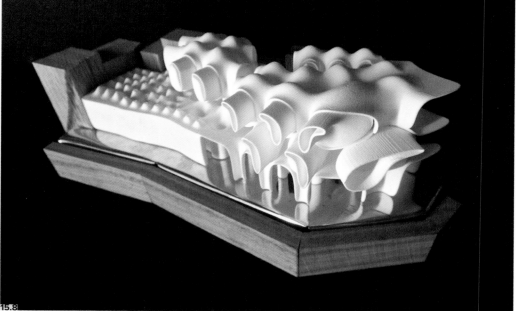

15.8

Fig. 15.7 Andrea Giordano, Y4, Argan Oil Hammam and
Capsule Hotel Scale 1:20 Sectional Model. Fibre-glass
reinforced plaster casted elements in CNC polystyrene molds,
vacuum formed walkway and 3D-printed furniture elements
sprayed with iridescent paint. **Fig. 15.8** Andrea Giordano, Y4,
Argan Oil Hammam and Capsule Hotel Scale 1:200 Site
Model. Hard wood, copper sheet, and 3D-printed elements.
Fig. 15.9 – 15.10 Amanda Moore, Y4, Cellular Honey Farm:
paper models exploring structures made from tubes.
Fig. 15.11 Amanda Moore, Y4, Cellular Honey Farm: view inside
a structure housing natural beehives which attach to the
concrete tubes. Hives are smoked by the beekeeper to calm
the bees before harvesting honeycomb.

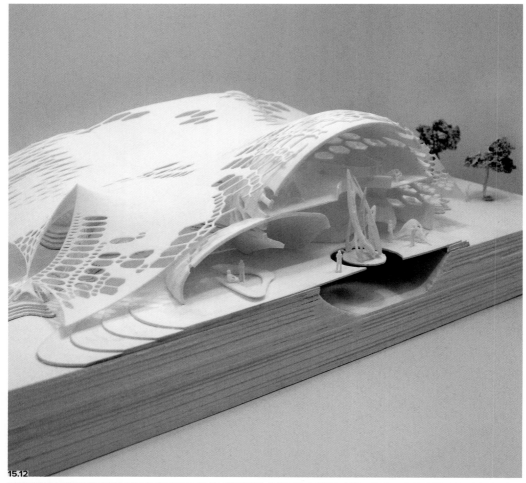

15.12

15.13

15.14

Fig. 15.12 Jihum Kim, Y4, Moroccan Textile Museum and Art Gallery, Marrakech, Morocco. The sectional model shows the different spatial qualities throughout the building. The apertures on the roof are adjusted according to the functions underneath. **Fig. 15.13** Jihum Kim, Y4, View of the public space between the building masses, showing the lighting conditions underneath the ornamental roof. **Fig. 15.14** Jihum Kim, Y4, Atrium Gallery Space, the main atrium is located in the centre of the gallery building. It connects the different exhibition spaces throughout in the building, thus acting as a focal point of the gallery's circulation. **Fig. 15.15** Kristoffer Mitchell, Y4, The Transition of a Watch. A stop motion display of how single elements are rotated along individual paths, negating discrete movements that can be extracted from the mechanism of a pocket watch. **Fig. 15.16** Jiyoon Bae, Y4, Weaving Architecture Initial Model. Initial physical model focus on showing how different timber panels structuring together based on the rule of the Ermine moth cobweb. **Fig. 15.17** Jiyoon Bae, Y4, Textile Exhibition Pavilion in Fez, Morocco, the project is an adaptive architecture based on the weaving tactic of the Ermine moth cobwebs. **Fig. 15.18** Rintaro Yoshida, Prototype_Eta: Fragment of Courtyard 'Atlas.' **Fig. 15.19** Rintaro Yoshida, Y4, Prototype_Delta: Repetitive Hyperplasia of Perforated Shells.

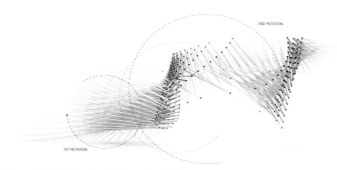

15.15

15.16

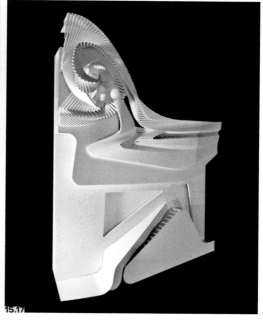

15.17

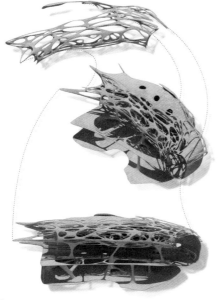

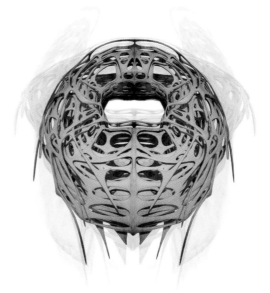

15.18

15.19

15.20

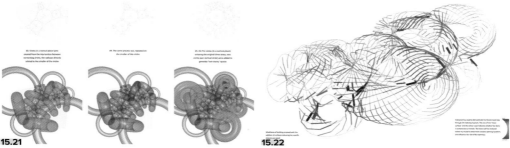

15.21 15.22

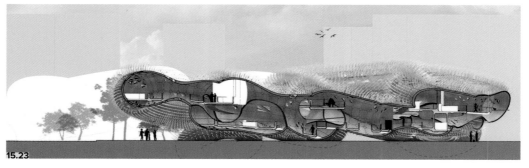

15.23

Fig. 15.20 Ka Lai (Kylie) Chan, Y5, School of Chinese Calligraphy, Creekside, London. Ornamentation is re-appropriated as an architectural language for people to learn Chinese calligraphy through spatial experiences. **Fig. 15.21** Stephen Johnson, Y4, Marrakech Film School, 'Modern' Marrakech, Morocco. Tests in the aggregation of tori over the project site focussing on the creation of omni-directional spaces at tori intersections, while maintaining public and private access across public plaza. **Fig. 15.22** Stephen Johnson, Y4, Analysis of compressive/tensile forces within individual composite panels of Design Realisation building project. The stress data was fed into an automated process which permitted varying size windows where individual panel stress levels permitted. **Fig. 15.23** Stephen Johnson, Y4,

Longitudinal section through the library and learning centre building. **Fig. 15.24** Ka Lai (Kylie) Chan, Y School of Chinese Calligraphy, Creekside, London, 2D calligraphic strokes evolve into 3D built form.

15.24

Utopias

Josep Miàs, Johan Berglund

The Bartlett School of Architecture 2013

'An underdose of utopia can be as dangerous as an overdose.' Reinier de Graaf, *Dezeen*, September 2012

'I do not want to talk to you about architecture. I detest talk about architecture.' Le Corbusier, AA after-dinner speech, 1 April 1953

Unit 16 exists in a close symbiosis between academic research and architectural practice. We prefer to make architecture rather than just talking about it. Our way of working is close to how projects are executed in our practices, with constant testing and 'reflecting through action', in order to challenge the limits of architecture. Our work is centered on the production of buildings, landscapes and spaces. We see architecture as an act of realisation; of making something real, which was only previously a brief thought, a vague concept, a utopian dream. Through this act we have the power to transform the world around us, and with that, the responsibility to make sure we leave something positive behind.

Legacy

This year, Unit 16 investigated the next summer Olympics, to be held in Rio in four years' time. The projects dealt with the political agendas and ideals that have shaped the idea of the Olympic games (and Brazil itself), as well as the often-problematic physical legacy that is connected to hosting the Olympics. What is left behind when the games are over, and who takes responsibility for it? By researching into the London Olympics, specifically the ideas surrounding the continued legacy project of the Olympic park area, we learnt from its successes and failures, in order to propose new and innovative ideas for the Rio Olympics, and for the life in Rio after the games.

The Growing Olympic Archipelago

The Olympics allowed us to think about the continuity of architecture in time. The world is seemingly acting in a global Olympic relay race;

every city is given the baton by the previous one. In this process, it is interesting to think about the transfer from one Olympic host to another. What can be understood and learnt from the previous one, so that the next Olympic games (and its legacy) can be improved? The projects of the Unit attempt to understand these political, geographic and spatial trips, where architecture is part of the baggage.

Permanence

We questioned the duration of the existence of our architecture, and encouraged the students to look at extremes. How do you build in an inventive and sustainable way for only three weeks, and how do you create buildings and cities that will last for millennia? We also questioned many things surrounding the production of architecture currently taken for granted, such as the assumed lifespan of new buildings, currently being based on guarantees given by material manufacturers and builders, as well as the absurd and unsustainable cost of building for short periods of time. We looked for inventive and utopian architectures, architectures that question permanence, duration, and temporality, architectural and urban spaces that can evolve and change rather than being demolished and replaced as they become outdated.

Unit 16 is part of a global network of research, related to the Olympic Architectural Project in Rio de Janeiro. The final projects will be displayed in Museo da Casa Brasileira in São Paulo. In September 2012, the Unit was invited by the Fargfabriken Art Foundation as one of five teams to propose ideas for the urban infrastructural development of Stockholm. The result of this work was exhibited at Fargfabriken in Stockholm in November 2012.

We would like to thank Nüssli, the main contractor for several of the temporary pavilions in London 2012, who have been our main sponsor for this year. We also extend our thanks to Dean Pike, our Design Realisation (DR) Tutor, for his energy and effort in teaching the DR report, and to Andrew Best from

Buro Happold for the very valuable technical support. Finally, a big thank you to all our visiting critics: Jack Newton, Jessam Al-Jawad, Damjan Iliev, Sarah Custance, Rhys Cannon, Kate Davies, Dorian Wiszniewski, Josep Grau, Martin Joos, Leon Smith, Pedro Gil, James O'Leary, Carlos Jimenez, Dr Markus Jatsch, Professor Murray Fraser, Katerina Dionysopoulou and Graeme Williamson.

Year 4

Benjamin Allan, Nathan Breeze, James Bruce, Robert Burrows, Natalia Eddy, Francis Roper, Louise Sørenssen, Richard Winter

Year 5

Jonathan Blake, Ione Braddick, Rachel Hearn, Etain Ho, Philip Poon, Oliver Leech, Samantha Rive

unitsixteen.com
42architects.com
miasarquitectes.com

16.1

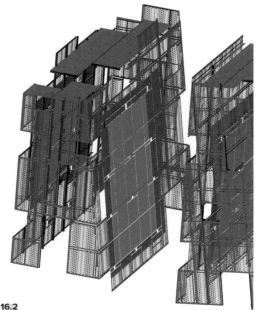

16.2

16.3

Fig. 16.1 Louise Sørenssen, Y4, Barra Coffee Farm, Rio De Janeiro. Model view. Louise's project criticises the current legacy masterplan for the proposed Olympic park in Barra, outside of Rio de Janeiro. As an alternative, she proposes a new masterplan of a productive landscape where local modes of cultivating the land is turned into community facilities to balance the current situation of gated communities and large anonymous condo developments. **Fig. 16.2** Richard Winter, Y4, Athletes On The Edge, Rio de Janeiro. Façade study. Starting with an interest in the history of the Barra area, Richard developed a counter proposal to the current plan for the athletes' housing. In an attempt to restore the eco-system of the area, he develops a typology of housing blocks to sit on the edge between the edge and the lagoon next to the

Olympic park, where the houses over time become more and more embedded in the mangrove ecology. **Fig. 16.3** Nathan Breeze, Y4, Sweetwater Trade School, London. Partial overview. A study of the relationship between the legacy developmen following the 2012 Olympics, and the neighboring Hackney Wick area, which currently houses the largest artist community in the UK. Linking the tradition of craft and skill, with the new developments in the area, Nathan proposes a trade school as a built framework, onto which the students can learn the trades of construction in a continuous cycle of building and unbuilding the site. **Fig. 16.4** Benjamin Allan, Y4, Olympic Power - The Exchange, Rio de Janeiro. Model view. Taking an early interest in the need to upgrade the electrical network and the various sub stations across the city, Benjamin proposes to

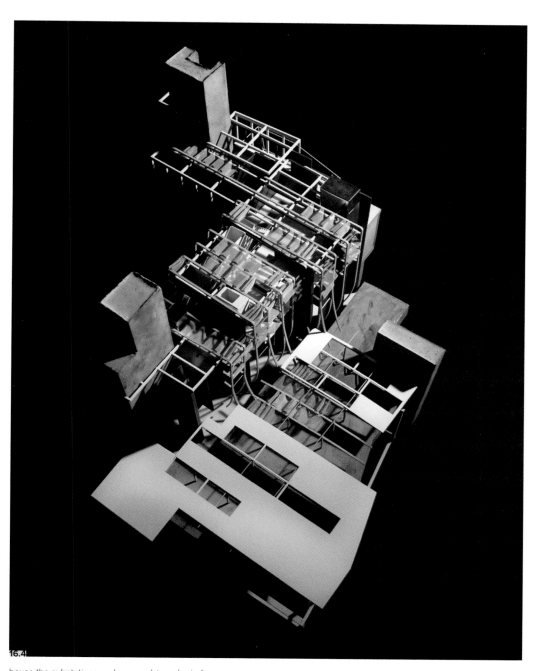

16.4|

house the substations underground, in order to free up space
for public use above. On one of these sites, he designs a mixed
use development comprised of a town hall, a market, and a
new metro station, with the intention of making the act of local
politics clearer and more engaging for the people.

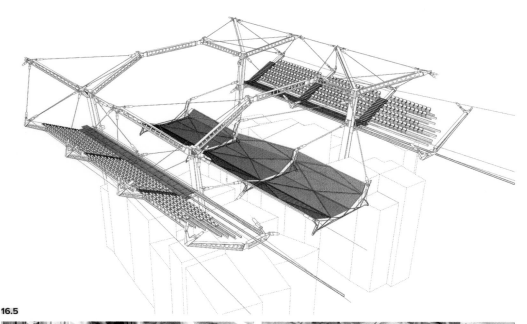

16.5

16.6

16.7

Fig. 16.5 Francis Roper, Y4, Favela BMX Venue, Rio de Janeiro. Detailed perspective. Francis began the year with a study that explored the possibility of a more integrated Olympic Games, instead of the typical reliance of an Olympic park, usually disconnected from the city life. The final result, a BMX events venue that weaves itself down through the roof scapes of Favela Rocinha, was conceived as a temporary, suspended structure, which would only exist for the duration of the games. **Fig. 16.6** Natalia Eddy, Y4, Barra Ferry Terminal, Rio de Janeiro. Rendered overview. Studying the relationship between the Olympic Games and water, Natalia re-invented the idea of the current Olympic park in Barra. Attempting to reinstate the original wetlands landscape, and housing the various venues within this water world, she ends her project with a detailed

study of one of the main entrance structures, a ferry terminal, that links the park with the rest of the lagoon area. **Fig. 16.7** Etain Ho, Y5, A neighbourhood library, Rio de Janeiro. Model view. Etain developed ideas for the various entrance structures that would be required during the Olympic games. Thinking of how they could have a continued use after the games, she designs them in a way where they can be re-assembled and clustered to form a new larger structure, which would contain a new library for the Barra area. **Fig. 16.8** James Bruce, Y4, Infrastructural Nodes, Rio de Janeiro. Model view. James' project investigates the possibility of an elevated pedestrian and cycle route, which would link the city with the highly disconnected Favela areas. Due to the usually difficult topography, James introduces nodal cores along the route,

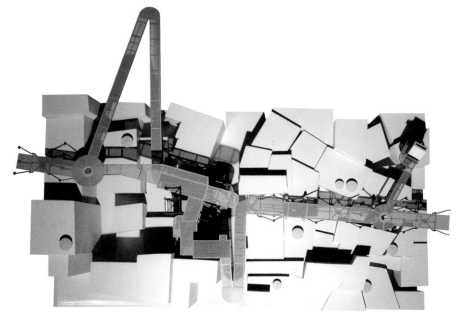

16.8

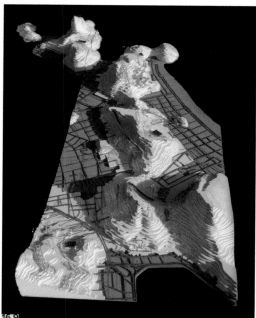

16.9

16.10

made from the temporary kiosk and small service structures used in the Olympic park. They serve as vertical connections down into the Favela, as well as a framework for various services, such as small libraries, launderettes, cafes and bike repair shops. **Fig. 16.9** Robert Burrows, Y4, Mountain Top Olympics, Rio de Janeiro, Masterplan model. Rob studied the possibility of housing the Olympic games within the centre of Rio, and proposed to situate the various venues across the hills and mountains that surround the city. Working with two methods of creating spaces, Rob first carves out the venues from the Gneiss granite rock, and then adds a lightweight and temporary layer of games mode infrastructure such as seating, lighting, service structures and media centres. **Fig. 16.10** Philip Poon, Y5, Virtual Olympics, Everywhere and nowhere,

augmented drawing. The project speculates on the idea of a placeless Olympics. Motion capture and film substitute the usually colossal and incredibly high budget builds, and instead the city is upgraded with technology that enables the user to scan, position and experience the Olympic events, taking place everywhere at the same time.

16.11

16.12

Fig. 16.11 Jonathan Blake, Y5, City Engines, Rio de Janeiro, Model view. Looking to solve the city's water supply problem, Jonathan uses the Olympics as a catalyst for developing a new set of infrastructures for the harvesting, cleansing and distribution of clean water. Situated in Guanabara Bay, the project is developed in two parts. The games mode, in which the sailing event is temporarily hosted in the bay, and the legacy mode, in which the remaining infrastructure continue to feed the city, long after the games are over. **Fig. 16.12** Ione Braddick, Y5, Carnival Of Construction, Rio de Janeiro, Model view. Ione wanted to develop a more local way of handling the Olympics, rather than the corporate, sponsored, and truly global event it currently is. Inspired by the famous carnival, she developed a design for the main stadium as a totally

temporary construction, with bespoke elements that could be re-assembled as a set of urban infrastructures, street furniture, temporary structures and permanent buildings.
Fig. 16.13 Rachel Hearn, Y5, Raining On Your Parade, London, Perspective view. Rachel's project dissects the legacy framework of the London Olympics, and attempts to fulfil the promise of improving the neighbouring host boroughs. She develops a strategy for recycling, cleansing and distributing water, and uses this process to create a public landscape where the thrill and poetics of water becomes the centre of attention.
Fig. 16.14 Oliver Leech, Y5, Favela Farm, Rio de Janeiro, model view. Studying the catering operation at the London Olympics, Oliver set out to offer an alternative way of urban farming to promote locally sourced produce and a community led

16.13

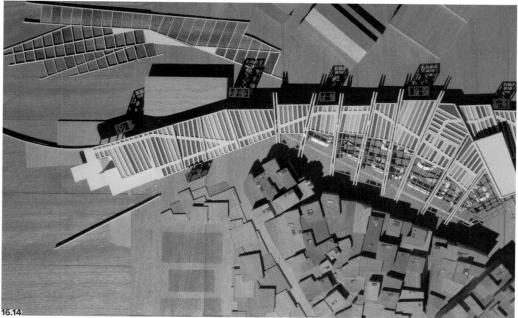

16.14

approach to food production. Situated at the edge of one of Rio's favelas, it straddles the border between the favela and the city centre, and as such become a connecting structure with the aim to bring the city together.

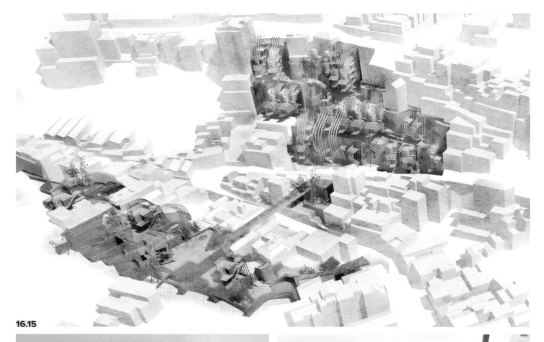

16.15

16.16

16.17

Fig. 16.15 – 16.18 Samantha Rive, Y5, A local Olympics,
Rio de Janeiro. Overview Image, model, rendered view
and plan fragment. Sam's projects starts with the challenge
of embedding the Olympic games into the fabric of the city,
and to celebrate sports as a culturally significant event. Through
a meandering route that takes the visitor from the Guanabara
Bay waterfront and up through the city, a series of programmes
are cleverly inserted into the currently vacant gaps in the urban
fabric. Terraces, cantilevering houses and public squares all take
advantage of the spectacular views below.

16.18

Materials: Ideas

Yeoryia Manolopoulou, Niall McLaughlin, Michiko Sumi

Unit 17 designs contextual buildings that interplay with the social, political and material cultures of specific places. Each project is research-based, aiming to construct an architectural thesis that is explicitly manifested in the design proposition. We are interested in the student's imagination and original voice, and seek diversity in the work produced by the Unit as a whole: projects complement and sometimes intentionally contradict each other to form a multi-layered dialogue about the nature of architectural thought and practice today. Design iteration through drawing and making is a constant activity that we encourage. Stimulating debates through open crits and tutorials, and a critical osmosis of ideas and techniques in the studio, are vital aspects of the Unit's culture. Field trips play an important role in the development of the work and we invest substantial energy in designing itineraries which include experiencing extraordinary places and cultures.

This year we visited rural and urban Russia to experience how places that physically embody a deep history of the tensions that occur between ideology and building. Our intention was to focus on the complex physical and political role that materials play in the production of architecture.

Materials have shaped architectural ideas throughout history and cultures. They are practical as well as intellectual tools which communicate powerful messages. Specific materials represent unique human values and achievements, and have socio-political meaning. They determine the structural logic and environmental performance of a building, but also the very essence of its space and its relation to experience.

Materials transform and dematerialise over time, creating ambivalences and paradoxes. We are interested both in the truth and fiction of materials: their ability to reveal and also to deceive. 'To fabricate' means to make by skill and labour, or by assembling parts or sections, but also to devise

a legend or a lie, to fake or forge a document. We find the idea of material metamorphosis and the ironic potential of fabrication inspiring for architecture today. We explore the extent to which materials can continue to reflect the geography and socioeconomic position of a site and look for material innovation which can transcend the limits of a place responsibly.

In the digital and post-digital era our material consciousness has changed. Virtual media and simulation deny the experience of physicality, biotechnologies change our sense of scale and solidity, and digital manufacture is redefining the building process. Mixing the manual and the digital in hybrid materialities is now the new norm. But in this post-digital era what is the potential of materials beyond just geometric form?

In the beginning of the year the students produced compelling architectural environments that were experienced spatially at large scales and evoked the extreme political and environmental conditions that have shaped aspects of the Russian building stock over time. These works were research-based and asked questions that were further explored in the field trip, where the students eventually found sites for their final building projects. Russia's vast land, declining industrial monotowns, remote islands and ice-bound wildernesses offered us a wealth of experiences. Our journey began in Moscow through the prefabricated micro-districts, the workers' clubs and experimental social housing schemes, the churches and heavily ornamented metro stations. From Moscow we took an overnight train through the winter Russian landscape to Petrozavodsk, flying to remote Kizhi Island in Lake Onega, where we explored the extraordinary seventeenth century timber churches of Karelia. Some of us ended our journey in St Petersburg, Russia's grand 'window to the west', with its Baroque buildings, Soviet factories, the constructivist avant-garde neighborhoods, and the Tsars' lavish summer palaces outside the city. Others made individual research field trips to the suburban dacha settlements in the hinterland of Moscow, the fortified Kronstadt on Kotlin Island, the port city of Murmansk within the Arctic circle, and the two declining monotowns of Pikalevo and Magnitogorsk, the last one in the inhospitable location of the Ural River deep within the Siberian steppe. These unique field trip experiences were crucial in determining this year's work.

For making our journey so informed and stimulating we are grateful to: architectural historian Nikolai Vassiliev from Docomomo, architect Inna Tsoraeva and graphic designer Mike Loskov who guided us through Moscow; Kuba Snopek and Eugenia Pospelova from the Strelka Institute; Yuriy Milevskiy from the Higher School of Economics in Moscow; and architects Denis and Katya Panfilova who helped us in Murmansk.

For their constructive criticism, special thanks to: Alessandro Ayuso, Johan Berglund, Peter Bishop, Anthony Boulanger, Barbara Campbell-Lange, Vasilis Constantatos, Bev Dockray, Will Hunter, Guan Lee, Tania Malysheva, Jack Newton, Sophia Psarra, Mary Ann Steane, Mike Tonkin, and Cindy Walters.

Design Realisation tutors: David Hemingway, Joanna Karatzas and Joseph Mackey, with Structural Engineer William Whitby, Arup.

Year 4
Alastair Browning, Joel Cady, Alicia Gonzalez-Lafita, Uieong To, Harry Tweddell, Mika Zacharias

Year 5
Alice Brownfield, Tamsin Hanke, Alexander Reading, Francis Hunt, Shu Wai (Charis) Mok, Ben Hayes, Hannah Sharkey

17.1

17.2

17.3

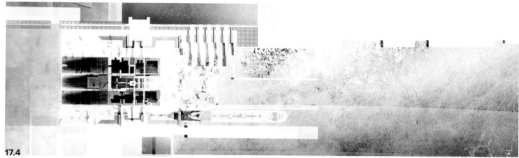

17.4

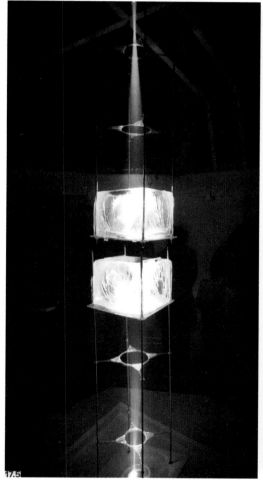

17.5

17.6

Fig.17.1 Alice Brownfield, Y5, Public Architecture Library and Kitchen, St Petersburg. The project is situated in Narvskaya Zastava, an area radically replanned in the 1920s as the centre of socialist Leningrad. It studies the ideologies of constructivist architecture and attempts to recharge the idea of the social condenser by considering the role of public libraries and kitchens in contemporary society. Montage is used both to destabilise perceptions and create incidents between the two programmes. Selected fragments of constructivist projects are retained, creating a space that is strangely familiar. **Fig. 17.2** (Left to right) Harry Tweddell Y5, Peski Airport, Petrozavodsk; Joel Cady Y4,, Klyazma Nursery School, Moscow; Uieong To, Y4, Collector's House, St. Petersburg. **Fig. 17.3** (Left to right) Mika Zacharias, Y4, Finland Station, St. Petersburg; Alicia

Gonzalez-Lafita Perez, Y4, Catherine's Portrait Hall; Alastair Browning, Y4, Khrushchev Housing, Petrozavodsk. **Fig. 17.4 – 17.6** Alexander Reading, Y5, Arctic Research and Political Faculty, Murmansk Technical University. Situated deep in the port of Murmansk, the proposal speculates an alternative version of the Arctic petropolis that Murmansk is shaping up to be. The project suggests a socially integrated approach to Arctic research and discourse, shifting Murmansk beyond the industrial and situating it in a new economic context that is focused on striking a balance with its delicate ecosystem. The architecture is conceived as an urban block, with narrow crevices that penetrate a thick and monolithic exterior to reveal a delicate and environmentally reactive interior, celebrating the movement of water and ice that encases the building.

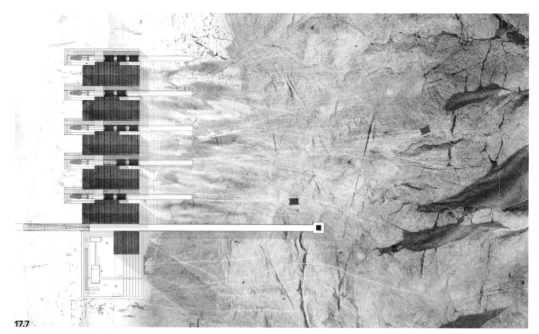

17.7

17.8

17.9

Fig. 17.7 Francis Hunt, Y5, Kronstadt Measuring Terminal, Kotlin Island, St Petersburg. By deploying portable micro-shelters across the frozen sea in Winter this outpost allows researchers to conduct ice monitoring and map stable tourist walking routes to Kotlin's ruined military islands. As these landscape instruments scratch thousands of pathways leading to the horizon, the project subtly memorialises the thousands of sailors fleeing the massacre of the Kronstadt Revolution of 1921. **Fig. 17.8 – 17.9** Hannah Sharkey, Y5, Reclaim Bahrain Reconnecting to the Sea. In response to the accumulating land reclamation that has privatised most of the coast of Bahrain and disconnected coastal villages from their coast, this project seeks to examine how the sea can once again be central to Bahrain, reconnecting Bahrain to its forgotten coast through a fish market and fish auction space. **Fig. 17.10 – 17.12** Shu Wai (Charis) Mok, Y5, Underground Public Square, Moscow. Moscow has an extensive underground network: the Moscow Metro partly built as a visual propaganda under Stalin, the secret Metro 2, newer metro lines and stations, and many underground rivers that crisscross to form a complex underground maze. The proposal focuses on the area of the Red Army Theater, extending the theatre and its square to the maze space below. Emphasis is given on public space and social interaction rather than efficiency of circulation. In certain parts weather, light and views are brought inside this underground labyrinth making strong visual connections to the sky and the city above.

17.10

17.11

17.12

17.13

17.14

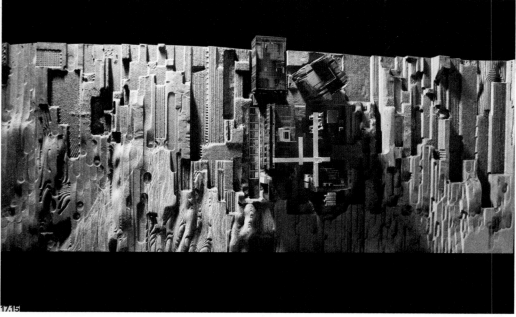

17.15

Fig. 17.13 – 17.16 Tamsin Hanke, Y5, Magnitogorsk: A study of Stalin's first and most significant 'monocity', which straddles the border between Europe and Asia on the eastern face of the Ural mountain range. Named after the 'magnetic mountain' from which its magnetite iron ore came, Magnitogorsk's existence is entirely built around the now privately owned MMK steel factory, which employs, feeds and infrastructurally supports the whole population of the city. The project looks at the history of the city from its design by Ernst May in 1929 to its current state as the stagnated spatial legacy of a construct deliberately designed to influence society to form a compliant new working class, instilled with the values inherent to a vision of utopia. Through this study, it establishes two main frameworks for the architectural project – firstly the importance of a financial disruption to the neoliberal capitalism which has replaced the communist economy locally; and secondly the necessity for a balance between top down order imposed as an intervention, and bottom up systems of self propelled change in the city. Through siting a location for the newly signed Russia China Investment Fund, it seeks to explore the potential for economic and cultural diversification within this single employer micro-dictatorship. The design spatially aims to use the mass of charred timber totems to define publically accessible voids beneath a cast iron roof. It plays with the idea of an opaque, primitive language through both analogue and digital technologies in order to try to find an architectural robustness able to both confront the existing condition and shelter a new function in the city.

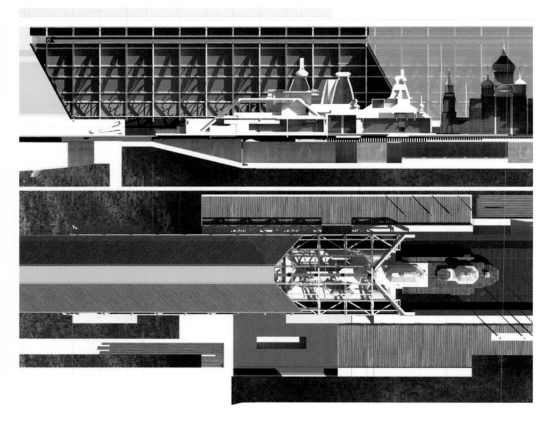

17.17

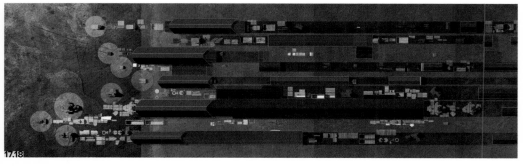

17.18

Fig. 17.17 – 17.19 Ben Hayes, Y5, Kizhi Island, Republic of Karelia, Russia. The project proposes an architectural intervention to facilitate the restoration and reassembly of 300 churches onto Kizhi Island in Northern Russia. These churches were once landmarks to their communities, however in contemporary Russia, these fragile, desecrated wooden structures will almost totally disappear in 10-15 years. The remote island of Kizhi is situated on Lake Onega and over time its image has been idealised and commodified as buildings have been relocated onto it. The project proposes a new type of open-air museum, a concept that was originally formed from the desire to preserve architectural heritage and aestheticise the past. This aesthetic approach to landscape grew out of the ideals of nationalism and romanticism, however, as shifting notions of culture and identity change in Russia, the role of the open-air museum in the future is uncertain. This project challenges how the island has been re-orientated towards the recreation of the 'aesthetic function' of monuments and inevitably reflects today's knowledge and aesthetic values, not those of the times when the monuments were originally built. The proposal addresses two problems: to protect and restore this fragile heritage close to extinction, and to radically redesign the visitor experience. A new restoration facility and open-air museum are proposed to facilitate the dismantling of surrounding timber monuments, their transportation to Kizhi, restoration and final deployment around the island. The landscape is treated as a repository for protected buildings, constantly transforming and challenging existing notions of heritage preservation and production.

1739

Crypto Phantom's Sensorial Materiality

Nannette Jackowski, Ricardo de Ostos, Manuel Jimenez Garcia

This year Unit 18, or *Generational Phantoms*, investigated concepts of cryptography to generate architectures with rich encoded social and material effects situated in the contentious territory of Jerusalem.

In many societies, secrets, mysteries, secluded knowledge and confidential information have been converted into codes, signs and symbols; their real meanings only being noted by those in the know. Cryptography as the art of encrypting information has been used for centuries in security protocols and military communication to securely transmit classified messages. The development of encrypting/decrypting methods alongside the arms races in the Second World War was the midwife of the digital computer, as testified in our visit to Bletchley Park, a secret code-breaking facility during WWII in the UK. At this moment students started to explore encryption and architecture as vents for design as a channel to processing codes of social practices and history into its armature.

Following the study of Alan Turing, one of the key cryptanalysts in Bletchley Park, and his exploration of what computational power can be and do, students developed their own process of encryption with the aim to create spatial structures and scripts. Here the notion of code was subverted from the well-known digital realm into analogue vocabularies of materiality. By generating methods of transforming information into matter, students created worlds where the computational is processed and 'saved,' not in bits, but in material grains and spatial scenography.

How could architecture as a vessel of spatial and material information further levels of social interaction? Could cryptography and its neurotic concern with security, codes and calculation power be utilised in architecture, not only to protect but also to create unconventional access to layers of interactive performance in buildings?

Moving to Jerusalem as a main context, students pursued the concept of diplomatic spaces placed in a sacred city filled with multi-layered beliefs, deep divisions and ancient religious practices. Where diplomacy, coexistence and access are key to understand the nuances of one of the oldest cities in the world, students mapped social practices, rituals, myths and symbol systems creating an architectural repertoire, positioning themselves and reacting to the tranquil and tense conditions found.

Investigating the Dead Sea Scrolls and their ambivalent interpretation, Anthanasios Varnavas problematised the notion of architectural meaning and digital language. Based on limestone extraction on site and the cultivation of knowledge the project is organised as a series of encrusted cave like spaces deliberately manufactured and encrypted by rough limestone drilling. The project unveils part of his experiential hypertext via a combination of wet surfaces and dry cactus, de-territorialising the contested landscape into a steaming primeval rock of opaque meaning.

Exploring the connection between encrypting generational codes, Anthony D'Auria regarded his project as a computational machine where materiality becomes the medium for social-historical integration. Here the secrets of Bletchley Park evolved into the history of a group of Ethiopian Jews called 'Beta Israeli' and their dramatic migration to Jerusalem. The outcome is an Amharic language institute situated on the armistice line in Jerusalem where the construction of the building becomes interwoven with a political and material context. Social codes are metamorphosed into a bullet spray, concrete formwork becomes a toolset of language degradation and light apertures slowly unveil a building under tension. Encryption becomes the means to morph the weak signals of culture.

What happens when ruins are territorialised, alienated from its users and disputed by religious driven politics? Set up in the City of David's archaeological site, Adam Casey investigated cryptography as the shadow noise between digital scanning and its mistranslation into a fluid construction site. Ruined arches and underground ornamented caves ooze into a new language of luminescent resins and light effects. The emerging structure is a digital phantasmagoria of scanned archaeological ruins manifesting against the backdrop of desert storms and religious conflict. Recognition is exchanged for discovery, symbolism for vestiges and the architecture figures ground for a reincarnated landscape of ambiguous formations. Visitors of this park of sorts may meander through sluggish spaces of incomplete arches, ornamented columns, reflective ceilings in search for hidden meanings and revelations.

Generational Phantoms is a think tank scrutinising the outcomes of digital interfaces in contentious territories. We speculate about the abnormal of 'situation normal' in war zones, divided geographies and contested territories reutilising the catalogue of beautiful monstrosities and the horrifically entertaining present in machine or human form. As spatial response the projects recreate what architecture can be in a world where the notion of the architect as a figure behind a desk is being substituted by an explorer of emerging environmental conditions. In this context cryptography is as much a digital design process as a protocol for socio-political engagement.

Thank you to our external consultants: Sara Klomps, Rob Partridge, Ricardo Baptista, Ruairi Glynn, Christian Derix, Stephen Gage and Jason Slocombe.

Thank you to our guest critics: Apostolos Despotidis, Ryan Dillon, Jeroen van Armeijde, Kostas Griqoriadis, Theodore Spyropoulos, Ruairi Glynn, Mollie Claypool, Theodore Sarantoglou Lalis, Marcos Cruz, Carles Sala, Tyen Masten, Brendon Carlin, Gilles Retsin, Filip Visnjic, Jose Sanchez, Christine Hawley, Alice Labourel, Tobias Klein and Robert Stuart-Smith.

Year 4
Anthony D'Auria, Sing Sun (Ryan) Cheng, Juhyung (John) Chun, Anna Maria Janiak, Alan O'Connell, Mahmetcan Sisman, Anthanasios Varnavas

Year 5
Adam Casey, Shao Jun (Susan) Fan, Anis Wan Kamaruddin, Alex Sanghwa Kim Saman Ziaie,

phantom18.co.uk

18.1

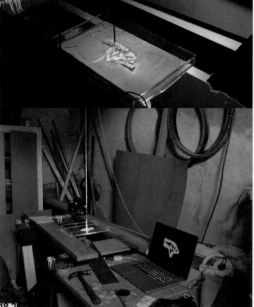

18.2

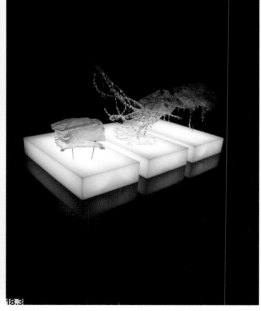

18.3

Fig. 18.1 Adam Casey, Y5, Translations of an Invisible Landscape. The initiation of a new archaeology based upon the hidden landscape of Jerusalem's contested past. Reconstruction revealing the translation from digital 3D scan to physical manifestation and the emergence of a new depiction of a digital landscape. **Fig. 18.2** Adam Casey, Y5, Translations of an Invisible Landscape. Process of manifesting the digital through the casting of light onto a UV curable material. **Fig. 18.3** Adam Casey, Y5, Translations of an Invisible Landscape; Material prototypes for the manifestation of the hidden archaeology, exposing the conditions for growth and the reconstruction through a light responsive medium. **Fig. 18.4** Adam Casey, Y5, Translations of an Invisible Landscape. Technological excavation of the hidden

pathways, cisterns and ossuary's beneath the surface of the old city of Jerusalem, and the extraction of the digital for the physical manifestation in the new archaeological park for the contested past.

18.4

18.5

18.6

18.7

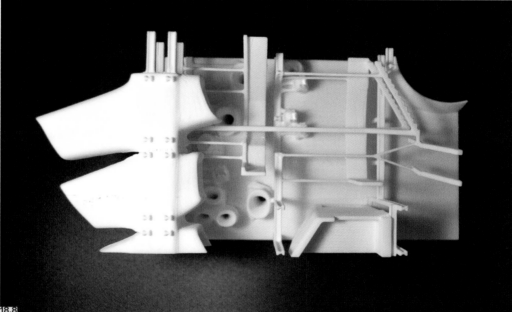

18.8

Fig. 18.5 Anis Wan Kamaruddin, Y5, The Essene Temples of Purity. In the quest for purity away from the politics of the sacred and an increasing anthropocentricity within Jerusalem, a cluster of Essene Temples slowly emerges from the receding Dead Sea. A section through the first level of ritual baths (mikveh) reveals the physical transformation it goes through as the water level recedes. The shape allows it to hold water long after it is fully exposed, allowing for crystallisation to take place, and for it to become a bath. **Fig. 18.6** Anis Wan Kamaruddin, Y5, The Essene of Purity. The descent into the Room of Feasts sits below a sequence of reading rooms overlooking the sacred space – its shape influencing the eventual crystallisation that will form on its underside, adorning the space below. Descent into the room is possible only when the cluster has completed its Jubilee cycle and the space is fully revealed. **Fig. 18.7** Anthony D'Auria, Y4, Amharic Language Institute. A hybrid materiality of 3D-printed bullets blasted into a concrete substrate encrypts recollections of the gruelling exodus of the Beta Israel people from Ethiopia to Israel. Encrusted bullets plug into the inner façade and act as expulsion vents for eclectic formwork secreted within the mass of the building. **Fig. 18.8** Anthony D'Auria, Y4, The Exodus of the Beta Israel. The language institute explores the social, cultural and linguistic displacement of the Beta Israel people by proposing a piece of cultural infrastructure to combat the gradual erosion and decline of their native Amharic Language in Jerusalem.

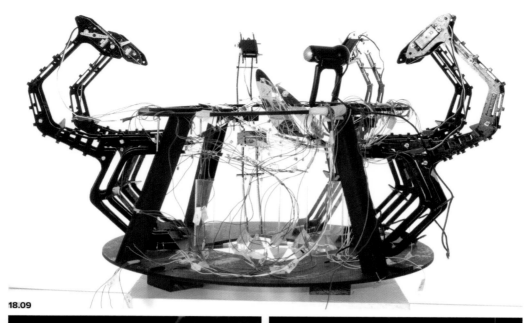

18.09

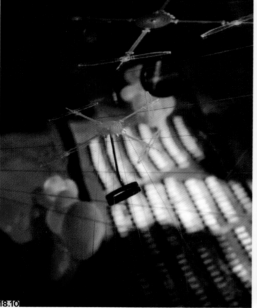

18.10

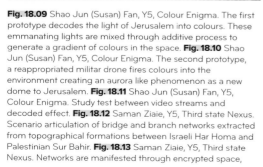

18.11

Fig. 18.09 Shao Jun (Susan) Fan, Y5, Colour Enigma. The first prototype decodes the light of Jerusalem into colours. These emmanating lights are mixed through additive process to generate a gradient of colours in the space. **Fig. 18.10** Shao Jun (Susan) Fan, Y5, Colour Enigma. The second prototype, a reappropriated militar drone fires colours into the environment creating an aurora like phenomenon as a new dome to Jerusalem. **Fig. 18.11** Shao Jun (Susan) Fan, Y5, Colour Enigma. Study test between video streams and decoded effect. **Fig. 18.12** Saman Ziaie, Y5, Third state Nexus. Scenario articulation of bridge and branch networks extracted from topographical formations between Israeli Har Homa and Palestinian Sur Bahir. **Fig. 18.13** Saman Ziaie, Y5, Third state Nexus. Networks are manifested through encrypted space,

hidden within a shell that camouflages the activity within. The concept of duality becomes integral to design, where two seemingly disparate elements harmonise with each other. **Fig. 18.14** Saman Ziaie, Y5, Third state Nexus. Digital painting study of entangled networks and appropriation of new peeled topography.

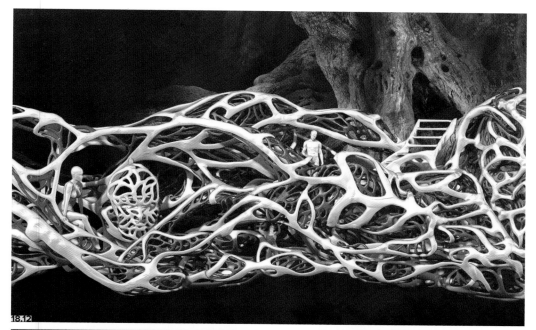

18.12

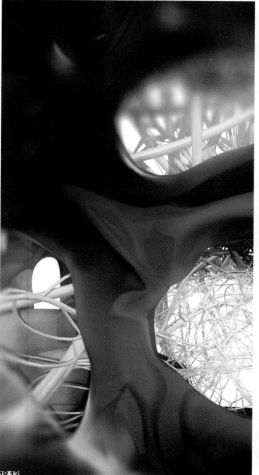

18.13

18.14

18.15

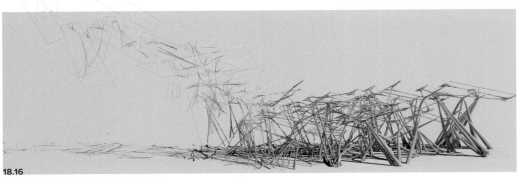

18.16

18.17

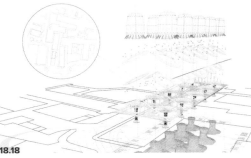

18.18

Fig. 18.15 Juhyung (John) Chun, Y4, Lighting Study of Shi-pai Village, Guangzhou, China. **Fig. 18.16** Anna Maria Janiak, Y5, (Top) Repository of Destroyed Buildings. The events of numerous terrorist attacks and bombings along Jaffa Road are encrypted in the 3D matrix of the building. (Bottom) Enchanted Forest. Intervention in Bletchley Park encrypts events from WWII into the forest of information. Lines encipher data of people killed during battles, countries participating in them and date of each event. **Fig. 18.17** Mahmetcan Sisman, Y4, Sonic installation in Bletchley Park. **Fig. 18.18** Sing Sun (Ryan) Cheng, Y4, Encryption of the decay. Spatial intervention in Hut 6, Bletchley Park utilising temperature difference and state change of wax as an encoding process for building envelope decay, consequently creating a deformation of spatial

and tactile experience over time as the notion of internal/ external gradually diminishes. **Fig. 18.19** Anthanasios Varnavas, Y4, Hermeneuticist's Embassy. The bridge of fear and courage. Expressing the innocence or danger of crossing between lines; the delicate artefact becomes referential to its urban context, augmenting the volatile nature of the 1949 Armistice Line and the place where it's torn to generate the No-Mans Land. **Fig. 18.20** Anthanasios Varnavas, Y4, Hermeneuticist's Embassy. Mining the rock, sourcing the materia prima. The building is constructed in a series of time-based phases of a choreographed machine performance which resembles even celebrates segregation. The rock is constantly sculpted, translating threshold lines into deep scars in the earths surface.

18.19

18.20

The Living Spaces of Algorithmics

Philippe Morel, Kasper Ax, Mollie Claypool

'We must turn our attention for a moment to something even more substantial than architectural design, and that is the question of how we live. [...] We must indeed admit that we do not live as we would wish to live, so that even more difficult question arises as how we want to live and what our ideals really are. In asking ourselves this question we have to be careful to define all three of its elements: we, want, live.' Constantinos A. Doxiadis, *Architecture in Transition*, 1963.

The question 'how do we want to live?' has driven our design research this year, coupled with a devotion to the utilisation of theories of computation, the philosophy of science and mathematics and new fabrication and construction technologies. The projects have taken this question and these tools to formulate an advanced theoretical approach in order to inform pragmatic investigations of what could be a *new analytic view of the house*. Unit 19 sees this question and computation as deeply interconnected, as computation has become more and more normative in our everyday lives: in the way we communicate, in modes of industrial production and in research and design. This paradigm is not novel, for the post-WWII Case Study House Programme in Los Angeles, signified the beginning of this evolution, with the shift from balloon frame construction to steel and other new materials and technologies.

The Case Study House Programme was a response to the context of post-WWII Los Angeles as an apogee for the war industry and laboratory for aeronautical engineering. This led to what *Arts & Architecture* editor John Entenza called a new kind of 'domesticity' of the post-war house. This new domesticity was made of high levels of performance, efficiency and hygiene in conjunction with low levels of cost that were seen as being inseparable from fabrication and construction. The banality of the house is countered by the notion that it could be the space for the synthesis of architect, engineer, designer, anthropologist and user into the making (design, fabrication/construction) process. Entenza therefore saw the house as singularly holding the potential for mass capitalisation on the revolution of industry and economy by the war effort. This was our starting point for the year.

In our first project, each student chose a Case Study House, which they found provocative, analysing it rigorously in terms of material, tectonics, construction, fabrication and social and cultural influences. This drawing exercise was countered with in-depth research into the evolution and dissemination of new technologies starting from post-WWII scenarios up until the present day. This research informed and was the driver for further drawing and modelling exercises beyond the initially selected Case Study Houses of each student, diversifying their projects – from research by Neil Keogh into the history of the plastics industry to inform his design of an affordable carbon fibre house; Shuo Zhang with the development of cybernetics and robotics from John Neumann onwards to confront the ever-more present issue of flexible working and living; or Stacy Peh tracing the breakdown of the post-war domestic model of the kitchen and our relationship to the automobile – making each student a specialist in their own right in a strand of architectural research from the last 60 years.

It has been our Unit's hypothesis this year that there is an inefficient and inconsistent relationship between initial idea, representation, production and execution in the architectural process. In order to reconcile this, we have implemented a working methodology that utilises various mathematical and computational tools to produce actual and virtual output in the form of physical models and prototypes – such as the use of cellular automata and fractal models by Matt Lacey in his project for an infinitely-expandable house for a growing family, the logic and mathematics of origami folding patterns by Mihir Benodekar to design a flat-pack housing system, or Stuart Colaco's work on optics and prisms to produce a prototypical wall system that manipulates user perception and experience of 'place'. David Ward's work on a 1:1 concrete component system and Jeffrey Lim's project utilising the corrugated surfaces of shipping containers to prototype a modular framework for social housing in Los Angeles tackled these issues from the opposite end of novel processes fabrication and construction, while Catherine Francis' project attempts to build a new framework for energy collection and consumption in areas of the United States most devastated by the recession of the last five years.

Our Unit's Design Realisation project was supported by robotics and software workshops with Research Cluster 5 of the MArch GAD programme and Manja van de Worp. Thibault Schwartz further informed our method of production, as did meetings with material scientist Justin Dirrenberger. A Unit trip to Los Angeles enabled us to not only have first-hand experience of many of the Case Study Houses which were the inspiration for the Unit this year, but also enabled us to meet with experts in Los Angeles housing such as UCLA Professor Mark Mack, partake in a review of Peter Testa's robotics studio at SCI-Arc and meet with Andrew Witt, Director of Research at Gehry Technologies.

Year 4
Stuart Colaco, Matthew Lacey, Jeffrey Lim, Stacy Peh, David Ward, Shuo Zhang

Year 5
Mihir Benodekar, Catherine Francis, Neil Keogh

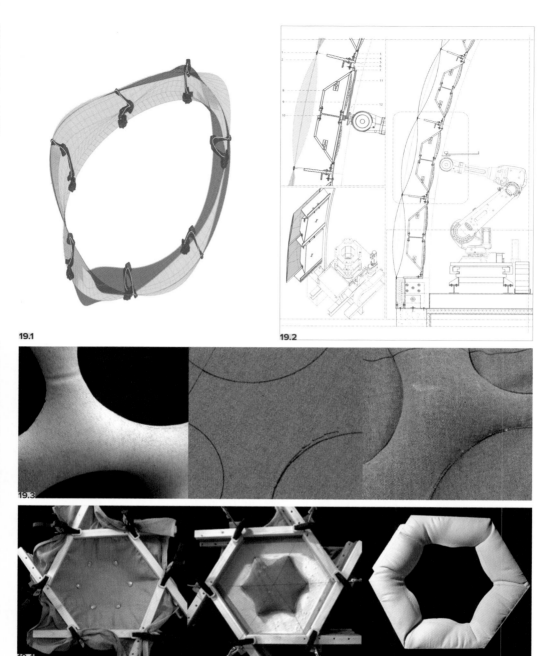

Fig. 19.1 Shuo Zhang, Y4, Tracing the robot trajectory as a path-finding experiment. **Fig. 19.2** Shuo Zhang, Y4, Reconfigurable envelope for a flexible live/work building. **Fig. 19.3** David Ward, Y4, Detail of David's Fabric formwork concrete façade components. **Fig. 19.4** David Ward, Y4, The fabric formwork jig and resultant façade components. **Fig. 19.5** David Ward, Y4, Fabric formwork concrete façade components.

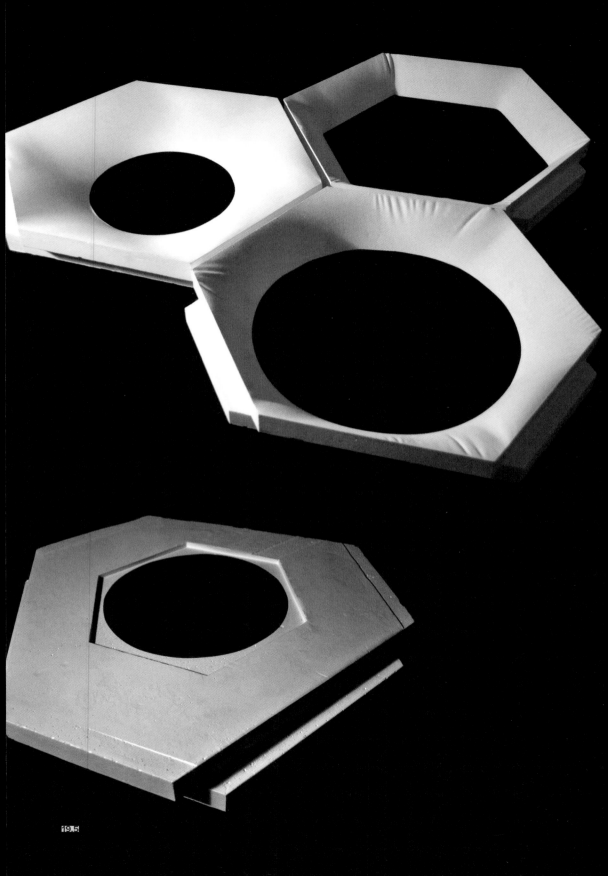

195

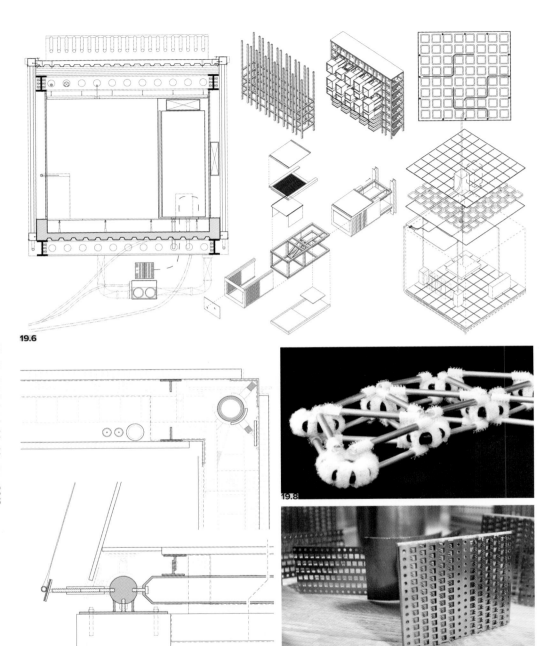

19.6

19.7

19.8

19.9

Fig. 19.6 Stacy Peh, Y4, Construction process of solar passive apartments by showing technical devices concealed in steel frame construction. **Fig. 19.7** Matthew Lacey, Y4, Detail drawings showing the lattice panel system of the unit component for infinitely expandable modular house. **Fig. 19.8** Matthew Lacey, Y4, Velcro model for simple expansion and reconfiguration of panel components. **Fig. 19.9** Matthew Lacey, Y4, Detail of panel component using Metaklett 'steel velcro' **Fig. 19.10** Catherine Francis, Y5, Design for a pneumatic roof that reacts to the sun, collecting water vapor in the air through a fog-catching fabric and mechanism, also providing shade.

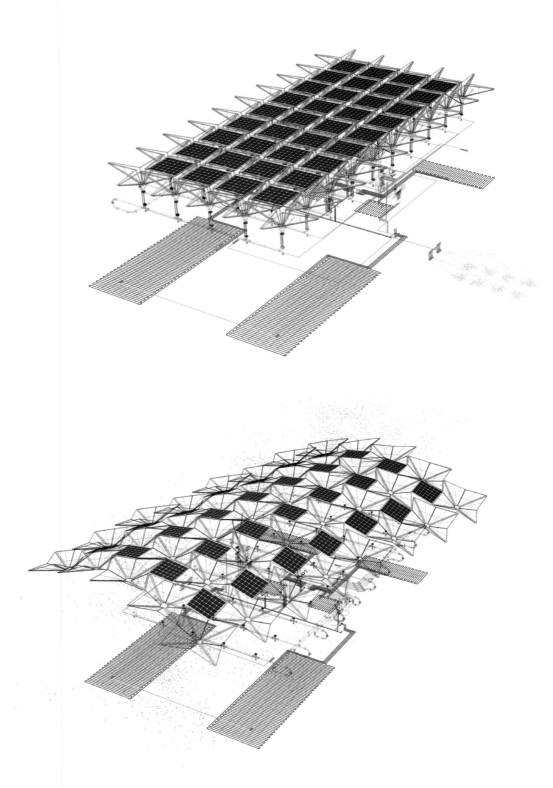

19.10

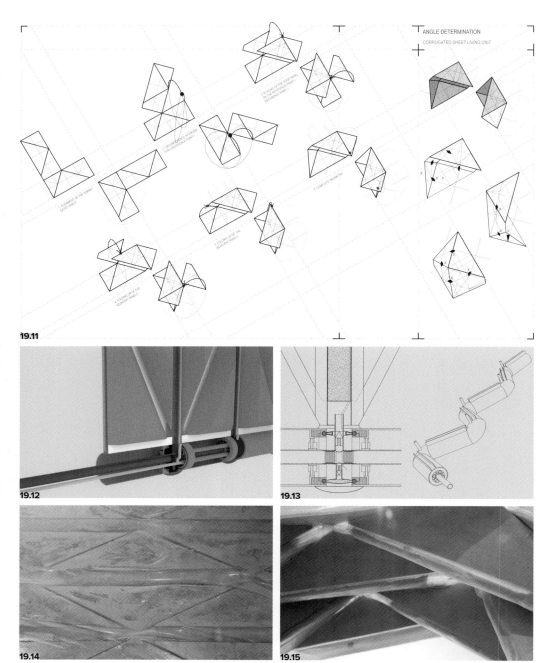

ANGLE DETERMINATION
CORRUGATED SHEET LIVING UNIT

19.11

19.12

19.13

19.14

19.15

Fig. 19.11 Jeffrey Lim, Y4, Determining the angles for a corrugated sheet metal panel system for Jmodular container house. **Fig. 19.12 – 19.13** Mihir Benodekar, Y5, The vacuumatic beam detail for house prototype for nomadic artists. **Fig. 19.14 – 19.15** Mihir Benodekar, Y5, Details of the 1:5 prototype of design for a flat-pack panelling system for the façade of his house prototype. **Fig. 19.16** Neil Keogh, Y5, search for a service core constructed of carbon fibre which twists along a ruled surface utilising the trajectory of the robot. The robot in red shows the automatic detection of an unreachable position by HAL 004.5 (for Grasshopper).

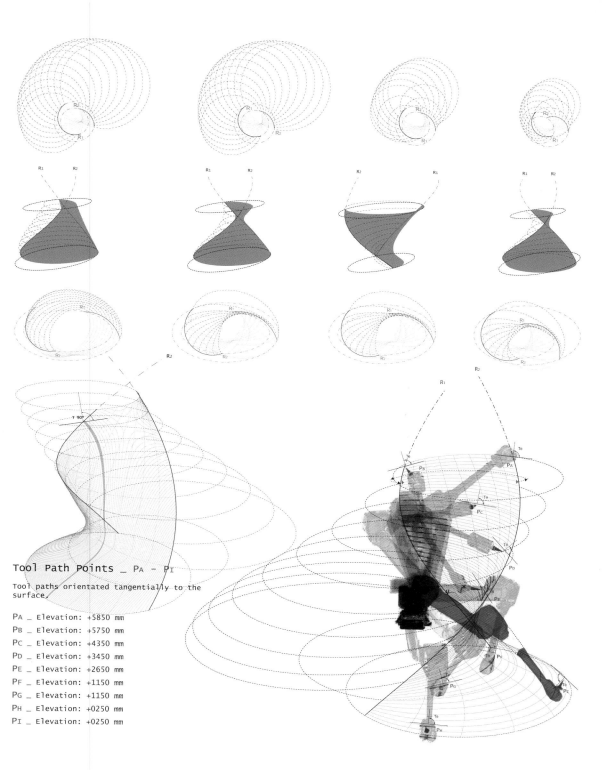

Tool Path Points _ P$_A$ - P$_I$

Tool paths orientated tangentially to the surface.

P$_A$ _ Elevation: +5850 mm
P$_B$ _ Elevation: +5750 mm
P$_C$ _ Elevation: +4350 mm
P$_D$ _ Elevation: +3450 mm
P$_E$ _ Elevation: +2650 mm
P$_F$ _ Elevation: +1150 mm
P$_G$ _ Elevation: +1150 mm
P$_H$ _ Elevation: +0250 mm
P$_I$ _ Elevation: +0250 mm

19.16

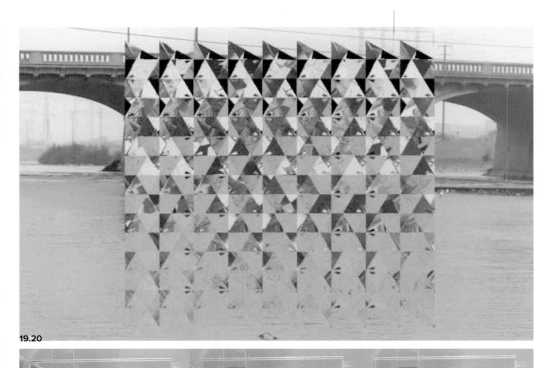

19.20

19.21

19.22

Fig. 19.20 Stuart Colaco, Y4, Façade simulation with a
geometrical component gradient looking out over the Los
Angeles river. **Fig.19.21** Stuart Colaco, Y4, Model experiments
for the design of refractive façade components utilising inverse
tetrahedrons filled with water in three phases. **Fig. 19.22** Stuart
Colaco, Y4, A 1:4 scale model of 1.5mm thermoformed right
angle tetrahedron moulds set inside an acrylic tank as part
of the design process for a house façade. **Fig. 19.23** Stuart
Colaco's, Y4, Photograph of 3D-printed model of perception
and vision-shifting façade for a house. **Fig. 19.24** Stuart
Colaco, Y4, A volumetric luminosity histogram of house.

19.23

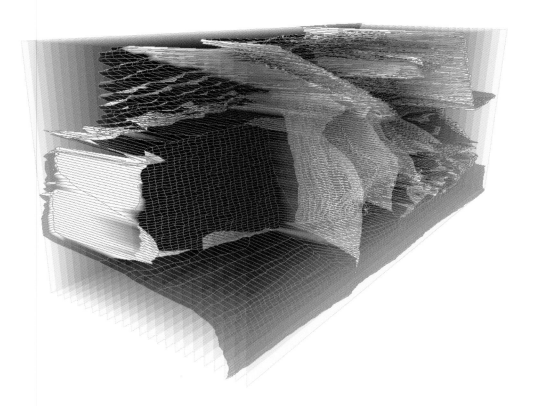

19.24

Porosity: A Material Shift Towards an Architecture of Permeability

Marcos Cruz, Marjan Colletti, Richard Beckett

Architecture has long been determined by its prime necessity of protection and permanence, which has in turn led to a sense of hardness, closure and inertia that still affects our buildings and cities today. In the early periods of the Modern Movement, architects proclaimed the liberation from heavy and massive constructions by turning to a much more open and free-flowing architecture. The Miesian fluidity of transparent space and Le Corbusian *Plan Libre* prophesised a new era in which society seemed to have gotten rid of its constraining mass. But the crisis of the Modern Movement and the emergence of Postmodernity exposed the fallacies of previous beliefs. Architecture went back to its former closure and inherently opaque dimension. Designers rediscovered their love of the physical presence of materiality and colour, indulging with the embedded nature of architecture in historic form and style.

Contemporary architecture overcame such dialectic positions (of either/or logics) by advocating more hybrid conditions that explore both three-dimensional depth and mass, as well as the ever-permeable condition of space, environment and matter. Profound transformations in our current society, new postdigital paradigms, and the emergence of an unprecedented environmental awareness are pushing architecture forward to discover a new understanding of social porosity and a new sense of materiality.

Social Porosity

The precincts of our information era have made our domestic environments in particular extremely exposed (even vulnerable?), pushing us to reflect on a new sense of intimacy and perception of space. The employment of new geometric, structural and material complexities is also allowing our cities to become physically, environmentally and technologically more sensitive and surely more pervious to cultural multilayering. The potential porosity of contemporary buildings is shifting towards an open architecture of ultimate permeability, including hybrid private-public

spaces, mixed internal-external areas, transitional enclosed-open voids, multi-layered façades etc.

Neo-materiality

It could be argued that the history of architecture is also a history of materials, material innovation, material assembly and fabrication and how they have drastically changed the discipline. In a contemporary debate, materiality as a driving force of innovation is reflected in a postdigital paradigm shift towards a new sense of materiality. Neo-materiality marks the ambition to escape from the virtual and cyber architectural visions of the early days of digital architecture, as well as from the standardised, off-the-shelf and environmentally and financially unsustainable architectural production methods of the past, towards innovative applied theories, techniques and technologies.

Students in Unit 20 explored new material conditions through a broad range of material studies. These included for example the experimentation with concrete, rubber, Polyfloss, 'sillycone', wax, 'foament' (foam and cement), nylon composites, milled stone and 'audio-bricks' (acoustic responsive bricks). By combining both analogue and digital processes, students embraced a variety of material/tectonic experiments, which created the underpinning conceptual structure of their projects. The implementation of new 3D rapid prototyping techniques and innovative CNC milling technologies also reflected (on) the advent of Neo-materiality.

Unit 20 investigated these conditions in the cultural context of Hong Kong and Macau; two places with a strong hybrid identity resulting from merging Chinese and Western cultures. Whilst analysing the extreme topographic, urban and social diversity of the river Delta, students researched new modes of private/public life in this part of the world, which is undergoing arguably one of the most rapid, fascinating yet problematic transformation processes occuring in human civilisation. Extreme urban sprawl is leading to an unprecedented form of verticality, density, (threat to) privacy, the proximity and/or segregation of wealth and poverty in these cities. By reinterpreting local habits, global typologies, old traditions and recent legislations, students developed projects that focused on contemporary domesticity and housing typologies, catering for an emergent open way of metropolitan living. Furthermore, the projects investigate how the sensorial presence of materiality can affect the generation and experience of space, both on a 1:1 bodily scale, as well as on a larger urban scale.

Thanks to Justin Nicholls for his invaluable commitment to supervising Year 4 students during the development of their Design Realisation report, and to all our critics: Jaime Bartolome, Kathy Basheva, Roberto Bottazzi, Matthew Butcher, Fernando Jerez, Marco Polletto, Yael Reisner, Stefan Ritter, Stefan Rutzinger and Marin Sawa.

Many thanks also to the Institute of Making, UCL for material sponsorship.

Year 4
Anahita Chouhan, Judith Shiow Yin Gillespie, Thomas William Hopkins, Wai Yue (Ruby) Law, Olivia Pearson, Sam Rigby, Javier Ruiz, Emily Yan

Year 5
Amittai Antoine, Steven Ascensão, Juhye Kang, Joanna Pawlas, Era Savvides

20.1

20.2

Fig. 20.1 Javier Ruiz, Y4, Dragonfly Colony. The residential project is sited over the Red Hill Peninsula, South of Hong Kong Island. The modular housing typology, developed through variable/iterative systems, focuses on circulation strategies for housing schemes. **Fig. 20.2** Thomas William Hopkins, Y4, Coast Line Thresholds. Using the study of thresholds to question conventional notions of space and challenge traditional distinctions between public/private and natural/built environments this housing project develops around a mangrove ecosystem along the coastline of Hong Kong, suggestive of a more porous and permeable architecture. **Fig. 20.3** Joanna Pawlas, Y5, Sonic Morphologies, The Compact Accommodation Tower. The proposal investigates ways of analysing and inhabiting the urban soundscape of Kwun Tong to generate controlled sonic environments through creation of site-specific, parametric geometry of reflective surfaces and levels of sonic permeability by means of natural acoustics.

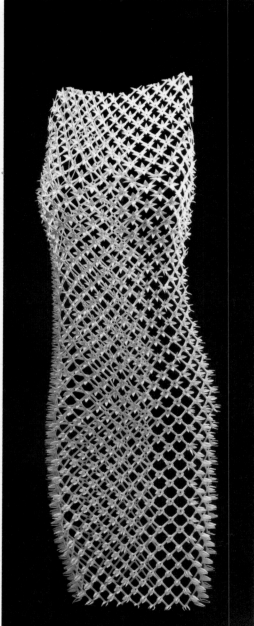

Fig. 20.4 Anahita Chouhan, Y4, Serendipitous House for Hong Kong. To stack and interlock housing equates to efficiency in the Mid-Levels of Hong Kong. There is a necessity for density and a growing urgency for verticality. This is maximised through the utilisation of the quintuplex apartment type, which focuses on fluidity of movement and circulation as the basis for its form. **Fig. 20.5** Ammitai Antoine, Y5, The Embellished Image. Full perspective of 1:1 selective laser sintered nylon dress. The project hopes to explore the subjective affect of the 'image'. This study accentuates the duality between the image one hopes to portray to the observer (through the dress), and the true condition of the body underneath, Dress of Petals.

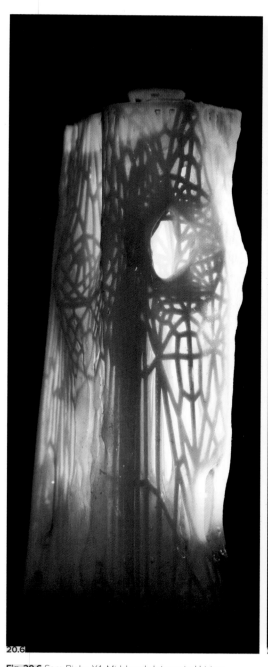

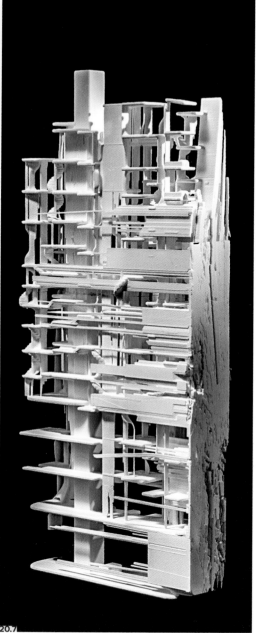

Fig. 20.6 Sam Rigby, Y4, Mid-Levels Introverted Living. Embedded silicone façade model testing light and density levels. The project reverses the local typological 'cage house' challenging traditional notions of space, light, adaptability and individuality. **Fig. 20.7** Juhye Kang, Y5, Innerforest, Tsim Sha Tsui District. Through considering the highly densified and destructive façade of Hong Kong, vertical service pipes develop the language of 'in-between' space, created as an inner forest with innovative self-foaming porous structures.

20.8

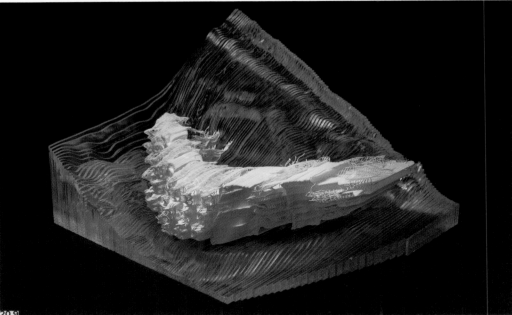

20.9

Fig. 20.8 Emily Yan, Y4, Inhabitable Thresholds, Undulating Apartments, Hong Kong. In response to the extreme densities of Hong Kong, the proposal develops a design system of maximised surfaces. The envelope creates tension between the interior and exterior. **Fig. 20.9** Olivia Pearson, Y4, The House of Denaturalisation, Investigating The 'Fibrous', Mount Davis, Hong Kong Island. The Dematerialising Residence begins to integrate a hybridity between the topographical context and the fibrous concrete proposal. Through material experimentation and investigation a stringy language of algorithms began to interpret and represent the delicate nature of the design proposal.

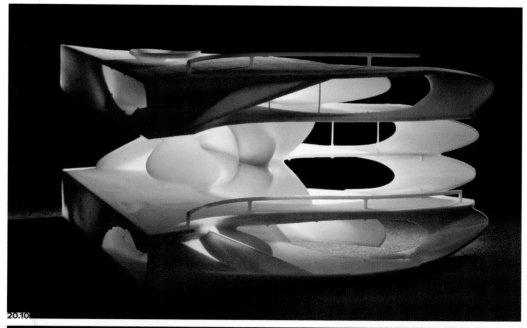

20.10

20.11

Fig. 20.10 – Fig. 20.11 Era Savvides, Y5, Digital Petrology.
The project wishes to uncover the parallels currently emerging
between the realm of digitality in architecture and that of
phenomenology, as interpreted within the current post-digital
context and through a primary focus on material poetics.
What begins as an open-ended enquiry into the porosity of
stone with a curiosity towards material translucency develops
into a propositional idea concerned with the potentialities that
arise from the synthesisation of various fabrication techniques
into a system, which uses a subtractive method to create
material for additive process.

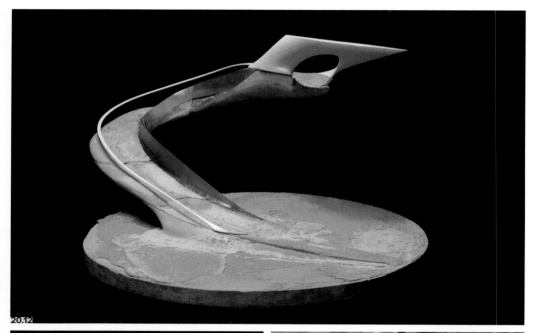

20.12

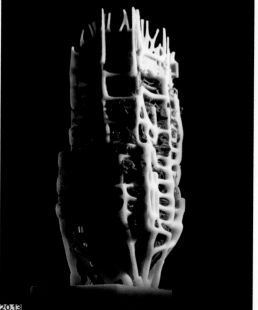

20.13

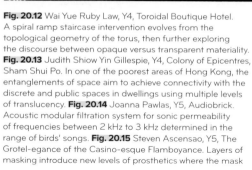

20.14

Fig. 20.12 Wai Yue Ruby Law, Y4, Toroidal Boutique Hotel. A spiral ramp staircase intervention evolves from the topological geometry of the torus, then further exploring the discourse between opaque versus transparent materiality. **Fig. 20.13** Judith Shiow Yin Gillespie, Y4, Colony of Epicentres, Sham Shui Po. In one of the poorest areas of Hong Kong, the entanglements of space aim to achieve connectivity with the discrete and public spaces in dwellings using multiple levels of translucency. **Fig. 20.14** Joanna Pawlas, Y5, Audiobrick. Acoustic modular filtration system for sonic permeability of frequencies between 2 kHz to 3 kHz determined in the range of birds' songs. **Fig. 20.15** Steven Ascensao, Y5, The Grotel-egance of the Casino-esque Flamboyance. Layers of masking introduce new levels of prosthetics where the mask

provides the user with greater capabilities reflected upon the architecture. The performance reflects the casinoesque nature of a habitable gateway in Macau's inner harbour; a connection point to mainland China. It uses the hybridisation of grotesqueness & elegance whilst embracing Chinese iconography as a figural language for the architecture. The two opposites interacts with one another where the soft, delicate fabric, penetrates the hard shell being left exposed and unprotected. This movement is also reflected upon the coexistence of the dragon and the phoenix is an important iconography for the Chinese culture as it symbolises the wealth and prosperity for the unity of polar opposites.

2015

Chronometrics

Abigail Ashton, Andrew Porter

Mercatorial projection is a translation between the curvilinear geometry of the surface of the earth and a two dimensional – or flat – projection. It is a deliberately false system that preserves the angles and meridians of the earth but presents it as a digestible tableau from which we can easily orientate ourselves. Since the creation of this geometric system in 1569 we have been conditioned to understand the world in this way; and it is ironic that after the world was largely established as spherical in the 15th century we have had such a predominantly 'flat earth' view since. Prior to the invention of satellite GPS; the dilemma between these two systems is exemplified by the history of the marine chronometer and the struggle to develop improvements in error correction (i.e. Harrison and the story of longitude).

This year the Unit continued to investigate such systems of slippage and distortion in the context of the translation between drawing and building. We developed a chronometric architecture that asked how you might represent time based and dynamic spatial systems or environmental datasets.

Panorama

By its very nature a panorama is artificial. It is a false view constructed from a series of views, which would ordinarily be unattainable with our natural cone of vision. In project one the Unit was asked to construct or draw a proposal that was optically panoramic or responded to a particular panorama of their choosing. They were asked to consider the scale of the panorama – for instance was it micro-scale rather than the conventional macro view? It could heave been a panorama of a normally hidden landscape or re-interpretation of what a panorama might be within contemporary culture. This first project was viewed as a tool to investigate initial ideas on the panoramic and the artificial, and how one might take these ideas forward into the year's work.

Pavilion

Tremenheere Sculpture Gardens in Cornwall is a garden that has only recently opened to the public. Amongst other sculpture pieces, it houses two of only five site sculptures by James Turrell in the UK. Turrell is one of the key references used by Robin Evans in his essay 'Translations from Drawings to Buildings' which the Unit drew inspiration from last year. Evans describes such translations as having the capacity to 'get bent, broken and even lost on the way' and this continued to preoccupy the Unit.

Tremenheere is located in Penzance and looks out onto Mounts Bay and St Michael's Mount; there is a 25-mile panoramic view out of the garden stretching from the Lizard Point to Lands End. The garden at Tremenheere is the work of one man who, over a fifteen-year period aided by a JCB, has remodelled and planted the new landscape that is apparent today. Whilst the scale of this undertaking and its obsession is reminiscent of the work of Simon Rodia in constructing the Watts Towers in LA, it is a project that is bedded in the history of the artifice of the English garden. In the manner of Stourhead it is a purely synthetic construct, shrouded in the picturesque. However it is an exotic scenario as the diverse global planting makes use of the warm microclimates found in Cornish valleys.

A series of new buildings are planned for the garden. The first, a visitor centre with a restaurant and shop, has just been completed. The next building planned is for a pavilion and this was the subject of the first building project of the year. It was a live project. The Unit held an internal competition and the intention was for Tremenheere to build the winner. Alex Gazetas project was chosen and he will be in discussions with Tremenheere and the local planning department shortly. This project was used as the basis for the fourth years Design Realisation document.

Tangier

In the New Year the Unit visited Tangier. It is an extraordinary city due to its geographic position. On the very edge of Africa and immediately adjacent to Europe it is a key portal between the two. Tangier looks inwards to the fast developing continent of Africa; and it looks outwards to Europe as a major trading partner. It is also at the gateway to the Mediterranean and is at the heart of an expanding shipping economy (both touristic and trading). Its ports are developing rapidly to cater for this. Historically, Tangier is obviously a densely layered culture with long traditions of both European and Arabic religious, political and mercantile systems. It is also more recently a draw for artists and writers and filmmakers. The Unit developed urban strategies and programmes based on their earlier chronometric research.

The fourth year also had the privilege of being invited by Kengo Kuma to participate in a competition to design a retreat in a rural area of Japan. Eight university teams were invited from all over the world.

Thank you to our critics: Professor Christine Hawley, Dr Rachel Cruise, Tom Holberton, Costa Elia, Godofredo Pereira, Professor Stephen Gage, Jonathan Kendal, Professor Peter Bishop, Theo Sarantoglou Lalis, Charlotte Bocci, Dr Neil Armstrong

Design Realisation Tutor: Tom Holberton
Unit Structural Engineer: Brian Eckersley

Unit 21 would like to give a special thanks to Tom Holberton and Dr Neil Armstrong for their support this year.

Year 4

Emma Carter, Naomi Gibson, Wai Hong Hew, Yu Chien (Wendy) Lin, Tess Martin, William Molho, Risa Nagasaki, Joseph Paxton, Simona Schroeder, Sayan Skandarajah, Antonia Tkachenko

Year 5

Alexander Gazetas, Sarah L'esperence, Shogo Sakimura

ashtonporter.com
ashtonporter.net

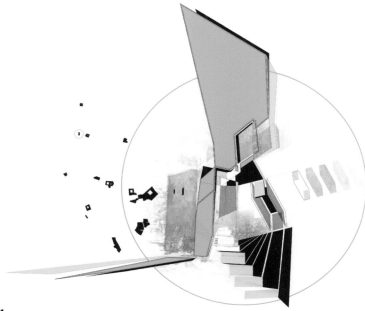

21.1

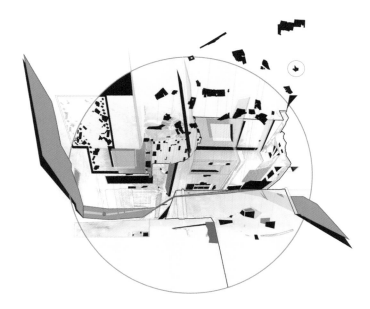

21.2

Fig. 21.1 – 21.2 Sara L'Espérance, Y5, Medina Parasite, Tangier. Inspired by the contrast between the tight, dark and winding streets of Tangier's Medina and the light and whimsical roofscape, the Medina Parasite seeks to bring public life to new heights as a hovering, expanding parasite in and amongst the roofscape of the old city. Developed as a flexible structure, the proposed parasite acts as a 'base' for future expansion as the need for public space increases. Moments from this base have then been re-appropriated elsewhere within the Medina as scale-shifted versions of their original function. These scale shifts not only change in size and orientation, but in their function as well: a lookout turns into a compressive prayer chamber, a dark stairwell into a viewing platform, thus recalling previous memories of past experiences.

Fig. 21.3 Sayan Skandarajah, Y4, Restituted Territories, Tangier. Spatial and temporal exchange is explored at the Tangier Medina wall; a threshold between opposing city conditions as well as between the foreign and local communities.

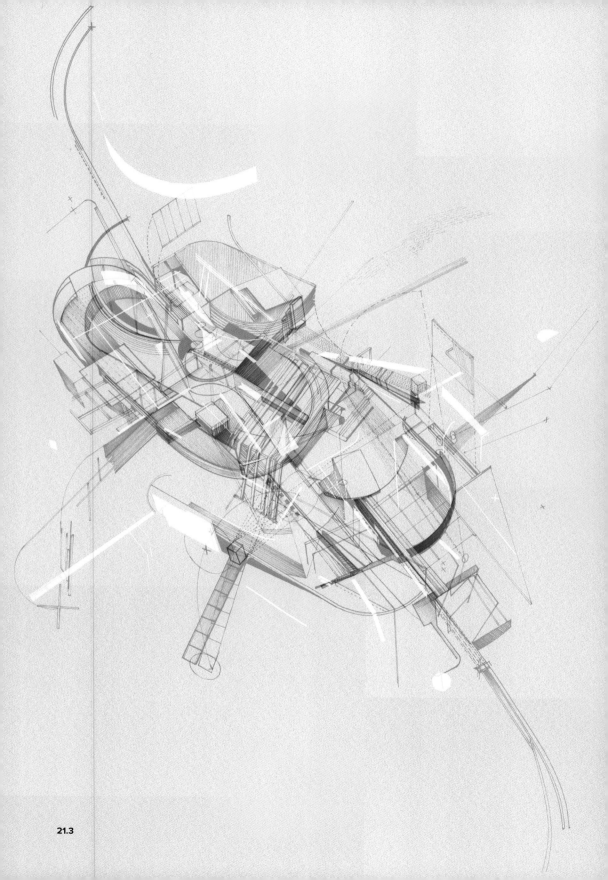

21.3

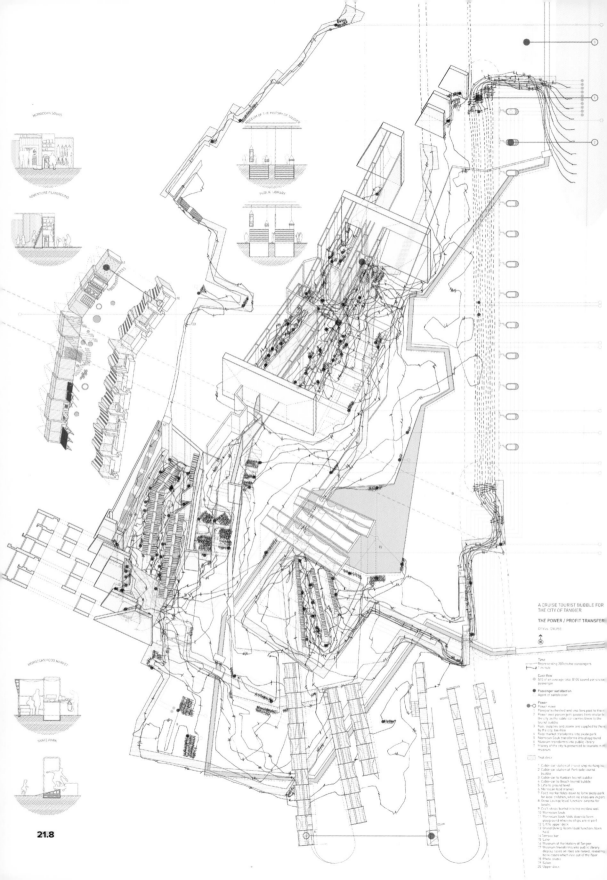

MOROCCAN SOUKS

ADVENTURE PLAYGROUND

MUSEUM OF THE HISTORY OF TANGIER

PUBLIC LIBRARY

MOROCCAN FOOD MARKET

SKATE PARK

A CRUISE TOURIST BUBBLE FOR
THE CITY OF TANGIER

THE POWER / PROFIT TRANSFER

CITY vs. CRUISE

21.4

21.5

21.7

21.6

Fig. 21.4 Antonina Tkachenko, Y4, Performative Flooding of Tangier Interzone. Proposed fluctuating levels of water flood the hyper-textural landscape and create a series of formal and informal performance spaces, bridging the boundary between the Medina and the Port. **Fig. 21.5** Sayan Skandarajah, Y4, Restituted Territories, Tangier. Spatial and temporal exchange is explored at the Tangier Medina wall; a threshold between opposing city conditions as well as between the foreign and local communities. **Fig. 21.6** Simona Schroeder, Y4, Tangier Roofscape Theatre. Bringing the tourists and travellers into the 'horizontal Medina' and creating spaces for communication with the people of Tangier. **Fig. 21.7** Wai Hong Hew, Y4, Tangier Folklore Museum. The Folklore Museum exhibits and documents the oral tradition of sharing stories, culture and

experiences of the Tangerines. A series of momentary experiences are intentionally composed and then spontaneously connected to one another to indicate a design and program that is intriguing, imaginative and story-like, and to complete the history of the Medina wall with the integration of the design as a wall façade. **Fig. 21.8** Tess Martin, Y4, The 6-Hour City: A Cruise Tourist Bubble for the City of Tangier. The development of the cruise tourist bubble proposes a reform of the way cruise passengers experience the city, and the way the city presents itself to the cruise industry, ultimately by changing the power / profit relationship between city and cruise company.

21.9

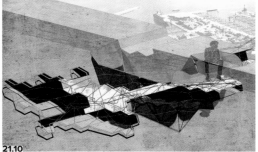

21.10

21.11

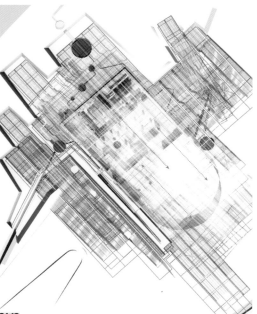

21.13

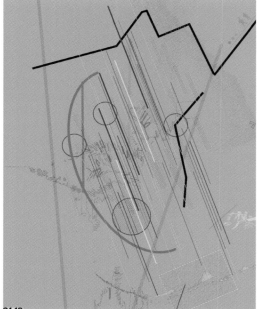

21.12

Fig. 21.9 Risa Nagasaki, Y4, Pixelated Topography, Cornwall: shift of focus and blurring the boundaries. **Fig. 21.10** Yu Chien (Wendy) Lin, Y4, House of Wisdom, Tangier. Tangier's public library is built as a continuation of the ancient Medina wall and introduces tourists (penguins) to Tangier's modern culture through subtle movements of the digital structure revealed at intervals. **Fig. 21.11** Tess Martin, Y4, The 6-Hour City: A Cruise Tourist Bubble for the City of Tangier. The development of the cruise tourist bubble proposes a reform of the way cruise passengers experience the city, and the way the city presents itself to the cruise industry, ultimately by changing the power / profit relationship between city and cruise company. **Fig. 21.12** Emma Carter, Y4, A [Cornish] Tropical Landscape, Cornwall. SpringTime - Carved microclimates choreograph seasonally

responsive routes through the landscape and provide optimum conditions for tropical plants to thrive all year round. **Fig. 21.13** Joseph Paxton, Y4, Tremenheere Kinetic Pavilion, Cornwall. The pavilion's design focuses on the interstitial zones created between the kinetic roof and the natural landscape below, providing perpetually transgressive states of opacity through multiple layers of ever-changing configured light modules. **Fig. 21.14** Emma Carter, Y4, B[r]eaching Tangier, Plage Municipale. Respectful interjections into abandoned and disused public spaces along the beach front in Tangier, aiming to rejuvenate an undeveloped and leftover area of a currently evolving, yet stagnant, city.

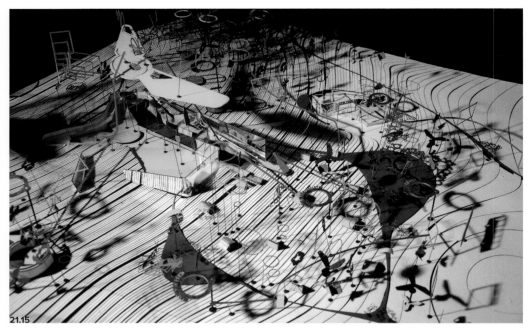

21.15

21.16

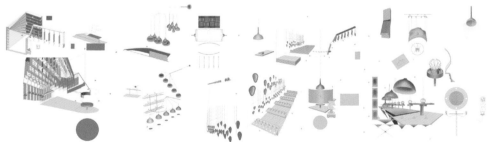

21.17

Fig. 21.15 Shogo Sakimura, Y5, Heterotopic Triarama, Cornwall. Framed views across the horizon are altered by a shifting landscape, which reflects and camouflages architectural moments. **Fig. 21.16** Alexander Gazetas, Y5, Light Cloud Pavilion, Cornwall. The form of the pavilion has been derived from light levels across the site in Tremenheere Sculpture Gardens, which were mapped and turned into point cloud data. This was then used to form the 'cloud-like' roof ceiling, floor, lighting, screening and structural elements. The intention behind the competition-winning pavilion is to manifest the world of hidden information into physical form. **Fig. 21.17** Naomi Gibson, Y4, The Unreliable Narrator's Stock Exchange, Tangier. Like the guides and verbal tales that permeate Tangier, the Unreliable Narrator's Stock Exchange is illusory and contrary, designed to disorientate visitors and never reveal the full story. It distorts and manipulates the trade and economic information created within it, questioning the boundary between fantasy and truth, presenting a false picture of the economic health of the city. **Fig. 21.18** Joseph Paxton, Y4, [Hydrodynamic] Landscapes of Liminality, Tangier. The Masterplan insertion deals with thresholds of old and new in the city of Tangier, creating a multilayered event of kinetic oscillations, fluctuations, fragmentary vision and perceptions of space, this is explored through the drawing of technological and experiential datascapes.

[HYDRODYNAMIC] LANDSCAPES OF LIMINALITY // COLLECTION 01_.

A map of kinetic oscillations and fluctuations and their interactions with the natural landscape. Showing a technological and experiential datascape
of perpetual transition between differing states. The time-based information highlights thresholds between the natural and artificial landscapes,
proposed and existing.

Wood And Fire: Towards a Definition of Mild Architecture

Izaskun Chinchilla, Carlos Jimenez

Unit 22 researches, among others things, how architecture can welcome users through small details and a soft and cosy understanding of materiality. For that reason, two material facts provided the title for the year: wood and fire. Wood was selected not only for its technical qualities but for its contextual dimension. Using local wood consciously implies understanding the structure of an ecosystem and managing geographical notions, while maintaining perception of memory, craft and biology. Placing real fire in our spaces has forced us to think about thermodynamic functioning while offering a place to gather and talk.

Wood and fire have been inspirations for the beginning of our year and the small details that welcome and empower users have been one of our major interests. But we quickly jumped out of a linear methodology to go deeper into the contextual implications of material and energy. In this process, the objective and subjective values of wood and fire have been melded together. The technical skills of the students, the details which serve as interfaces to users, and a deep contextual reflection, have met.

If we began the year wondering around what 'mild architecture' could be, we now have new words and definitions providing a wider frame to architecture for its future.

Folk
Academic architecture typically avoids an association with folk. Architecture has been decontextualised and abstract languages and materials have provided the aesthetic. It is now time to look at human rituals, daily life and communal celebrations. In those episodes, space, objects and material systems reassemble the human figure and restructure community. Many of our students have researched ancestral rituals from different areas of the world. The decoration of the floating boats and platforms made by the Bajau Laut tribe in Semporna, Malaysia, for their annual festival; communal bathing rituals in Greece, Russia and Japan; rice

transportation in Kerala, India; craft activity in Beijing Hutongs, China or the puppet theatre in Indonesia have been part of the reflection of Akmal, Megan Townsend, Joanne, Lulu and Kirsty. Within their designs they have challenged the tradition in which technical aspects command the design process. Their architecture does not fundamentally follow an abstract function or occupy a structural frame. Their drawings and models take the footprint of human activity, assume its vernacular precedents and shape this activity in a soft materiality that wraps the inhabitants and occupies the place between their body and their shelter. Technical elements have to find their place and scope within this folk nature.

Cute
While Western cultures encourage women and children to value 'cuteness' there is also a real masculine tradition of fighting it. Architecture, as part of a masculine domain of knowledge and practice, has systematically refused cuteness as a major value. One obvious yet evident effect of this battle has been the colourblind tradition affecting architecture throughout the last century. Meanwhile Claire has placed sky blue tiles in her Coventry project, Akmal has been daring with pink chimneys, delicate star patterns cover Kirsty's skins and embroidery gives character to Clarissa's textiles. These students have found that part of the charm of British medieval cities can be underlined by bringing fairytales to visitors' minds or that delicate embroidering can challenge the significance of digital fabrication techniques in the construction industry. Cuteness may have a strategic communication value in future decades; it is already used by advertising agents, pop singers and food brands.

Alive and Vibrant
The methodology of the year was planned to make the students aware of the types of life architecture has to preserve. The main project, 'harbour', forced students to face an open definition of the built

environment. Open air facilities, infrastructures, landscape treatment, links and connection between architectural objects have been framed in each exercise. Each project helps architecture to meet and organise different environmental levels. The architecture of many of our students presents exceptional continuity with its surrounding landscape. Many details have been designed to flow with the wind, to keep moving during their lifespan, to change with the rhythm of seasons and tides – to create an architecture that breathes. The roof over Lilian's floating architecture swings slightly with the rainwater, helping its collection and its direct use. Jose Ignacio has learned from tropical architecture to keep his designs open to natural flows; he has even learned to knot them. Water is storage; it evaporates, forms cloud and mist, and softly condenses in Megan Townsend's indoor bathing landscape. To use Megan Smedy's hotel facilities one needs to cycle and walk. The movement around the landscape and its surroundings helps users find comfort and beauty.

A Bigger Pattern

Unit 22's design core implies a strategic vision of architecture. Therefore we have encouraged students to propose specific combinations of sites and projects with strategic intentions. Many of our students split the project across several locations or transform a whole urban area in the frame of a new institutional activity. Most of the projects include benefits for locals and visitors. Some create typologies that can be replicated. All of them try to think on how architecture can help make a life. All act within a larger pattern. These principles can be found in the collaboration that Lilian established between Cambodian medicine, floating architecture and income coming from tourists. They are also crucial to how Clarissa has understood the participation of Tunisian workers in Sicilian agriculture. This sensibility has enabled Freya to distribute her student location tactically in Cartagena de Indias, enabling students and businesses to work together. This vision is the one

helping Lulu imagine Beijing Hutong can be an architecture school and a local necessity, with reinforced income ensuring not only preservation but a respectful upgrade.

This year Unit 22 has been generously supported by Vidal Associates and Roca.

Pedro Gil has supported the Unit as a Practice Tutor for Design Realisation. Roberto Marin has been our Structural Consultant. During the year Catrina Stewart, Hugh McEwen, Felipe Mesa, Miguel Mesa, Nerea Calvillo, Felipe Hernández, Nacho Martin of Mi5 architects, Carlos Arroyo, Nuria Lombardero, Curro Canales, Yael Reisner, Luis Vidal, Max Dewdney and Chee-Kit Lai have participated in our intense and deep crits.

Our fieldtrip to Colombia was especially amazing for the support of MAMM Museum in Medellin and the direction of Felipe Mesa or Plan B Arquitectura. Medellín Digital, Mesa Editores and Universidad Bolivariana de Medellin were also some of the welcoming institutions.

Year 4
Akmal Azhar, Georgia Follet, Jiang Dong, Yuen Sar (Lillian) Lam, Jose Ignacio Ortiz-Muñoz, Joanna Preston, Kirsty Williams

Year 5
Victoria Bateman, Freya Cobbin, Le (Lulu) Li, Megan Smedy, Clarie Taggart, Megan Townsend, Clarissa Yee

Fig. 22.2 MAMM Pavilion, Medellín. 1:10 scale prototype of the outdoor pavilion comissioned by Museo de Arte Moderno de Medellín (Colombia). Design was developed by Unit 22 together with students from Universidad Pontificai Bolivariana de Medellín directed by Felipe Mesa (Plan B arquitectos, UPB), Jorge Pérez Jaramillo (UPB) and Miguel Mesa (Mesa Editores, UPB). It is composed by six detachable units inspired by local palafito villages allowing them to be relocated in the future. Sponsors: Mamm, U.P.B, The Bartlett School of Architecture, Cluster de Energía de Medellín, Restaurante Blanco, Área Metropolitana de Medellín, Medellín Digital. **Figs. 22.3 – 22.4** Le (Lulu) Li, Y5, Scale 1:10 model for Hutong Architecture School drawing studio. The model study aims to reintroduce paper as architecture material and test how paper can be used together with wax to create temporary architectural elements fit for the culture and weather, through a combination of craftsmanship and contemporary digital fabrication.

22.3

22.4

22.5

22.6

22.7

22.8

Fig. 22.5 Joanna Preston, Y4, Chimney Dwelling: A dwelling for a Local Historian, Batley. Sited at a local vantage point and drawing upon the mechanisms used in the local textile industry, the structure unfolds to become a gathering place where storeys about the towns prosperous history can be shared. **Fig. 22.6** Kirsty Williams, Y4, Theatre for traditional Indonesian shadow art, Wayang Kulit. Sited on the Citarum River, widely acknowledged as the most polluted river in the world, it also incorporates a water treatment centre. **Fig. 22.7** Akmal Azhar, Y4, A Fish Market for the Sea Nomad in Borneo, Malaysia. The fish pickling aquarium details; the external façades of the aquarium are made out of boat sails that are recycled from the annual Regatta Lepa festival. The sails will be propped open when the pickling process is done to exhibit the product to the visitors. **Fig. 22.8** Le (Lulu) Li, Wax and paper reading table designed for the 'Hutong Architecture School' library, to test the idea of revealing through time, and fire as the main source for lighting and heating.

22.9

22.10

22.11

22.12

Fig. 22.9 Claire Taggart, Y5, Start-Up City (Coventry). Adaptable live/work business incubation unit structure for temporary inhabitation in empty high street retail units. **Fig. 22.10** Freya Cobbin, Y5, Harbour of Exchanges (Cartagena). Single cut pop-up technique enabled development of an inhabitable terraced roofscape. **Fig. 22.11** Megan Townsend, Y5, Bow Creek Cultural Bath House, sited on a derelict outcrop in East London, is a new community and experience driven proposal, for social interaction within London's modern urban fabric. **Fig. 22.12** Yuen Sar (Lilian) Lam, Amphibious harbour: Traditional Khmer health care centre, Cambodia. Sited next to the Tonle Sap which constantly floods its surrounding areas, the design proposes a new approach to deal with climatic changes and re-establish people's links to their use of water within the architecture.

22.12

22.13

Figs. 22.12 – 22.13 Kirsty Williams, Y4, Theatre for traditional
Indonesian shadow art, Wayang Kulit. Sited on the Citarum
River, widely acknowledged as the most polluted river in the
world, it also incorporates a water treatment centre. **Fig. 22.14**
Clarissa Yee, Y5, New Migrant Journeys, Sicily. A typology,
to house migrant Tunisian agricultural workers in Sicily.
The dwelling design draws upon Sicilian and Tunisian culture,
each migrant worker is given a house, which is transported by
lorries to agricultural lemon and almond picking sites, forming
clusters of seasonal accommodation.

22.14

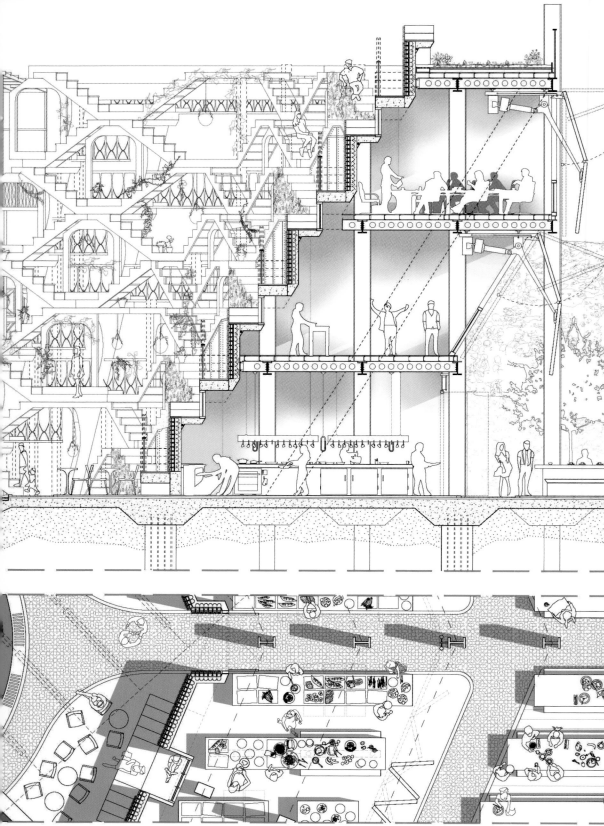

22.15

22.16

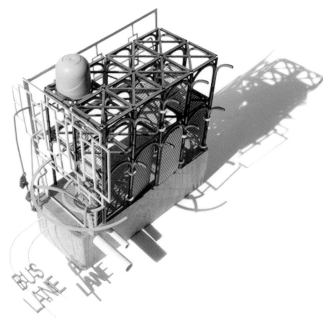

22.17

Fig. 22.15 Freya Cobbin, Y5, Harbour of Exchanges: National Apprenticeship Centre, Cartagena. Section and Plan. Implemented over three sites within the city, the proposal draws together both informal and formal spaces for learning and living in response to Cartagena's vibrant street life and urban activity, fostering the process of knowledge interchange. **Fig. 22.16** Megan Smedy, Y5, Eco-Hotel and Tourist Route within a South African landscape. The two main drivers for the design project are temporality (deconstructability) and a relationship with the natural environment. A series of functional carts have been designed to meet specific needs alongside the railway. These can be moved or deconstructed, as and when seasonal demands change. **Fig. 22.17** Clarie Taggart, Y5, Start-Up City (Coventry). Adaptable live/work business incubation unit structure for temporary inhabitation in empty high street retail units.

Unit 23
Acts of Deception

Emmanuel Vercruysse, Kate Davies, Bob Sheil

In Unit 23 we make things. We make things that make things up. We fabricate fabrications. We are devious, irreverent and not to be trusted. This year the Unit continued its re-appropriation of reality, constructing precise scaffolding for the imagination as we revelled in the skilful artistry of make-believe and dabbled in the dark art of manipulation. Our architectural constructs exist both live and mediated, with and without make-up, and the true site of the work exists in the no-mans-land between fact and fabrication.

Reality in the 21st century is increasingly defined by the untrustworthiness of its representation. Seeing is deceiving. Whether for artistic, commercial or political ends, images mediate our understanding of the world, conjuring powerfully convincing secondary narratives that can serve to reveal truth, obscure it or reinvent it entirely. Reality is constructed from what we are given to believe and all, it seems, is not as it seems.

The photographic document, data visualisation and the scientific image play a critical role in the accurate representation of events, objects and spaces, whilst at the same time cinematic tools, staged photography and theatrical techniques embroider and manipulate reality to support leaps of the imagination. We began the year with a series of explorations using a variety of representational and imaging technologies such as film, photography, 3D scanning and digital simulations to reimagine, remodel and rework reality, crafting a series of reconstructions, deceptions, acts of manipulation and make-believe. The act of observing was our focus for the year as we applied an acute eye for detail. We took inspiration from test facilities that employ precise modes of observation – ballistics, forensics, crash-tests – and from a rich tradition of cinema and theatre which use technique and artistry to creatively deceive. The Unit's fabrications oscillate between figuring, disfiguring and reconfiguring. Our architecture emerges from the meticulous task of composing, staging and rebuilding. Throughout the year, we alternated between acts of revelation and obfuscation in order to forge instruments of imaginative and elegant fabrication.

In the winter term, the Unit embarked on a road trip through California, from San Francisco to Los Angeles, visiting film studios, movie towns, silicon cities, ghost suburbs and military sites in search of fabricated places and spaces that have been invented or reinvented through cinema and mass media. The Unit focussed the major project of the year around the title 'House of Fabrication' and the projects explore design and proposition as a complex act that operates across a multiplicity of sites, spanning physical and digital realms and manifesting in a rich variety of guises.

Unit 23 is a forum for in-depth design investigation. We pride ourselves on our hands on approach to design through making and direct experimentation. Closely aligned with the Bartlett's advanced fabrication labs, it spans the gulf between the speculative and the tangible and places a strong emphasis on the exploration of ideas through elaborations of craft, rigorous physical testing and experimental production in order to test and explore directly the material consequences of our inventions. The Unit's work is diverse and personal and is driven by individuality and flair. It exists in twin digital and physical states. It is handcrafted, emerges from code and dissolves into point cloud. It lurks at the edges of perception and interferes within distortions of the senses. It sets its own terms of engagement, deploying active transgressions across the fertile territory between the apparent and the actual.

Special thanks to our critics and guests:
Paul Bavister, Johan Berglund, Matthew Butcher, Mark Campbell, Nat Chard, Mike Dean, Ilona Gaynor, Ruth Gibson, Bastian Glassner, Ruairi Glynn, Penelope Haralambidou, Robin Jenkins, Birgir Jonsson, Simon Kennedy, Madhav Kidao, Guan Lee, Yeoryia Manolopoulou, Josep Mias, Ed Moseley,

James O'Leary, Jose Sanchez, Rupert Scott,
Matt Shaw, Misha Smith, Tom Smith, Will Trossell,
Peter Vaughan, Graeme Williamson, Simon Withers.

Year 4
Kairo Baden Powell, Yanyi (Gladys) Ching, Tom
Farmer, Sarah Firth, Rory Keenan, Thomas Pearce,
Eliza De Silva

Year 5
Kevin Chen, Jacob Down, Benjamin Gough,
Kaowen Ho, Tom Svilans, Michelle Young

23.1

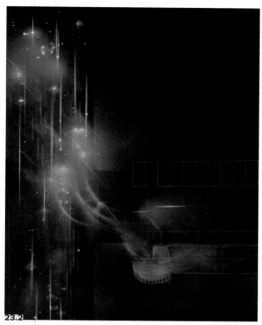

23.2

23.3

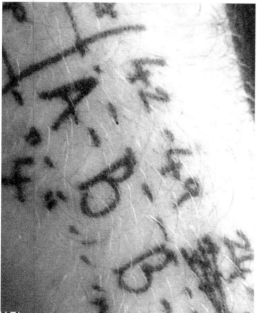

23.4

23.5

Fig. 23.1 Michelle Young, Y5, Waiting for Requiem. What type of evidence and how much of it is needed to convince you to fully understand something? Established from the claim that the presentation of objects of evidence is the making of fact through narrative fabrication, the project is framed both within the anticipation and aftermath of a fictional narrative to bring home the Hubble Space Telescope. **Fig. 23.2** Yanyi (Gladys) Ching, Y4, A Nocturne. '... brief sharp movement against a background of static visual fields...' J.G. Ballard. The project draws on evocative descriptions of cities at night, in literature, film and photography. The architecture constructs the spatial adaptation of a series of novels, by harvesting the ambient light of the city surrounding it. **Fig. 23.3** Sarah Firth, Y4, Meteorological Sirens. A study of physical lines of sight from the coastal outpost of a weather station. The architecture constructs a dense disorienting space that draws on the deceptions of inclement weather at sea, as a Siren on the pacific coast. **Fig. 23.4** Rory Keenan, Y4, Invisible Choreography. The code, written on the body instructs a hidden performance piece in the city. It marks the times and spaces between moving security cameras and is accompanied by an empty piece of film footage as seen from through the lens. **Fig.23.5** Tom Farmer, Y4, Act 00. One of a series of photographs constructed without digital manipulation. The first instinct of the digitally literate is to disbelieve an image. The work probes our notions of authenticity, featuring a series of visual illusions created by physical apparatus constructed in the camera's blind spots.

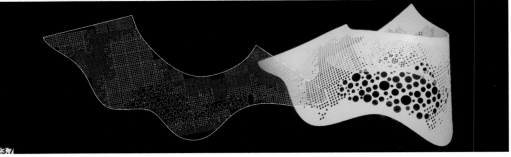

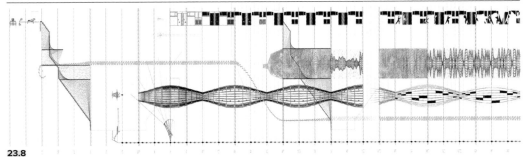

Fig. 23.6 Kairo Baden Powell, Y4, House of Fabrication. A performative architectural prosthetic for the Golden Gate bridge, responding to the seismic landscape of San Francisco and the harmonic vibrations of the bridge, the intervention reinforces it structurally and reinstates it as an inhabitable public space. **Fig. 23.7** Eliza De Silva, Y4, Unfolding Views. The project constructs a series of spaces for observing human behaviour and obscuring those doing the observing. The model shows the development of a series of perforated carbon fibre veils. **Fig. 23.8** Thomas Pearce, Y4, Decoding Brutalism. In an automated procession, a set of Paranoiac Players harvests the Alexandra Estate's surfaces, converting textures to sound and composing a syncopated Ballad of Brutalism.

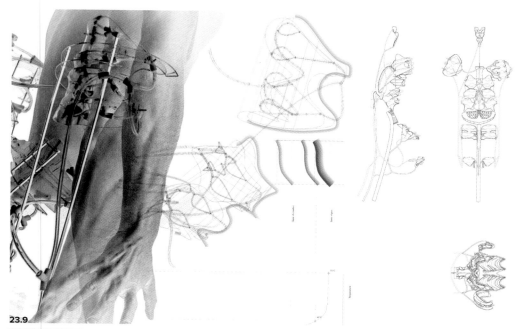

23.9

23.10

23.11

Fig. 23.9 Kevin Chen, Y5, The Garden of Earthly Delights. Inspired by Bosch's eponymous triptych, The Garden borrows from the utopic vision of a sensual paradise depicted in its central panel, as well as the tortures of the Hell scene, to propose a garden of heightened sensual and synaesthetic encounters that appeal to the breadth of human sensation and straddle the ambiguous thresholds between pleasure and pain. Situated in a domed biosphere, the Garden is a hybrid landscape of technological interventions, controlled microclimates and natural vegetation. **Fig 23.10 – 23.11** Benjamin Gough, Y5, A Frenectic Architecture: Frenectic, a term derived from the surgical procedure the Frenectomy, the reconfiguration of a biological organ restraint. The project investigates the concept of an architecture where a slow,

86-year movement is choreographed by restraining and directing environmental forces in order to choreograph spatial components. An inhabitable clock, components are initially laid out orthogonally and then slowly contort and reconfigure to create floors, surfaces and walls. Investigated primarily through models, spatial restraints embody the force of their environment through their reconfiguration and distortion over time.

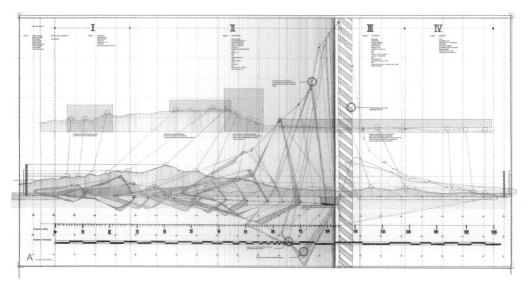

23.12

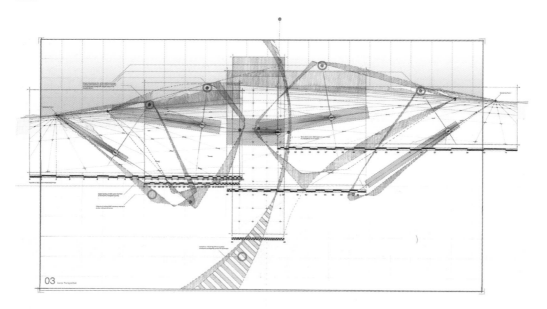

23.13

Fig. 23.12 – 23.13 Kaowen Ho, Y5, Drawing Supersonic.
Set within the Black Rock Desert of Nevada, the project
deconstructs a Land-Speed Record attempt focusing on the
experience of the desert at speed and the resulting distortions
of a series of spatial and temporal elements. Through
analytical drawings exploring the understanding of this
distinctly American landscape at Mach 1 and the inherent
dichotomy between geological time and supersonic time,
the project proposes a series of architectural insertions that
begin to immortalise both the event and the landscape in
which it takes place by attempting to capture and prolong
the phenomena of the sonic boom.

23.14

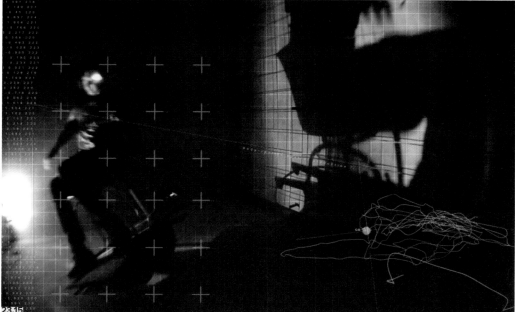

23.15

Fig. 23.14 Jacob Down, Y5, Institute of Bio Spatial-Mechanics: Body-centric Trajectories. The project probes a unique set of spatial characteristics induced by extreme bodily motions. A series of rigs were built to explore directly a set of ineffable qualities evoked through forces exerted on the body, ones that are impossible to represent through conventional forms of architectural representation. The proposal explores the territory between thrill and the extremes of human endurance. **Fig. 23.15** Jacob Down, Y5, Multiple G-Terrain. Rotating at 1.2789 [rad./s] an artificial gravity is induced within the 107 .108m horizontally rotating structure. Occupants are centripetally pulled to the g-terrain's inside surface defying gravity's vector, but occupants are able to freely explore g-spaces of varying magnitude as they roam. The further

an occupant deviates from the centre of rotation, larger the magnitude of g-force induced on the body. Additional spaces include constant g-platforms, and the g-module. **Fig. 23.16** Tom Svilans, Y5, The Bradbury Transcripts. The fragmentation of the Bradbury Building into an'architecturalised film sequence' seeks to address the continuity between actual and implied space, and the slippery territory between fact and constructed fiction. As the camera moves from set to set, changes of scale, virtual extensions and anamorphic geometries constantly seek to disorient the viewer and displace his or her assumptions of what is real and what is not. Similarly, actual events, recorded fictions, and imagined happenings are compressed and overlapped, further blurring the boundary between truth and deception.

23.16

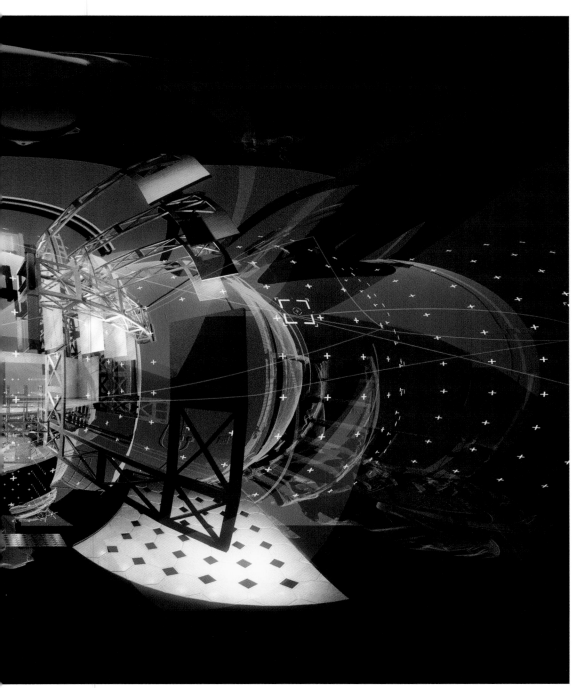

Collisions

Simon Kennedy, Michael Chadwick

'Americans may have no identity, but they do have wonderful teeth.' Jean Baudrillard

Unit 24 employs film, video and animation techniques to generate architectural propositions, operating consciously and conscientiously within the globalised, decentralised, desensitised territories of media.

The Unit recognises the current absence of a dominant socio-political architectural and design regime. We aim to celebrate this freedom and draw from popular artforms: cinema, television, photography, literature and computer games can be analysed and utilised to form hybrid and synthetic spatial propositions.

Collisions

We inhabit unique times of tumultuous transition. Encroaching digital technologies collide with analogue and chemical technologies (nowhere more strikingly than in the construction industry). Cyberspace collides with and infiltrates built fabric. Iconic images collide with their own dissemination. Globalisation collides with everything. The Unit attempted to interpret the collision as a force of positive change, and sought to experiment with its potential use as an instrument of architectural investigation.

Beginning the year with a series of short, moving-image-based projects, students outlined a conceptual position while refining the skills required to examine their own architectural collisions. Intensive workshops were held during this phase of the year in key techniques for digital animation, editing, production and compositing.

We then travelled to the source of the spread of globalisation, armed with iconic images and film, with the intention of testing the power of such iconography against its origins. As part of a field trip to California, the Unit studied the Case Study Houses and works by Frank Gehry, Eric Owen Moss,

Morphosis and Coop Himmelb(l)au, the LACMA Stanley Kubrick exhibition, and Hollywood. Visiting the Sony Animation Studios, students were treated to a 3D and compositing workshop where they recreated a scene from The Amazing Spiderman. A visit to SCI-Arc also enabled students to experience SCI-Arc's cutting edge Robotics & Simulation Lab.

Fourth year students then resolved their early speculations into a cinematic building proposition informed by filmic-spatial investigations, translations and notions of genre. Fifth year students defined a personal spatial and artistic practice, while constructing a speculative architectural thesis proposition, also with the moving image as a key parameter.

Creative Practice

Unit 24 benefits from a broad network of associated professionals working in sectors ranging from architecture to film, animation, sound design, motion graphics, urban design and contemporary art. Contributions from these professionals serve as a critical pedagogic counterpoint to the conceptual and theoretical discourse within the Unit, as well as providing inspiration and practical guidance – students are encouraged to consider their potential as practitioners while still studying at the Bartlett.

Unit 24 arranged a series of lectures covering all aspects of setting up a creative and commercial practice in today's economy and, importantly, maintaining creativity and conceptual development throughout the process. The Unit welcomed speakers such as David Chambers and Kevin Haley of Aberrant Architecture, Zoe Chan and Joao Gameiro Neves from Atelier ChanChan, Alex Scott-Whitby at Studio AR, George Thompson of Visitor Studio, Pedro Gil of Studio Gil, Jenny Fleming and Alessio Cuozzo of JAA, Rob Small of Lotsmorehere and Ed Soden.

Many thanks to our critics: Diana Cochrane, Hal Currey, Andrew Gancikov, Alexis Germanos, Christine Hawley, Ephraim Joris, Jerome Keam, Patrick Lewis, Kim Quazi, Reza Schuster, George Thompson. Unit 24 has benefited from its relationships with a network of practising architects and construction industry consultants, and so would like to thank practice tutors Kim Quazi and Hal Currey of Arup Associates, Structural Engineers Michael Thomson and Timothy Snelson, also of Arup Associates and Environmental Engineer Ali Shaw of Max Fordham.

Year 4
Ai Deng, Daniel Cotton, Liam Davis, Khadija Durbar, Muhammad Zhlfiker Enayet, Jonathan Holmes, Steven Howson, Keiichi Iwamoto, Edward Mascarenhas

Year 5
Ruben Alonso, Isaac Eluwole, Douglas Fenton, Sasha Smolin

24.1

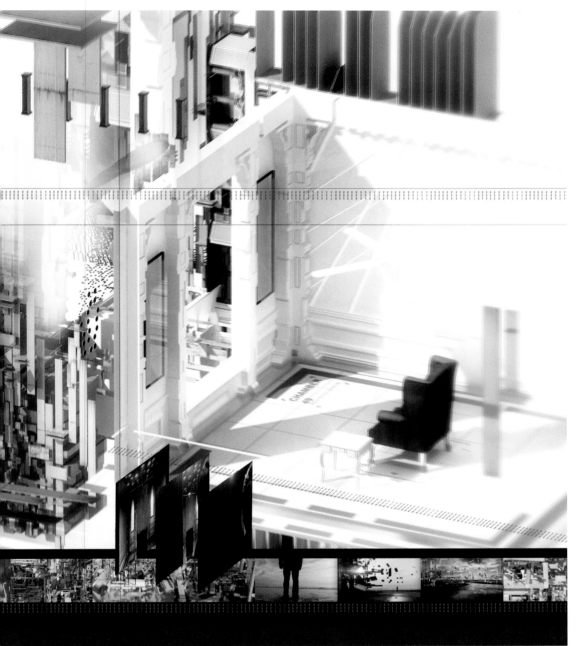

Fig. 24.1 Douglas Fenton, Y5, The Post-Human Experiment. Based on a theoretical view of the consciousness as a pattern of information which might be held within a digital substrate, the project explores the relationship between architectural environments and the duality of the mind/body that experiences them. The image describes a sequence within the film, *The Post-Human Experiment*, where the protagonist enters geometries and abstracted spaces generated by a digital version of consciousness. By representing this 'mindscape', the project speculates on the perception of 3D space and juxtaposes this against the abstracted spatiality held within the subconscious and in dreams, where time, space, place and event merge into one another, shifting and changing.

24.2

24.3

24.4

24.5

Fig. 24.2 Jonathan Holmes, Y4, Super Supper, film still.
Normative shop-based activities are gamified with hilarious
results, subsequently enabling new commercial potentialities.
Fig. 24.3 Ruben Alonso, Y5, Southbank, photo-collage:
'The production of reality no longer depends on the direct
relationship with reality, but with a represented reality.'
Fig. 24.4 Douglas Fenton, Y5, The Post-Human Experiment,
spatio-temporal graphic depicting the procession through
the Post-Human Experiment Tower. **Fig. 24.5** Douglas Fenton,
Y5, The Post-Human Experiment, spatio-temporal graphic
showing the filmic journey from entering the Tower
to emerging into mental geometric constructions.

Fig. 24.6 Ai Deng, Y4, Bricolage, A Three-Dimensional
Collision, film still. **Fig. 24.7** Edward Mascarenhas, Y4, Colliding
Chairs, graphic storyboard. Set in the City of London, the film
speculates on an infestation of banal office-derived objects
and examines the surreal results. **Fig. 24.8** Sasha Smolin, Y5,
Market Stall Typologies, film still. Beginning with a process of
intensive data gathering, the project generates a series of
opportunistic typological interventions derived from the
multiple cultures inhabiting Caledonian Road, London. These
are combined to form dynamic and sympathetic new urban
spaces. **Fig. 24.9** Sasha Smolin, Y5, Market Stall Typologies,
Eritrean typology. The Nda Mariam temple is Asmara is
transformed via projection, drawing and modelling.

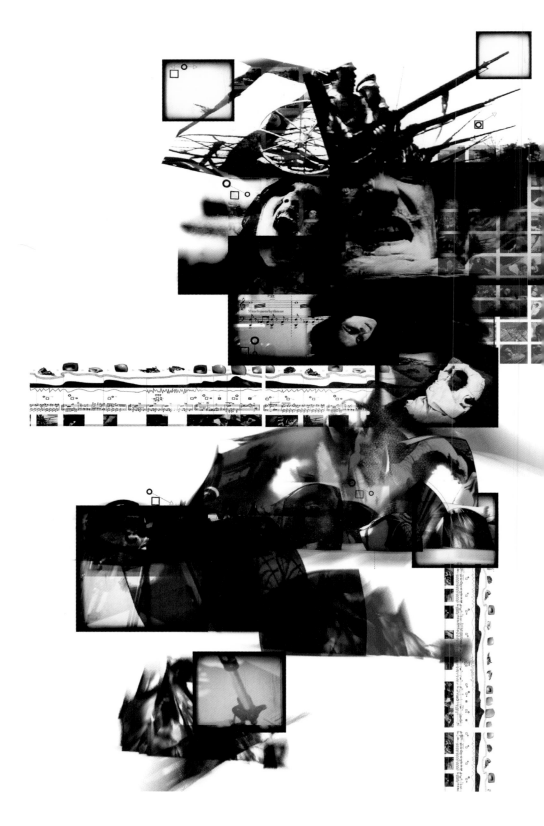

24.10

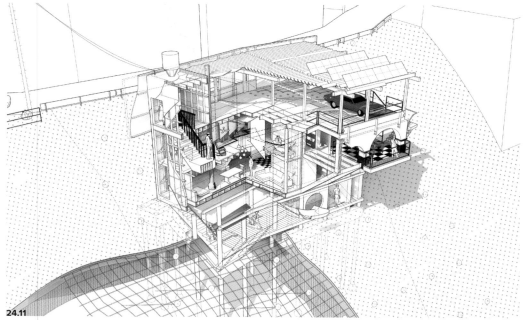

24.11

24.12

24.13

Fig. 24.10 Liam Davis, Y4, Collage: Film to Form, spatio-temporal graphic. The project seeks to generate architectural space via the analysis of filmic montage techniques. Here, Sergei Eisenstein's *Battleship Potemkin* is analysed graphically, sonically and temporally, giving rise to a system of notation, which is then used to drive software-based parameters, allowing the construction of new spaces and filmic architectures. **Fig. 24.11** Daniel Cotton, Y4, Transitions: The Marlowe House, Hollywood, California. The project seeks to derive architectural space from filmic transitions between virtual and cinematic space, and footage filmed with a custom-designed steadycam. Transitions are mapped into three-dimensional habitable spaces which form a residence for the fictional detective, Phillip Marlowe. **Fig. 24.12** Steven Howson, Y4, The Thirty Second City, film still. The project describes the near-instant formation of a hyper-dense fictional urban amalgamation. **Fig. 24.13** Keichi Iwamoto, Y4, The Restoration of the London Baths – conceptual graphic. Following an investigation into London's historic red-light districts, the project suggests a controlled collision between eastern and western cultural modes.

Fig. 24.14 Isaac Eluwole, Y5, The Quotidian Utopia, Aaron's Undercroft, film still. The project seeks to reappraise forgotten and maligned Modernist spaces, countering preconceptions then inverting them with counter-cultural augmentations and interventions. Beginning by photographing and modelling each site in meticulous detail, the spaces undergo software-based transformations, from which each intervention is generated. A study of the prejudices surrounding the site, actual and perceived uses, and historical occurences gives rise to the intervention's programme. **Fig. 24.15** Isaac Eluwole, Y5, The Quotidian Utopia, The Memorial spatial construct, film still. **Fig. 24.16** Isaac Eluwole, Y5, The Quotidian Utopia, The Memorial in construction, film still. **Fig. 24.17** Jonathan Holmes, Y5, The Stahl House, a constructed image of a mythological artefact at the boundary between reality and fiction.

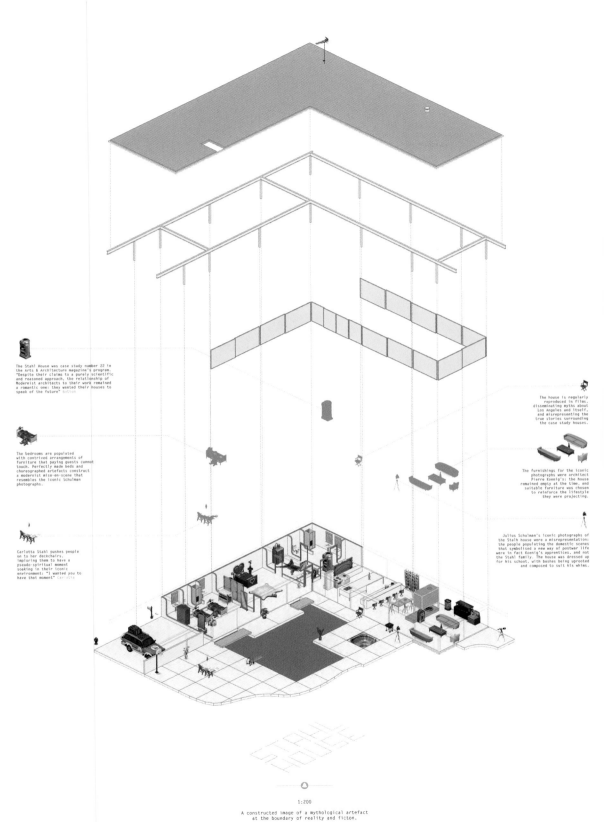

The Stahl House was case study number 22 in the Arts & Architecture magazine's program. "Despite their claims to a purely scientific and reasoned approach, the relationship of Modernist architects to their work remained a romantic one: they wanted their houses to speak of the future" Botton

The bedrooms are populated with contrived arrangements of furniture that paying guests cannot touch. Perfectly made beds and choreographed artefacts construct a modernist mise-en-scene that resembles the iconic Schulman photographs.

Carlotta Stahl pushes people on to her deckchairs, imploring them to have a pseudo-spiritual moment soaking in their iconic environment: "I wanted you to have that moment" Carlotta

The house is regularly reproduced in films, disseminating myths about Los Angeles and itself, and misrepresenting the true stories surrounding the case study houses.

The furnishings for the iconic photographs were architect Pierre Koenig's: the house remained empty at the time, and suitable furniture was chosen to reinforce the lifestyle they were projecting.

Julius Schulman's iconic photographs of the Stahl house were a misrepresentation; the people populating the domestic scenes that symbolised a new way of postwar life were in fact Koenig's apprentices, and not the Stahl family. The house was dressed up for his schoot, with bushes being uprooted and composed to suit his whims.

1:200

A constructed image of a mythological artefact
at the boundary of reality and ficton.

Year 5
MArch Thesis

Peg Rawes, Mark Smout

The thesis is the place where Year 5 students have the opportunity to develop a series of focussed research questions that underpin their design work. These questions may be informed by disciplines such as, architectural history, physical and biological sciences, cultural theory, technology, literary theory or philosophy. As a result, a reflexive relationship is created between the portfolio and thesis, each informing the other.

Alice Brownfield
A Moment of Danger
Tutor: Professor Jane Rendell

At first glance Narvskaya Zastava is an unassuming place. It lies southwest of central St Petersburg and north of a very large proportion of the populated world. The district originated around the Pulitov Works as an industrial area in the mid 19th Century. In 1924 Narvskaya Zastava became the development centre of socialist Leningrad and was radically replanned by Stroikom, the Russian Building Committee, as an exemplary urban area for the rest of the USSR. Its Constructivism demonstrates the focus of 1920s Soviet architecture on creating a new *byt* (daily life).

Meanwhile, under the coalition's Big Society in the UK, housing provision, school design standards, changing attitudes to food consumerism, tenders for healthcare services, and public institution reforms, are all enacted under a reassuring rhetoric of community cohesion and social progress yet increase the role of a deregulated private sector. We now find ourselves in a moment of danger where public services and long-standing components of the welfare state are threatened with privatisation, disguised behind Big Society rhetoric which claims to support the improvement of daily life: promising affordable housing, improved education and a notion of care in the community.

The thesis is interested in the role architectural analysis can play in exploring potential disparity between Big Society rhetoric and action. Inspired by Walter Benjamin's method of dialectical thinking, it proposes the constructivist district of Narvskaya Zastava is a vital dialectical image, appearing at this moment of danger. Five architectural typologies constructed under the social modernism of 1920s Leningrad are juxtaposed alongside counterparts within contemporary neo-liberal Britain, each of which have been, or are being, privatised.

One thousand, seven hundred and seventy two miles sit between my desk on Gordon Street and the foot of the main square in Narvskaya Zastava. This geographical distance is coupled with the dislocation of writing about a period of social modernism that was already being dismantled 80 years ago.

Images: Tractornaya Street: the first public housing project in the Soviet Union

Alisan Dockerty
The Riparian Resort America
Tutor: Oliver Wilton

Historically the Kissimmee River Basin is at the heart of the Everglades watershed existing as a complex, slow-moving hydrological system. The area became frequently inundated with prolonged flooding during the wet season (summer) supporting kilometers of wetlands, which was later controlled in the 1960s by the U.S. Army through 'channelisation'. The floodplain is now dried out pasture, which seeps contaminants into this new, fast-flowing canal, polluting this delicate ecosystem. Privatisation of Northern parts of the floodplain is the beginning of a government restoration project where backfilling the canal aims to reinstate the natural meandering form of the Kissimmee. As a result of privatisation and restoration many resorts and ranches have been dissolved, therefore eliminating this new 'nature' which been developing within the floodplain since 1958. This deteriorating Riparian landscape is taken as the environmental setting to be seasonally inhabited by North American retirees, who annually travel to the Florida for the winter months in RVs ('Snowbirds'). Florida's economic reliance on tourism and huge annual influxes of visitors intent on living 'the good life' is fuelled by notions of freedom for lifestyles without regret or thought for ecological damage. This thesis reviews the specific problems surrounding this over-consumption, and gives detailed studies of the river's declined ecosystem to achieve a hyper-nature.

Technological design solutions – *Flow Manipulating Infrastructures* (FMIs) – strike a balance between the fragile ecology of the river and the coexistent fuel-dependent RV community by using the river basin as a renewable energy resource. The flow manipulating infrastructure works in companion with a vegetative strategy to reinstate a type of controlled river landscape. Creating a complex masterplan of quasi-natural riparian edged streams, the FMIs slow down the river's flow, providing an alternative future for Floridian tourism in an environmentally conscious resort.

Image: Model of the resort lido which utilises the high level energy storage pools. When the water level drops due to high energy consumption, diving is prohibited.

Jacob Down
The Art of Surfing and its Spatial Engagements
Tutor: Professor Iain Borden

Large lumps of solid ocean swell dissipate their power and energy on reefs and beaches of our coastline. Born naturally from low pressure weather systems acting on the ocean's surface, undulating rhythms of energy are transmitted through saltwater over thousands of miles before exploding on our coastline in truly unpredictable and highly complex spatial forms. The insertion of the human body into this emergent context, and its immersive ability to read, reconfigure and adjust to the tune of these liquid spaces, are explored here.

The study is tailored towards the spatial engagements produced from advanced levels of (shortboard) surfing ability whereby the rider has developed high degrees of skill, balance, posture, visual sensitivity, haptic feedback, muscular control, power, hearing, strength, flexibility, fluidity, agility, stamina, timing, technique, style, and ocean knowledge; enabling the human body to experience unique spatial characteristics that would be unattainable to an 'unconditioned body' (Bourdieu, 1990). At this advanced level of conditioned ability surfing may be understood as an art form because it establishes the surfer as a 'craftsman' (Sennett, 2008) who reads space and produces body-centric spatial representations.

The thesis blends theorised interdisciplinary studies, personally written accounts, visual-based work, as well as moments of comparative analysis. Surfing-related secondary sources range from small scale online film edits, mainstream Hollywood films, books, magazines, and surfing scholars, to primary research methods including quantitative body-centric spatial data collection, personal accounts and qualitative interviews with professional surfers and surf film producers.

Section one sets out the intimate relationship between human body and surfboard in an analysis of surfboard design and performance the extent of this body-board relationship. For the duration of a glide, the surfboard is transformed from an inanimate artefact of foam and fibreglass to a material extension of the human body. Section two examines the advanced surfer as a craftsman in reading space; in tune with shifting macro-spatial conditions out of the water, and engaged in a kinespherical structure with water. Finally, once the complexities involved in catching, standing up on, and reading a morphing liquid space are understood, a specific set of body-centric motions and the respectively induced spatial productions are examined.

Image: Body-Centric Trajectories: the incarnation of unique spatial characteristics.

Stephen McCloy
EU: The Gardens of Fantastica
Tutor: Oliver Wilton

In this project the present is the future, where the past is revisited and 2013 is reconsidered in an alternate history. The thesis asks: What if we had cared about sustainability in 1945? What would the European Union be like if sustainability was its founding medium and driving force? Looking back, we might imagine a position where European cities are required to be self-sufficient in food and energy.

The project began with storyboards to illustrate a speculative archaeology, examining an article about the fictional world 'Fantastica' extracted from *The Dictionary of Imaginary Places* by Manguel and Guadalupi. Fragments of the article begin to define a set of rules with which to speculate this alternate history. Clues of gardens, art and culture are traced to Paris, home of Surrealism.

The events leading up to the foundation of the EU after WWII are reimagined, where concerns about sustainability: Energy, Food and Cultural Security, become key policies, and each states 5 year leadership term showcases both the aims of the EU and enables special focus on national concerns.

Paris undergoes rapid change during its term hosting the EU, leaving a legacy of infrastructure and knowledge that will continue to improve and safeguard the city until the EU returns in the future. Grand projects, such as those undertaken in Paris by President Mitterand are reimagined, and the nature of landmark architecture and cultural palaces within the modern day city, from the point of view of energy, food and community sustainability are proposed.

Through a literary review and research of historical contexts and technologies, combined with design, the thesis investigates an allegorical situation in an effort to deal with some of the major issues of the 20th century and suggest futures for 21st century politics and cities. It notes other architectural visionary works for Paris, from Haussmann, through Le Corbusier and Yona Friedman, to the present day.

Image: A squadron of artificial clouds oversee the daily operations of the new Parisian food and biomass infrastructures.

MArch Design Realisation

James O'Leary, Dirk Krolikowski

The Bartlett School of Architecture 2013

The MArch Design Realisation (DR) course provides the opportunity for all Year 4 students to consider how buildings are designed, constructed and delivered. Students are asked to reflect upon their relationship to technology, the environment and the profession. This is explored through an iterative critical examination of the major building design project taught within the context of individual design Units in Year 4. The course is supported by an extensive lecture series, seminars, and cross-unit crits. The course forms bridges between the world of academia and practice, engaging with many internationally renowned design and consultancy practices. A dedicated practice-based architect, engineer and environmental designer support each design Unit, working individually with students to develop their work throughout the duration of the programme.

This year we inaugurated the Design Technology Prize for the project with the most potential for developing innovative processes and systems in architectural design. Prizewinners were provided with financial and in-kind support from The Bartlett to extend the scope of research initially developed through the Design Realisation programme, culminating in an exhibition at The Bartlett in October 2012. This year Viktor Westerdahl and Tom Svilans shared the prize. Viktor explored an emerging technological application for energy harvesting known as the piezoelectric effect, studying the transfer of kinetic energy in load bearing structures. His prototype generates electricity from deformation in engineered ceramic discs. Tom Slivans explored the idea of digital craftsmanship, constructing a prototype that demonstrates an integrated process that spans the virtual / real divide: between virtual modelling, numerical analysis and physical making. The work explores virtual 3D 'sketching', highly precise CAD and CAE tools and new methods of digital production.

We would like to thank our lecturers for 2012-13: Justin Nicholls, Make; Damian Eley, Arup Structures; James Thonger, Arup Services; Joanna Pencakowski; Hareth Pochee, Max Fordham; Katerina Dionysopoulou, Heatherwick Studio; Felix Weber, ARUP Materials; Sara Klomps, Zaha Hadid Architects; Xavier de Kastellier, Foster + Partners; Cristiano Ceccato, Zaha Hadid Architects; Susan Ware, The Bartlett; Dean Pike, David Chipperfield Architects; Nathalie Rozencwajg, RARE Architecture; Simon Allford, AHMM; Viktor Westerdahl and Tom Svilans, Design Technology Prize Winners 2012; Dirk Krolikowski, Rogers Stirk Harbour + Partners; James O'Leary, The Bartlett.

DR Practice Tutors 2012-13: Simon Dickens, Youmeheshe Architects; John Lyall, John Lyall Architects; Carl Vann, Domi Oliver, Pollard Thomas Edwards Architects; Daniel Wright, Rogers Stirk Harbour + Partners; Peter Vaughan, Asif Khan; Dean Pike, David Chipperfield Architects; Maria Fulford, David Hemingway, Joanna Karatzas, Niall McLaughlin Architects; Sara Klomps, Zaha Hadid Architects; Justin Nicholls, Make; Pedro Gil, Studio Gil Architects; Hal Curry, Kim Quesi, Arup; Tom Holberton, Rick Mather Architects; Manja van de Worp.

The Bartlett School of Architecture
M.Arch Design Realisation Programme 2013

Featuring
AHMM
Arup
Ben Godber
Buro Happold
David Chipperfield Architects
Foster & Partners
Heatherwick Studio
John Lyall Architects
MAKE Architects
Max Fordham
Niall McLaughlin Architects
Pernilla & Asif
Price & Myers
Pollard Thomas & Edwards
Rare Architecture
Rick Mather Architects
Rogers Stirk Harbour + Partners
Soma
Studio Gil
Youmeheshe
Zaha Hadid Architects
and staff from The Bartlett UCL

DR.1

Fig. DR.1 Poster announcing the current MArch Design Realisation academic programme 2012-2013, featuring the architectural and engineering practices which provide tutorial or lecture support for the course. Photo: Renzo Piano's Shard under construction - Courtesy AP **Fig. DR.2** Andrew Walker, Unit 14, Design Realisation Process for a Homeostatic Brewery in Camden Town. Exploded axonometric detail of a 'self-aware' refractive screen; a device designed to dislocate observers and blur the boundaries in which they find themselves. **Fig. DR.3** Andrew Walker, Unit 14, Atmospheric lighting models are used to test superimposed live projections, which generate an immersive, interactive, "uncertain" architecture of constant instability and misperception.

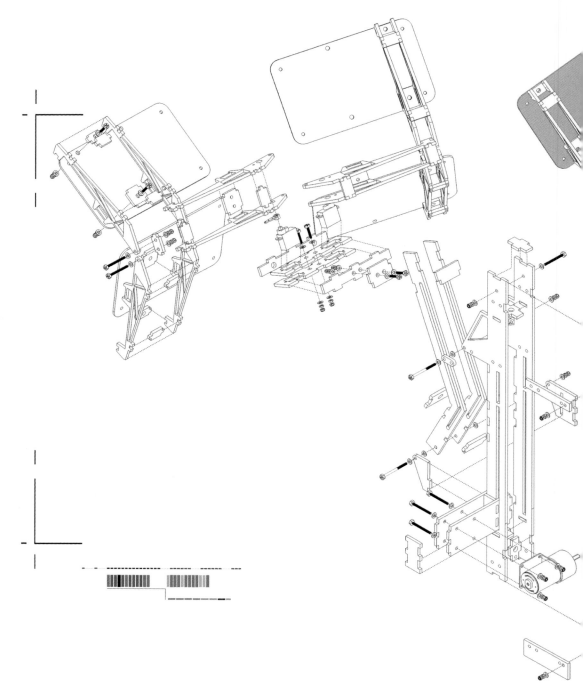

DR.2

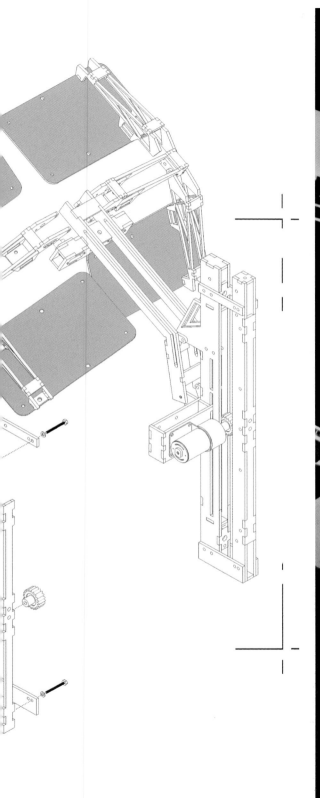

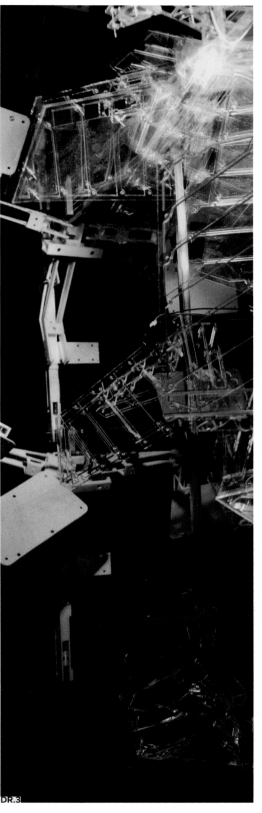

DR.3

Smartgeometry 2013 workshop at The Bartlett

Bartlett Alumni Korea exhibit at Seoul City Hall, Korea

Bartlett alumni exhibit at the Shaikh Ebrahim Centre in Bahrain

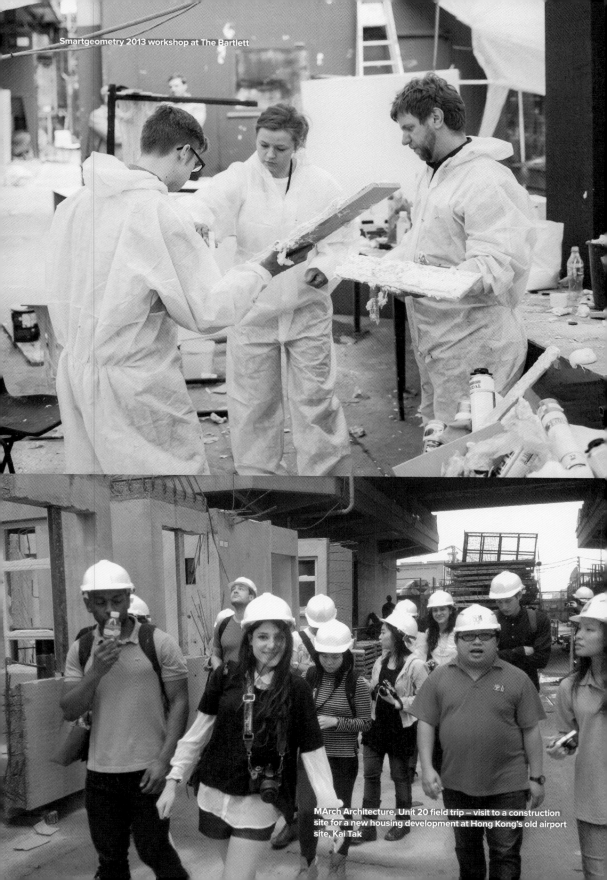

Smartgeometry 2013 workshop at The Bartlett

MArch Architecture, Unit 20 field trip – visit to a construction site for a new housing development at Hong Kong's old airport site, Kai Tak

ARB/RIBA Part 3

Postgraduate Diploma in Professional Practice & Management in Architecture (ARB/RIBA Part 3)

Susan Ware

The Bartlett School of Architecture 2013

The new modular Bartlett Part 3 programme has now been running successfully for a year and is designed to meet the new ARB and RIBA criteria for Part 3 and the new practical experience requirements.

This six-module part-time programme can be taken over 12, 18 or 24 months to suit students' employment and work/life commitments. The programme is made up of five modules, each delivered over a six-week period, and which can be taken in any order; each module is assessed in a different format. The sixth module is composed of a case study, career appraisal and evidence of work experience. Each student's experience of learning and development in professional practice will differ, depending on the type of project, type and location of practice and management processes undertaken, and the preparation for the examination must therefore be approached in a structured way, whilst recognising the diversity of the profession and the construction industry. Module 6 is delivered through one-to-one tutorials where students have the opportunity to explore, analyse and reflect upon their professional education and experience with their tutor.

We aim to educate a generation of architects who are equipped to practice in an increasingly challenging environment. We do this by providing teaching and learning which encourages students to develop the skills beyond those required at threshold level by the professional criteria through reflection, appraisal, critical enquiry and research. We ask students to examine the role of the architect in the changing global construction industry to examine the effect of politics and economics on the design and procurement of the built environment in future practice.

The programme is delivered through a comprehensive series of 50 lectures given by experts from practice and from within the Faculty. In addition, the teaching in each module is led by a director who is either a member of the Professional Studies team or an expert from practice. The school draws extensively from long standing connections with practice and the construction industry.

The programme aims to provide students with the skills to be competent to practice and demonstrate the knowledge, ability, judgment and integrity needed to fit an architect for his or her professional duties and to understand how an office organisation is managed for this purpose. Professional criteria are used to establish evidence of candidates' fitness to practice, demonstrated through their professional, procedural and technical awareness, understanding, knowledge and ability and have achieved a threshold of competence (in terms of knowledge and ability) and professionalism (in terms of conduct and responsibility) that is consistent and relevant, and will safeguard clients, building users and society.

Continuing Professional Development – CPD at the Bartlett

A series of 50 + lectures take place on Tuesday evenings from January to May as part of the Part 3 programme, these lectures are available either as a full CPD update course or as groups of themed lectures. The lectures cover the key topics required by ARB and the RIBA for the maintenance of competence to practice.

Bartlett 3+3 Programme

These Friday afternoon CPD events take place twice a year and are aimed at those who completed their Part 3 three or more years ago. Experts in planning, energy, contracts, employment law and so on present a number of short update talks covering legislation and practice matters which have changed in the last three years or so. The event is followed by an opportunity to network and discuss informally.

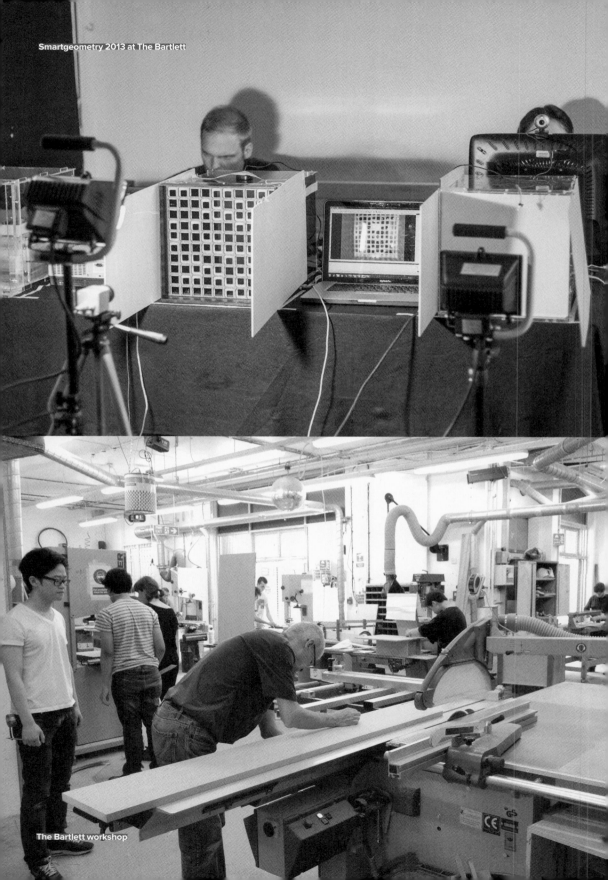

Smartgeometry 2013 at The Bartlett

The Bartlett workshop

Students at work in The Bartlett workshop

B>PRO

Frédéric Migayrou, Andrew Porter

Bartlett Prospective or B>PRO is the new structure for the post-professional Masters Programmes at the Bartlett School of Architecture. It is directed by the Bartlett Professor and Chair of the School, Frédéric Migayrou.

Post-professional programmes include the MArch Graduate Architectural Design (GAD), the MArch Urban Design (UD) and the MA Architectural History (AH). All programmes are 12 months full-time. In the first phase of the B>PRO the MArch GAD programme was redesigned in the 2011-12 academic year. This has been joined by the MArch UD programme for the 2012-13 academic year. For 2013-14 the MA AH will also be redeveloped as a B>PRO programme.

B>PRO is an umbrella structure for prospective architecture, urbanism, design and theory at an advanced level. Students on the B>PRO programmes will develop research and speculative design that is underpinned by contemporary design theory. There is a particular emphasis on the impact of digital theory, politics and culture within the contemporary city and their influence on the conception and production of architectural space.

Research and design throughout B>PRO extends from the tools of spatial and demographic analysis, to the software of creation and production, the hardware of digital fabrication and manufacture through to the organisation, infrastructure and choreography of the contemporary city.

Both the MArch GAD and UD programmes are driven by research clusters. Each cluster develops its own manifesto for design and employs strategies and techniques that are unique to their pedagogy and particular design ethos. Within the GAD programme the clusters predominantly focus on a number of ways to deploy computational tools, digital techniques and their connection to tools of fabrication. The UD programme clusters develop their differing approaches through both the lens of

various themes such as politics, archaeology and ecology and the challenges posed by particular cities within in the lands of the Mediterranean basin.

Since September 2012 B>PRO has been housed within a new annex to The Bartlett School of Architecture at the Royal Ear Hospital (REH) in nearby Capper Street. This is the first new building occupied by the School since they took up residence in Wates House in 1975. Within the REH large open plan studios have been created to house both the GAD and UD programmes. It is the first time the Bartlett has been able to offer a studio culture for an entire programme and this marks a significant change in student space. In addition, the REH is a new hub for evening lectures, seminars and exhibitions.

B>PRO Structure
B>PRO Director: Professor Frédéric Migayrou
B>PRO Deputy Director: Andrew Porter

MArch GAD Programme Leader: Alisa Andrasek
MArch UD Programme Leader: Adrian Lahoud

Image: The Talented Mr. Ripply (2012)
Design: Marjan Colletti, Guan Lee, Tea Lim
Fabricated at Grymsdyke Farm.
Design assistants: Vasileos Chlorokostas, Muhammad Hissaan Awaiz Randhawa.
Photo: Sydney Zuellig

B>PRO
MArch Graduate
Architectural Design

Alisa Andrasek

Design (GAD) is a 12-month full-time post-professional course, leading to a Masters of Architecture (MArch) degree. The programme emphasises the key role advanced design plays in complexities of acute context. The programme is structured around eight Research Clusters curated to deliver diverse yet focussed strands of speculative research.

Design plays an important role in the accelerated convergence of matter and information. While data visualisation exposes the hidden beauty, and complexity of observed systems, data materialisation can produce such beauty and complexity within new synthetic fields. The boundaries of disciplines are increasingly porous, giving architecture and design an expanded agency at the centre of open synthesis applicable to a myriad of complex domains.

GAD addresses adaptation and enrichment of local cultures, complex natural and constructed environments, and active rethinking of design as an extended ecology. The programme recognises the synthetic power of design at the core of complex ecologies, and its ability to bind a plethora of agencies.

Current Research Cluster interests include: the latest approaches to robotics, simulation and computational physics, generative design, interactivity, advanced algorithms, extensive material experiments and links to material science. GAD engages critically with such developments, which are already radically changing the landscape of architecture, its social and economical role and its effectiveness as an active agency particularly within urban ecologies. Through computational resources, architects have increased access to the physics of materials and structures at orders of scale. These physics of matter are embedded in the design-search process, incorporating the constraints and inputs of manufacturing and constructability. Alongside cutting edge research, this year GAD

hosted series of public events, including the 'Material Matters' and 'Effective Knowledge' lecture series, the Nexus Project, as well as being involved with Smartgeometry 2013.

The programme is structured so that students are introduced to theoretical concepts through lectures and initial design projects supported by skills workshops in the first part of the course. During the second stage students work in small teams or individually, according to the methodology of each Cluster, allowing the student to focus on their individual interests in advanced design research and the development of a design project. There is a continuous discussion of work via tutorials with regular design reviews organised between Clusters which include external critics. The programme culminates in an exhibition curated by Professor Frédéric Migayrou and Alisa Andrasek.

B>PRO Director: Professor Frédéric Migayrou
B>PRO Deputy Director: Andrew Porter
Programme Leader: Alisa Andrasek
Report Coordinator: Stephen Gage
Research Cluster tutors: RC1 - Alisa Andrasek, Daghan Cam, Maj Plemenitas, RC2 - Marjan Colletti, Guan Lee, RC3 - Ruairi Glynn, RC4 - Xavier de Kestelier, RC5 - Philippe Morel, Thibault Schwartz, RC6 - Luke Pearson, RC7 - Jose Sanchez, RC8 - Daniel Widrig

GAD.2

GAD.3

Fig. GAD.1 Francois Mangion, Shuchi Agarwal, Ran Yan, Ali Zolfaghari, RC2, Star Rot 1. Caustic analyses through the Star geometric shape of curvature, recording the shift in the projected caustic curves, with respect to the movement of the light source. **Fig. GAD.2** Amirreza Mirmotahari, Joanna Theodosiu, Shahad Thamer Al-Thadity, RC1, Sets of agents that manipulate the porosity of the structure and retain structural stability together with sphere packing depending on some specific arrangements for construction. **Fig. GAD.3** Iro Karantaki, Dimitra Angelopoulou, Vassia Diamanti, RC7, Wire Flies. The project explores new building blocks of architecture working around the collection of energy and its distribution. By using patterns they can intuitively redefine the topology of the circuits that run through the building fabric.

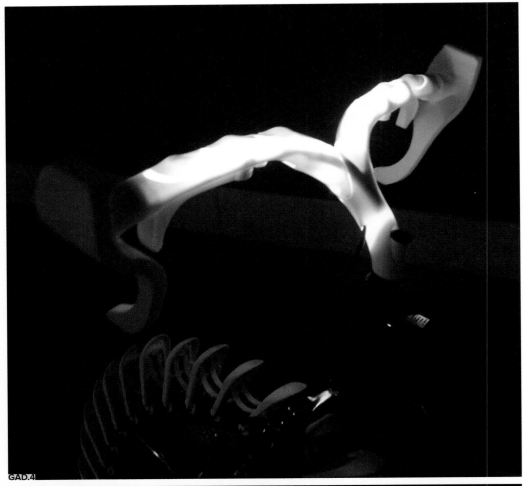

GAD.4

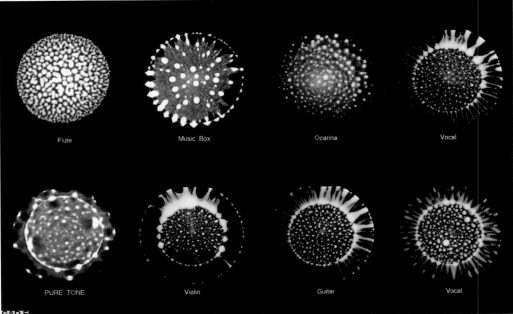

Flute

Music Box

Ocarina

Vocal

PURE TONE

Violin

Guitar

Vocal

GAD.5

GAD.6

GAD.7

GAD.8

GAD.9

Fig. GAD.4 RC4 Group project. **Fig. GAD.5** Eva Lui, RC3, Studies in Fine Silicon Fluid Behaviour to Sound. **Fig. GAD.6** Robotic cutting of EPS foam blocks with HAL. 0.04.5, during RC5 robotic workshop #3 (4-8 March 2013), with guest tutors Eng. Lucia Mondardini and Eng. Arch. Martina Presepi and additional tutor Tristan Gobin. **Fig. GAD.7** A view of the intrados of the final dome made of 126 ashlars assembled through a nexorade logic during RC5 robotic workshop #3. This type of reciprocal structure is inspired from the flat vaults developed by Joseph Abeille (XVII Century). **Fig. GAD.8** Stefan Bassing, Efi Orfanou, Matthew Martensen, Qiuying Zhong, RC8. **Fig. GAD.9** Bernardo Dias, Lauren Diaz, Sowmya Mahesh, Chiaki Yatsui, RC8. **Fig. GAD.10** Yuchen Liu, RC6, Through simulating the processes of controlled demolition, the project suggests momentary architectures that form as part of a visceral and dynamic act. These formal elements leave traces in the landscape, starting to define an archaeology of destruction. **Fig. GAD.11** Mo Wang, Shengchen Yang, Alex Wang, RC1, The elevation of the column reveals not only evolve and massive trend of the structure, but local detail texture and intricacy as well.

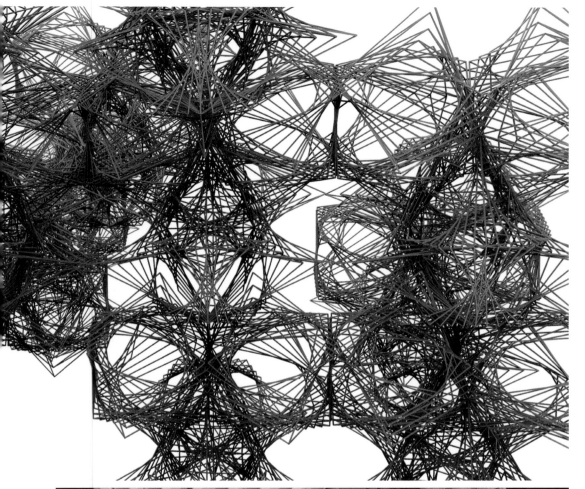

GAD.10

B>PRO
MArch Urban Design

Adrian Lahoud

The MArch Urban Design is a 12-month full-time postgraduate course that sets out to transform existing paradigms of urban design education. The programme sees urban design as a practice without obvious boundaries spatially, culturally or in terms of other disciplines. It aims to open inquiry into social, anthropological, economic and ecological concerns in a context where the political, moral and ethical responsibility of the designer is seen as fundamental. A sustained and comprehensive engagement with the realities of urbanisation is cultivated through extensive research and fieldwork, providing a rigorous platform for design experimentation.

The programme is structured into seven Research Clusters, bringing together a new generation of designers and thinkers from across the world in order to provide rich and challenging spaces for long-term research on urbanisation and design. Every three years a single geo-political region will act as a common object of inquiry for the entire programme. Individual Clusters work collaboratively on projects located within this region. For the period 2012-2015 the programme will focus on the cities of the Mediterranean basin including: Athens, Algiers, Beirut, Marseille, Reggio Calabria and Messina, Tangier and Tunis.

Working on a common regional scale for three years offers a number of important benefits. By extending the length of engagement the programme is able to build a knowledge archive on the cities in question as well as the Mediterranean as a whole, simultaneously developing longer-term relationships with institutions, practitioners and other stakeholders. The result of this engagement is a richer and more meaningful form of design research.

Believing that urban design has no natural scale, the integration of seven diverse studios within a common regional structure allows for a multi-scalar dialogue to take place across the different clusters, this allows students to range across a wide variety of concerns from a soil sample in the Tunisian desert to the dominance of a single architectural type in Athens. Working in this way also creates a strong sense of collectivity within the programme as common methods, problems and ideas emerge across different sites of inquiry. Today the Mediterranean is a unique theatre of political and spatial transformation, the revolutions taking place in North Africa and the Arabic speaking world seize our attention, likewise the crisis of capitalism and its impact on the Mediterranean countries of Southern Europe.

Athens
Yannis Aesopos and Ross Exo Adams attempt to reimagine the possibility of city currently built around a single dominant typology – the polikatoikia. Symptomatic of the state's strategic withdrawal from civic affairs and leading to a hyper-individualised scale of development, this studio explore ways of re-connecting these elementary pixels in the hope of generating new scales of collective activity within the city.

Algiers
Beth Hughes and DaeWha Kang attempt to reformulate the basic conventions of mass housing in a context beset by housing shortages and cheap, poorly built tower typologies.

Beirut
In the Lebanese capital of Beirut, Sam Jacoby and Aristide Antonas enter into disputes over public space through the lens of education, in a context of a weak state and poor provision of social services, the studio proposes education as one of the last avenues in which public space can be delivered through private means.

Marseille
Camila Sotomayor and Platon Issaias lead a project that explores the way in which the city has been shaped by a series of distinct spatial and political ideas about migration and trade.

Reggio Calabria and Messina

In Southern Italy on the facing cities of Reggio Calabria and Messina, Luca Galofaro and Davide Sacconi propose a radical inversion of the North-South axis in which the South is always conceived in terms of its under-development – instead reclaiming not only 'the South as a resource of human energy, memories and relationships' but also architecture which has lost its fundamental role in imagining new common spaces.

Tangier

Peter Besley, Hannah Corlett and Jonathan Kendall explore the ways in which sprawl, tourist infrastructure, markets and special economic zones place unique and often contradictory pressures on this emerging city.

Tunis

In the urban and semi-urban periphery around Tunis Marco Poletto and Claudia Pasquero engage with itinerant and sedentary forms of agricultural practices exploring possibilities for new forms of energy harvesting and economic activity.

What unites these different projects is an attempt to see through the visceral impact of recent events, to peer beyond the day-to-day turmoil of politics and render visible the slower, long-term conventions, norms and protocols that shape our cities and the lives we lead in them.

Programme Leader: Adrian Lahoud
Research Cluster Tutors: 1. Marseille – Camila Sotomayor and Platon Issaias, 2. Reggio Calabria and Messina – Luca Galafaro & Davide Sacconi, 3. Beirut – Sam Jacoby and Aristide Antonas, 4. Tunis – Claudia Pasquero and Marco Poletto, 5. Algiers – Beth Hughes and DaeWha Kang, 6. Athens – Yannis Aesopos and Ross Exo Adams, 7. Tangiers – Peter Besley, Hannah Corlett and Jonathan Kendall.

London Project: Professor Peter Bishop
Design Workshops: Elia Zenghelis
Report Tutors: Ross Exo Adams, Sam Jacoby, Graciela Moreno, Godofredo Pereira, Lorenzo Pezzani

UD.1

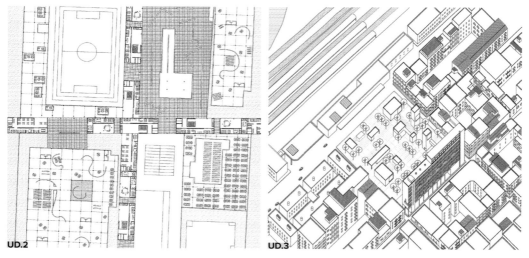

UD.2

UD.3

Fig. UD.1 Robin Liu, Monument to Debt. Cluster: Athens.
Fig UD.2 Yingnan Chu, Domestic Frames. Cluster: Marseille.
Fig UD.3 Christina Varvogli and Lily Tsolakidi, Archipelago of the Common. Cluster: Reggio-Calabria and Messina. **Fig. UD.4** Workshop reviews in studio with Platon Issaias and Adrian Lahoud.

UD.4

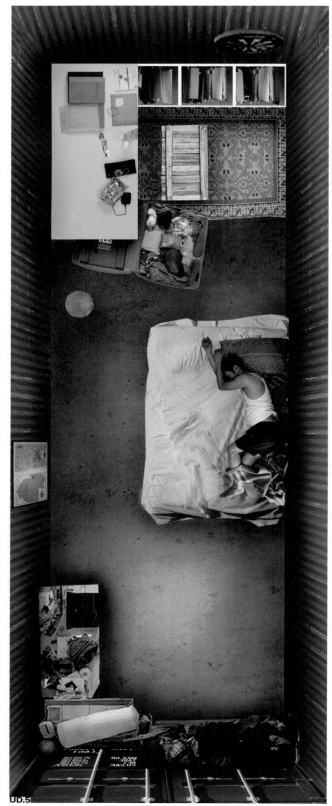

UD.5

UD.6

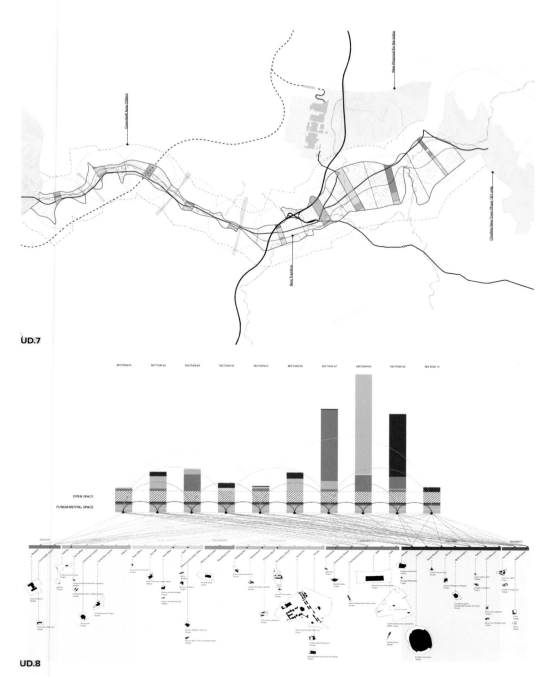

UD.7

UD.8

Fig. UD.5 – UD.6 Constantinos Marcou, Thresholds of
Knowledge. Cluster: Reggio-Calabria and Messina. **Fig. UD.7
– UD.8** Young Joon Chung, Uneven Tangier. Regional strategy
and program matrix. Cluster: Tangier. **Fig. UD.9** Ruowe Song,
Edible Landscape Montage. The montage simulate an iteration
of the Edible Landscape with the key parameters indicated.
The simulation is adapted from Ant Colony Pheromone
Simulation which imitates the food sourcing behaviour of
ants. Cluster: Tunis. **Fig. UD.10** Ting Wen, Edible Lanscape
Montage. The model shows the overlays of the different
ecological, agricultural and social layers which influence the
food production network in SidiBouzid, Tunisia. Cluster: Tunis.
Fig. UD.11 Zi Wang, Operation fields drawings – agri-urban
terrain – Bizerte – Tunisia. Cluster: Tunis.

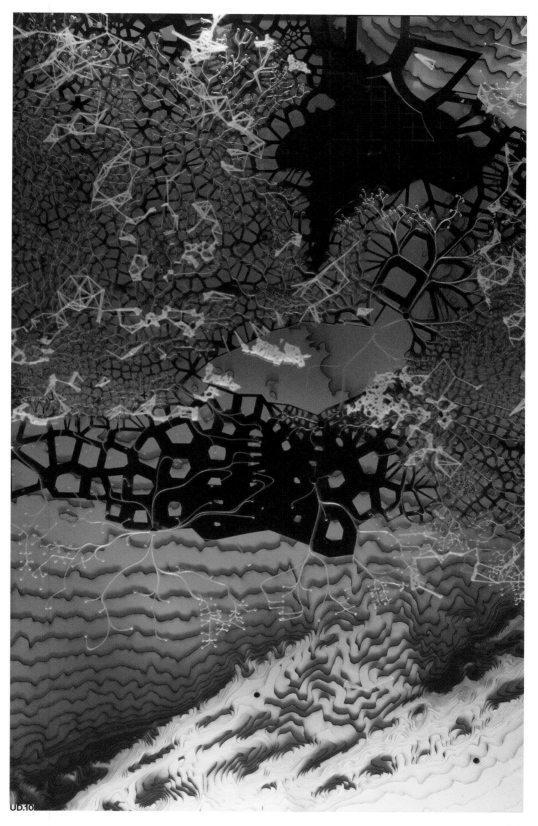

UD.10

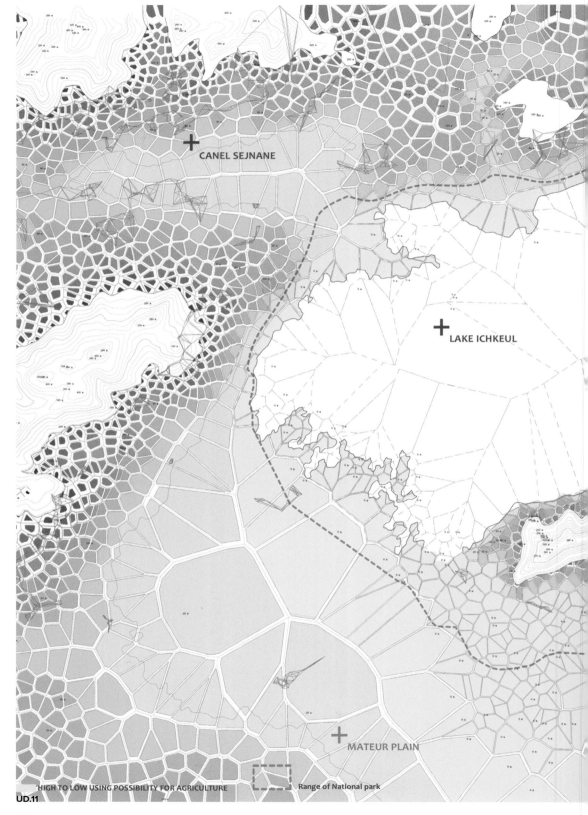

CANEL SEJNANE

LAKE ICHKEUL

MATEUR PLAIN

HIGH TO LOW USING POSSIBILITY FOR AGRICULTURE

Range of National park

UD.11

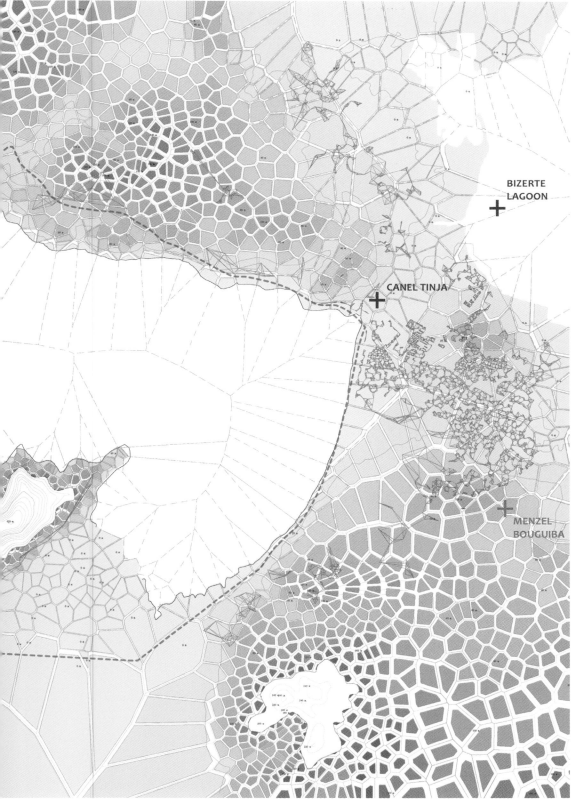

BIZERTE
LAGOON

CANEL TINJA

MENZEL
BOUGUIBA

MA Architectural History

Adrian Forty

Architecture consists not only of buildings and projects, but also of the life that takes place within them, and of the ideas and discussions that they give rise to. It is the business of the MA Architectural History to interrogate these discussions, to extend them, and possibly to reframe them in terms of broader debates about culture, history and politics.

We encourage our students to be experimental, to try out ideas from different fields, and to see whether bringing them to bear on architecture changes the way we think about buildings, cities and the life within them. Each one of the projects listed here is a small experiment, in which some particular architectural phenomenon has been put under the microscope and examined in the light of a particular theory or set of ideas, to see whether our view of it might change – or, alternatively, whether a theory might need to be reassessed.

The one-year Masters programme in Architectural History, which has been running for 30 years, is partly a taught programme that prepares people for research, and partly a research programme, in which people undertake a self-selected and self-directed research project – two examples are included here.

2011-12 Reports

Ana Baeza
Performing Whiteness: The Imperfect Case of Chinese-American Cultural Rebirth in San Francisco Chinatown, 1906-1920s
Lucy Dunn
Truth and Fiction: The Barbican and Postmodernism
Reenie Elliott
Berlin Observation Towers: the Collapse of Power and Vision
Jenine Hudson
Imaging the King's Cross Gasometers, 1988-2012
Rebecca Lane
Constructs of Home and Identity in Public Policy and the Psychic Realities of a Long-term Homeless Hostel
Tatjana Leboff

The Geographies of the Soho Prostitute: locale, gender, and mobility
Runa Matthiesen,
The Use and Abuse of Heritage in Brandscaping: Place-making of Carlsberg's Our City Townscape in Copenhagen
Maksymilian Fus Mickiewicz
Copeland Industrial Park: Culture, Community and Urban Change
Adam Nemeth
Architecture, Urban Planning and State Power in the late Eighteenth Century Habsburg Monarchy: the case of Pest
Dafni Papaemmanouil
The Image of the Parthenon, An Exploration of its Various Uses
Isabelle Priest
Coming Clean: In Search of Le Corbusier's Cleaners in his Parisian Domestic Architecture, 1922-1934
Claudia Rath
Food in Kitchen Representations: Good Housekeeping Magazine
Catherine St Hill
Big Jim in Runcorn: Urban Memory and the Demolished Southgate Estate
Yuki Sumner
Angels and Demons of History: the Architects of Air
Freya Wigzell
Pleasure's Follies

Catherine St Hill
Big Jim in Runcorn: Urban Memory and the Demolished Southgate Estate

This is a study of a building that has been physically forgotten and edited out of the canon; the story of how one architect's bold experiment to create 'a new garden city' became tainted by problems, seemingly loathed by its residents, but then several decades later reminisced about fondly with a sense of nostalgia and loss by those I interviewed. The Southgate Estate seems universally acknowledged as unsuccessful, yet it was designed by one of Britain's most successful architects. This is about our perception of post-war state housing, and about how the absence of a building can be more of a provocation to architectural history than if it was still here today.

Commissioned in 1967, and split into two phases, the Southgate Estate was conceived as a high-density, low-rise solution to the overspill of slums in Victorian terraces in Liverpool. By 1989, a little over a decade after the final phase was completed, the Runcorn Corporation went into administration, and their successor demolished the estate in 1990, replacing it with red brick 'Noddyland' housing just two years later. This is a story told in reverse, where a bold vision for the future was displaced for a safer vision of the past. [...]

The grand façades of the concrete squares with their porthole windows, inspired by Georgian terraces, characterised Phase 1 of the Southgate Estate, completed in 1975. *Casabella* described this stage as 'powerful classical macrostructures that creates a stronger overall image than even Aldo Rossi's Gallaratese Quarter in Milan' – a view reiterated by the Japanese journal *A+U*: 'The effect of the giant order is most telling when the façade is lit by raking sunlight except that the first four storeys seem to disappear entirely behind the pillars, giving the building a Rossian air of contrast that is unusual in an English building'. When I interviewed Julian Harrap, who was working in Stirling's office at the time, he echoed this sense: "It was such a dream when it was first opened for us. It's very grand to say, but when you see the western light falling on the concrete, and we went from square to square, it was like walking around Verona at night. We had, in our terms, created a little vision of the Bath that had been our inspiration – to create a new urban landscape in a wilderness of left-over land from a motorway, linked to what should have been the heart of the town of Runcorn." There was something about the first phase of the Southgate Estate that had a monumentality, with its non-domestic scale and almost neoclassical order, that made the building seem otherworldly, as if it didn't quite belong in Liverpool.

Image: Demolition of The Southgate Estate, Runcorn, 1990

Isabelle Priest
Coming Clean: In Search of Le Corbusier's Cleaners in his Domestic Architecture, 1922-1934

The cleaning of buildings is a mostly invisible activity. Who are the cleaners, what are their practices?

The enquiry looks at cleaners historically, in the early twentieth century, when issues of hygiene converged with architectural design. And it takes the canonical works of one of the founders of the new style, an architect famous for cultivating the beauty of cleanliness: Le Corbusier.

Geographically, the study leads us to the city with the greatest concentration of Le Corbusier's buildings from the 1920s and 1930s - Paris and its environs - and to his domestic architecture, because that contains the most surprises.

For whatever reason – the low status of cleaners in society, their invisibility and the difficulty of tracing them – and despite the acknowledged importance of the rhetoric of cleanliness for Le Corbusier, none of the existing scholarship on his domestic architecture deals with how the buildings were cleaned, or by whom. The report, therefore, draws upon new primary research in Paris - at the houses themselves, at the archives of Fondation Le Corbusier, of the , and at the Bibliothèque Nationale.

What becomes apparent from the primary sources, however, is that we are dealing with another subject entirely. Although subtitled 'In Search of Le Corbusier's Cleaners,' we find, in fact, that there are no cleaners at all. Instead cleaning was absorbed into the multiple tasks of domestic servants, of whom it turns out there were many. Ultimately, because of the inherent invisibility of cleaning processes, this essay concentrates on the spaces provided for the people who cleaned.

Given the alleged 'enlightenment' of Le Corbusier's clients many of whom made a virtue of cleanliness and hygiene in commissioning such architecture, it is surprising they employed so many live-in servants. Servants' quarters amount to a quarter of the houses' total area, yet in all of the secondary literature, the servant accommodation has been predominantly left, so to speak, 'off plan'. The astonishing neglect is even repeated at the houses themselves. At Maison La Roche, where the concierge and kitchen were first publicly opened in 2009, the pamphlet guide makes no mention of these areas - and the same applies at Villa Savoye and Le Corbusier's own flat at L'Immeuble Molitor.

When asked about the spaces and people who worked in these buildings, the tour guides' responses, if they had any, were reliant on anecdotal evidence: that the two domestic staff who lived with Raoul La Roche, for example, remained at his house after he was transferred into a nursing home, and allegedly until after his death when the Fondation Le Corbusier took over.

The representation of Le Corbusier's houses as servant-less may not only be the result of collective amnesia. Evidence suggests that Le Corbusier wanted people to believe that his buildings magically maintained and cleaned themselves – that this was their principle characteristic and advantage.

As no doubt part of 'the machine for living in' agenda, no contemporary descriptions or photographs of the servants or of their quarters exist. The most striking evidence comes from a letter Le Corbusier wrote to his mother, that Colette Sidonie Gabrielle (1873-1954) wanted to live in a 'Corbusière' as she believed it would allow her to dismiss her servants, whom she described as 'vampires.'

This attitude does mark a point of departure from nineteenth century conceptions of domestic service and dirt. Whilst the majority had been invisible, some servants – butlers and footmen – were for public visual display. It was acknowledged that a well-kept home with time-consuming-to-clean decorative schemes was a symbol of the family's social prestige because it demonstrated they could employ large numbers of competent domestic staff.

Gabrielle believed, on the contrry, that if one removed complicated decorative orders, one automatically removed the need for servants. This rveals how far employers were from the reality of dirt - for, paradoxically, the effect was probably the reverse. Dust and dirt sit visibly on white, shiny surfaces, rather than being hidden by the colours, patterns and deep pile of fabric, and hence they become more 'blatant and inexcusable': modern design created the need for an even more obsessive cleaning programme.

Servants would have been, and are still, incompatible with Le Corbusier's self-professed progressive clients. To appear 'intellectual and moralistic,' one had to deny the existence of one's servants: rendering them even more physically, socially and architecturally invisible.

It is my belief that these spaces have continued to remain invisible so as to perpetuate the hegemonic historical interpretation of 1920s Western Europe as the era of female emancipation, socialist ideals, intellectualism and joie de vivre. My argument is in the domestic realm, these experiences were experienced only by the few of the middle and upper classes. Life for the rest remained as burdensome as before. Le Corbusier's dwellings are a microcosmic image of the era: more limitedly progressive than they appear.

Despite the lack of concern in France towards service areas, Le Corbusier did pay some attention to them. His servant quarters are not 'undesigned' – on the contrary they are very 'designed.' They are not left-over spaces, but they are the result of some deliberate design decisions. Nevertheless, most interestingly, they contain a different character to the rest of the house in size, position and access, window types, materiality, light and colour. This report identifies these differences whilst considering possible explanations. What emerges is that Le Corbusier simultaneously and contradictorily displayed both a care for and a disregard towards domestic workers. Furthermore, the distinctive characteristics of service areas have in general meant that they are unsuited to alternative uses and remained unabsorbed into the home. Although acclaimed for his flexible, efficient architecture, effectively they are a waste of space. This calls for a revision of Le Corbusier.

PhD Architectural Design

Jonathan Hill

Leading to a PhD in Architecture, the MPhil/PhD Architectural Design allows especially able and reflective designers to undertake research within the Bartlett School of Architecture's speculative and experimental ethos. The first to be established in the UK, the Bartlett MPhil/PhD Architectural Design is internationally recognised as one of the most influential doctoral programmes dedicated to architectural design.

The programme draws on the strengths of design teaching and doctoral research at The Bartlett, encouraging the development of architectural research through the interaction of designing and writing. An architectural design doctoral thesis has two interrelated elements of equal importance – a project and a text – that share a research theme and a productive relationship. The project may be drawn, filmed, built, or use whatever media is appropriate.

UCL's multidisciplinary environment offers a stimulating and varied research culture that connects research by architectural design to developments in other disciplines, such as anthropology, art, digital media, geography and medicine. This academic year, we began a collaboration with the doctoral programmes at the Royal Academy of Music, allowing students to present in each institution. The PhD Architectural Design programme is intended for graduates of architecture and other disciplines who wish to pursue research by architectural design. 50 students from over 20 countries are currently enrolled.

The Bartlett School of Architecture's two PhD programmes organise a number of annual events for doctoral students. PhD Research Projects, an exhibition and conference with presentations by current practice-based PhD students in UCL, is held during the second term. Invited critics in 2013 were Dr Victor Buchli, Anthropology, UCL; Dr Sarah Callis, Royal Academy of Music; Professor Nat Chard, University of Brighton; Dr Neil Heyde, Royal Academy of Music; and Dr Despina Stratigakos, State University of New York, Buffalo. Throughout the year, PhD Research Conversations seminars are an opportunity for doctoral candidates to present work in progress.

Programme Coordinator: Dr Penelope Haralambidou

Supervisors: Dr Camillo Boano, Professor Iain Borden, Dr Victor Buchli, Dr Ben Campkin, Dr Marjan Colletti, Professor Sir Peter Cook, Dr Marcos Cruz, Professor Penny Florence, Professor Colin Fournier, Professor Murray Fraser, Professor Stephen Gage, Professor Ranulph Glanville, Dr Penelope Haralambidou, Professor Christine Hawley, Dr Neil Heyde, Professor Jonathan Hill, Dr Adrian Lahoud, Dr Yeoryia Manolopoulou, Jayne Parker, Dr Barbara Penner, Dr Sophia Psarra, Dr Peg Rawes, Professor Jane Rendell, Professor Bob Sheil, Dr Hugo Spiers, Professor Phil Steadman, Professor Neil Spiller, Professor Phil Tabor

Current students: Adam Adamis, Yota Adilenidou, Nicola Antaki, Rachel Armstrong, Alessandro Ayuso, Jaime Bartolome, Katy Beinart, Joanne Bristol, David Buck, Niccolo Casas, Emma Cheatle, Ines Dantas, Catja De Haas, Bernardita Devilat, Pavlos Ferreos, Pablo Gil, Ruairi Glynn, Polly Gould, Mohamad Hafeda, Popi Iacovou, Christiana Ioannou, Nahed Jawad, Tae Young Kim, Felipe Lanuza Rilling, Constance Lau, Guan Lee, Tea Lim, Jane Madsen, Igor Marjanovic, Matteo Melioli, Malca Mizrahi, Ollie Palmer, Christos Papastergiou, Maria Pereira Pestana, Henri Praeger, Felix Robbins, David Roberts, Natalia Romik, Luisa Silva Alpalhao, Eva Sopeoglou, Camila Sotomayor, Ro Spankie, Theo Spyropoulos, Ben Sweeting, Cindy Walters, Stefan White, Michael Wihart, Alex Zambelli, Seda Zirek, Fiona Zisch

Polly Gould
No More Elsewhere: Antarctica through the Archive of the Edward Wilson Watercolours
Principal Supervisor: Professor Jane Rendell, Subsidiary Supervisor: Dr Victor Buchli

No More Elsewhere is a practical and theoretical project, which takes the encounter through the archive with the extreme environment of Antarctica as a departure point for making art and investigating an eco-ethical aesthetic. I aim to apply feminist theory, anthropology, philosophy, and art practice methods of copying and distortion, to the understanding of contemporary representations of Antarctica. How are techniques of vision and ethics of positionality informed by the multifaceted interpretation of no more elsewhere?

'No more elsewhere' is a polysemic phrase. It can refer to the end of the Heroic Era of Antarctic exploration, or to the imminent future disappearance of the melting icecaps and to the time when the evidence of their existence is preserved in climate-controlled air-conditioned archives. As an exercise in art making and in writing, it indicates a poststructuralist approach to criticism in which there is no outside of the text or artwork, while exploring, to the contrary, ways in which writing and art create 'elsewhere' as part of their effect.

This research is undertaken in the context of contemporary art practices featuring Polar landscapes that are either predicated on the artist 'being there' (Cape Farewell, SPRI Artist Residencies) or, in contrast, are derived from secondary mediated encounters with the landscape (Eliasson, Neudecker). Making watercolours in Antarctica and in the archive are both activities subject to climate; Antarctica's climate limits due to freezing temperatures, the archive due to institutional restrictions enforced for the sake of conservation. What can my archival encounter with the Antarctic watercolours of Wilson tell us about the contemporary envisioning of extreme environments? My encounter is explored through practical making of artworks, such as the *Anamorphic Landscape* series of handblown mirrored glass globes on watercolour paintings of anamorphic inverted panoramas, each titled after a Wilson watercolour.

Ollie Palmer
Mind Control in Architecture
Principal Supervisor: Professor Stephen Gage, Subsidiary
Supervisor: Dr Peg Rawes, Subsidiary Supervisor: Dr Hugo
Spiers

My work explores the role of architect as designer of
environments, drawing on speculative fictions created
by theatre, cinematography and hard science.

In particular, my interest lies in control systems and the use
of paranoia as a means to alter behaviour. These principles
have long been the subject of architectural investigation
(such as Bentham's Panopticon, 1785), fiction (as in Orwell's
Nineteen Eighty-Four, 1948), as well as being tested through
large-scale social engineering experiments during the Cold
War (1945-1991). However, where it is unfeasible – and
unethical – to experiment with humans, my project uses
ants, whose colonies can be safely disrupted, dissected
and experimented with.

I construct a series of environments as small-scale
architectural installations, which invite viewers to reflect on
issues of control. The installations then serve as metaphors
for the human environments that they represent and are fed
back to observers.

My work to date includes the 'Godot Machine' – a Sisyphean
device which monitors and controls the movements of a
single ant, causing her to follow her own trail indefinitely, and
the 'Ant Ballet' – an attempt to choreograph an entire colony
of ants through use of robotics and specially synthesised ant
communication pheromones. The work is presented as film,
installation, performance and text.

David Roberts
Empty Words Build Empty Homes: Language, Politics and Participation in the Pursuit of Public Housing
Principal Supervisor: Professor Jane Rendell, Subsidiary Supervisor: Dr Ben Campkin

The history of housing the working population in Britain has a predictable circularity in architectural form; one generation's panacea becomes the next generation's problem, only to be reappraised with remorse after it has passed. My thesis is a practical and theoretical investigation into this cycle. It follows the life of an east London housing estate to allow its inhabitants to reflect on the utopian promises of public housing in order to reclaim the principles of equality, dignity and security at its foundation.

I focus on the Haggerston West Estate built in the late 1930s by the London County Council Housing Department which is to be demolished in 2013 and replaced by a mixed tenure and mixed use development typical of contemporary regeneration programmes. The accelerated retreat of social welfare under austerity measures has paved the way for a dismantling of public housing in ideal and form. This has catalysed a groundswell of renewed interest in housing estates from academics and practitioners seeking to mend their conceptual, built and social fabric. I draw from the work of Ravetz, Phillips and Watt, and the socially critical practice of Rendell, Watkins and Pearson to create an interdisciplinary dialogue.

My thesis examines how changes in the theory, design and representation of public housing are expressed in language. I use methods of archival research, discourse analysis and oral history alongside participatory practices to take the ideals of public housing back to the sites –plans, manifestos and spaces – and subjects – architects, politicians and residents – from and for which they were conceived. The outputs to date include a documentary/fiction film, public photo-installation and site-specific performances each devised and written collaboratively to enable residents and the public to develop their own lines of enquiry into these critical debates.

MPhil/PhD Architectural History & Theory

Barbara Penner

The Bartlett School of Architecture's MPhil/PhD Architectural History & Theory programme allows students to conduct an exhaustive piece of research into an area of their own selection and definition. Great importance is placed on the originality of information uncovered, the creativity of the interpretations made, and the rigour of the methodological procedures adopted.

Approximately 20-30 students from around the world are enrolled at any one time for MPhil and PhD research in this field. The range of research topics undertaken is broad, but most explore the history and theory of architecture and cities from c. 1800 to the present day, with an emphasis on the critical reading of these subjects from cultural, political and experiential viewpoints.

The MPhil/PhD Architectural History & Theory programme draws on the expertise and experience of the Bartlett School of Architecture's team of architectural historians and theorists, who are recognised internationally for their contributions to the field. The programme itself is very dynamic with an active series of talks, seminars, and conferences. Inkeeping with UCL's multidisciplinary ethos, connections between architectural research and other fields are encouraged, and there are active collaborations with the Departments of Anthropology, Fine Art and Geography, and UCL Urban Lab. We have also conducted research exchanges with the Royal Academy of Music and Cornell University.

Programme Coordinator: Dr Penelope Haralambidou

Current Supervisors: Dr Jan Birksted, Professor Iain Borden, Dr Ben Campkin, Professor Adrian Forty, Professor Murray Fraser, Dr Penelope Haralambidou, Professor Jonathan Hill, Adrian Lahoud, Dr Barbara Penner, Dr Peg Rawes, Professor Jane Rendell, Dr Sophia Psarra

Other Supervisors: Dr Julio Davila, Bartlett Development Planning Unit; Dr Victor Buchli and Dr Ruth Mandel, UCL Anthropology; Dr Stephanie Schwartz, UCL History of Art

Graduating Students: Ricardo Agarez, Suzanne MacLeod, Pinai Sirikiatikul

Current Students: Wesley Aelbrecht, Tilo Amhoff, Kalliopi Amygdalou, Sabina Andron, Pinar Aykac, Tal Bar, Eva Branscome, Eray Cayli, Stella Flatten, Stylianos Giamarelos, Nicholas Jewell, Kate Jordan, Irene Kelly, Thomas-Bernard Kenniff, Torsten Lange, Claudio Leoni, Abigail Lockey, Kieran Mahon, Nathan Moore, Dragan Pavlovic, Brent Pilkey, Matthew Poulter, Regner Ramos, Sophie Read, Sarah Riviere, Ozayr Saloojee, Maria del Pilar Sanchez Beltran, Huda Tayob, Amy Thomas, Nina Vollenbroker, Danielle Willkens

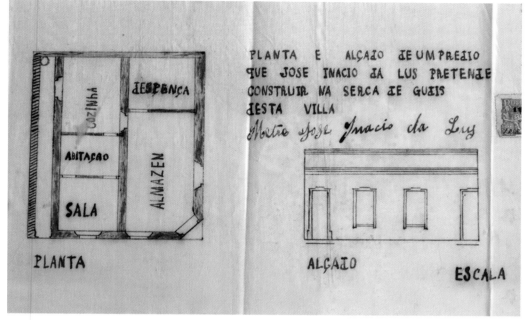

Dr Ricardo Costa Agarez

*Regionalism, Modernism and Vernacular Tradition
in the Architecture of Algarve, Portugal, 1925-1965*

Principal supervisor: Professor Adrian Forty;
second supervisor: Dr Jan Birksted

This thesis looks at the contribution of real and constructed local traditions to modern building practices and discourses in a specific region, focusing on the case of Algarve, southern Portugal, between 1925 and 1965.

By shifting the main research focus from the centre to the region, and by placing a strong emphasis on fieldwork and previously overlooked sources (the archives of provincial bodies, municipalities and architects), the thesis scrutinises canonical accounts of the interaction of regionalism with modernism. It examines how architectural 'regionalism', often discussed at a central level through the work of acknowledged metropolitan architects, was interpreted by local practices in everyday building activity. Was there a real local concern with vernacular traditions, or was this essentially a construct of educated metropolitan circles, both at the time and retrospectively? Circuits and agents of influence and dissemination are traced, the careers of locally relevant designers come to light, and a more comprehensive view of architectural production is offered.

Departing from conventional narratives that present pre-war regionalism in Portugal as a stereotype-driven, one-way central construct, the creation of a regional built identity for Algarve emerges here as the result of combined local, regional and central agencies, mediated both through concrete building practice and discourses outside architecture. Post-war regionalism appears as more than a sophisticated re-appropriation of vernacular features by cultured architects to overcome the shortcomings of both modernist orthodoxy and official stylistic conservatism: the thesis shows how Algarve's traditional features allowed modernism to be pragmatically restyled as locally sensitive and keep its fundamentals unquestioned; and the architects' authority to be reasserted where non-architects dominated. Tradition became the key to architecture's future. Regionalism, a consistent undercurrent of 20th century architecture, resurfaced and was morphed by modernism, with mutual benefit. In Algarve, vernacular tradition and regional agency appear as not mere footnotes in the narrative of modernism, but as part of its main text.

Image: House in Cerca do Júdice (Rua Sacadura Cabral), Olhão. Dec 1917. Câmara Municipal de Olhão planning office

Dr Pinai Sirikiatikul
Constructional 'Theory' in Britain, 1870s-1930s
Principal Supervisor: Professor Adrian Forty;
second supervisor: Professor Iain Borden

Unlike spoken and written theories, the constructional 'theories' explored in this thesis are drawn essentially from 'practice'. While occasionally drawing upon what architects said and wrote, the thesis investigates the extent to which architects have worked out their theoretical propositions within the practical aspects of building, without necessarily articulating them verbally.

Of the recent discussions on the relation of architectural theory to building practice, Kenneth Frampton's *Studies in Tectonic Culture* (1995) stands out; but Frampton's book is limited by his anti-post-modernist framework, his mode of argument that largely attributes the value of architectural works to a theoretical dimension, his treatment of construction as a constant and passive given, and his disregard for the entirety of British architecture. This thesis criticises *Studies in Tectonic Culture*, arguing that British architecture offers some alternatives for thinking about the dialectics of 'theory' and 'construction'. The way in which some British architects of the late 19th and early 20th centuries worked – experimental, craft-based and treating the process of construction as integral to the process of design – indicated that for them construction was more than simply a medium through which an architect's ideas are expressed;

and out of their calculated employment of construction could emerge a certain 'implicit intellectuality', which was no less a 'theory' than verbally articulated statements existing prior to construction.

The aim of this thesis is to recognise as 'theory' intelligent building practices, which take place within well understood processes, but are usually understood in terms of 'pragmatism'. The constructional 'theory' that this thesis puts forward is of an intellectual understanding, implicit in, and occurring in parallel with, practical action, its aim a more comprehensive anticipation of the work of construction than that customarily occurring. It is not theory that dictates construction, but rather that 'construction' itself can be a 'theory' in the process of becoming. In opening up possibilities for thinking about constructional 'theory', the thesis suggests the removal of an assumed theory/ practice distinction, proposing instead 'practice' as essentially an indispensable body of 'immanent theory' as an alternative to Frampton's theory of the *Tectonic*.

Image: Construction workers standing at the main arches of the Royal Horticultural Hall under construction, Westminster, London, 1927

Postgraduate Certificate in Advanced Architectural Research

Stephen Gage

Architecture and engineering have a history
where research and practice go hand in hand,
where many great practices have grown as a result
of fundamental research and where many research
projects arise from groundbreaking design. This is
especially true during periods of economic inactivity
when recent models of working are called into
question and new modes (sometimes based on
rediscovered historical precedent) are established.
This can lead to the formation of innovative practices
and to the start of academic careers in research
and teaching.

The Postgraduate Certificate in Advanced
Architectural Research gives students with
appropriate graduate degrees the opportunity to
take their work to a further stage development.
Part of its production are group exhibitions, such as
Constructing Realities held at Arup's Phase 2 Gallery
in 2011, curated by Stephen Gage and Ruairi Glynn,
and designed by Nick Westby. It showed how some
of the best Masters portfolios and thesis contain the
seeds of serious design research proposals, and
how these might be taken forward to create new
types of place, novel interactive building elements
and new façade and structural systems.

BLOOM _ Crowd Sourced Garden by Alisa Andrasek and Jose Sanchez (Biothing)

House of Flags by Yeoryia Manolopoulou and Anthony Boulanger (AY Architects)

Universal Tea Machine by Laura Allen and Mark Smout (SmoutAllen), Luke Pearson and Sandra Youkhana (You+Pea), and Iain Borden

Tr(ee)logy by CJ Lim, John Chang, Samson Lau and Martin Tang

The Alga(e)zebo by Marjan Colletti and Marcos Cruz (marcosandmarjan)

Summer Foundation

Sabine Storp, Carlos Jimenez

Architectural Innovation for a Social Revolution

The Bartlett Summer Foundation is a new course created to introduce and prepare students for a future career in architecture and architectural education. Running for eight weeks over the summer, the programme provides students with a unique creative platform to improve their design and communication skills, as well as their individual conceptual and critical thinking. Participants are of varying ages and differing backgrounds, including prospective Bartlett students, international students, secondary school students and those who have a career change in mind and want to use it as a testbed to see if they are suited to a university degree in architecture.

As well as critical design skills and conceptual thought processes students are also introduced to disciplines related to architectural design practice as a means to expand their understanding of architecture. These include contemporary art practice, theatre design, fashion, drawing and photography. During the course students are also encouraged to explore London, to read widely, to visit galleries, exhibitions, concerts and to listen to lectures.

The School offers two separate routes within the Summer Foundation. The first of these runs for five weeks from late July and focuses on developing key design skills and critical thinking. The second route offers an additional three weeks, which allows students to develop not only skills but also additional and more advanced modes of conceptual thinking which enhance their creative learning.

Students on this course develop ideas of innovative architecture and design, as tools to improve the world. To inform these speculations they are asked to investigate London's transformation within the present economic climate. Students aim to reclaim the role of design to develop scenarios to promote and celebrate a diverse and sustainable future environment.

Tutors: Sabine Storp, Carlos Jimenez, Anne Ryan, Catrina Stuart, Antoine Hertenberger

Image: Ali El Hashimi, Theatre Project, Summer Foundation

Summer School

Bill Hodgson

Outdoor[s in] London

A visit to London in 1970 would have found a fraction of the number of occupied outdoor spaces in comparison to today. Britain now boasts a culture of outdoor cafes, public spaces designed for outdoor events, temporary theatres and pleasure gardens. In 2013, the Bartlett School of Architecture's annual Summer School explores the outdoor life of London with participants recording what they find and developing architectural responses. Proposals may be small interventions or larger projects. Using the Bartlett's excellent workshop and studios and University College London's associated facilities we will stage a practical symposium to survey, speculate and construct.

Each year we accommodate a group of up to 80 participants of varying ages and differing backgrounds, including prospective university students, international students, secondary school students and those who are simply keen to develop their interest in architecture and the Bartlett School of Architecture.

Participants produce a range of work including drawings, models and large-scale installations. Students will work in groups, and individually under the instruction of The Bartlett's teaching staff. Previous years have produced boats, bridges, shadow puppet theatres, as well as a range of projects at multiple scales.

ScanLAB workshop in the Kielder forest – Tom Pearce, Zenshi (Tracy) Xiao, Aleksandra Cicha and Anton Boganskyi, Stormy Beacon

ScanLAB workshop in the Kielder forest – Iulia Fratila, Ben Hayes and Deng Al. A Road to Nowhere

Smartgeometry 2013 exhibition at The Bartlett

Smartgeometry 2013 exhibition at The Bartlett

Lectures

The Bartlett International Lecture Series
features speakers from across the world. Lectures in
the series are open to the public and free to attend.
This year's speakers included:

Rob Adams
Ben Addy
Yannis Aesopos
Ben van Berkel
Aaron Betsky
Iain Borden
Benjamin Bratton
Mario Carpo
Peter Cook
Nat Chard
Raffaello D'Andrea
Graham Harman
Jonathan Hill
Luca Galofaro
Giuseppe Longo
Kengo Kuma
Winy Maas
Gurjit Singh Matharoo
Achim Menges
Nicholas de Monchaux
Gianni Pettena
Dominique Perrault
Wolfgang Rieder
Joseph Rykwert
Philippe Rahm
Casey Reas
Jenny E Sabin
Bob Sheil
Kristina Schinegger and Stefan Rutzinger
Tezuka Takaharu
Timothy Wray and Andrew Higgott

A new range of smaller lecture series' attracted over
50 speakers to our Royal Ear Hospital building.

Bartlett Nexus
Maj Plemenitas, Gennaro Senatore, Ezio Blasetti,
Paul Nicholls, Tobias Klein, Madhav Kidao, Jack
Munro, Michail Desyllas, Gregory Epps, Kate Davies,
Slub, Catrina Stewart, Tom Betts, Matt Johnson, Ollie
Palmer, Manja van de Worp, Marcus Wendt and
Vera-Maria Glahn, Memo Akten, Mollie Claypool,
Ines Dantas, Niccolo Casas, Martin Dittus, Cohen
Van Balen, Vlad Tenu, Gilles Retsin, Ryan Mehanna,
Tom Smith

Effective Knowledge
Emilie Hergott, Nicolas Bredeche, Justin
Dirrenberger, Andrew Witt, Lucia Mondardini,
Niccolo Baldasssini

Material Matters
Daniel Bosa, Enrico Dini, Matt Wade, Ollie Palmer

B>MADE

The Bartlett has extensive studios, workshops, seminar and lecture rooms, exhibition spaces, computing facilities and environmental laboratories. Specialist facilities in the School of Architecture include DMC London, Media Hub, an advanced computing cluster with printing/plotting and scanning (CADCAM), robotics and an exceptional workshop. All are staffed by teams of exceptionally skilled and experienced designers, makers, teachers and technicians. As of 2013 all these facilities are being brought together under one new identity – Bartlett Manufacturing and Design Exchange. B>MADE consists of:

Digital Manufacturing Centre (DMC)
DMC London is the Bartlett School of Architecture's state-of-the-art digital manufacturing centre. The centre's advanced 3D modeling facility brings together key technologies in 3D printing, including two ZCorp 3D printers, two Selective laser Sintering (SLS) printers, and an Object Connex 500 multiple polymer printer.

Media Hub
The Media Hub is the central resource within the Bartlett School of Architecture for photography, audiovisual, moving image and 3D scanning. The facility offers tuition in and access to equipment and techniques central to the production and representation of architectural ideas. Principal equipment, tooling and facilities include wet darkrooms, lighting studio, new 3D scanning support, 4D animation.

CADCAM & Robotics
The Bartlett has invested over £1.5m in state of the art equipment for B>MADE in recent years, including two large CNC milling centres, a large CNC flatbed router, three industry standard laser cutters, a large vacuum former, two desktop robotic arms, and one large robotic arm. Orders for a waterjet cutter and more robotics have been placed for next academic year.

Workshop
The Bartlett workshop, run by a team of craftsmen and architects, plays a crucial role in design education and research. The workshop contains a wide range of machinery for modelling wood, plastic and metal. The workshop's principal equipment consists of: one table saw, two band saws, one planer, one wood lathe, four pillar drills, two TIG welders, two metal lathes, one milling machine, one vacuum former, one plastics bender, an extensive stock of hand tooling and 15 workbenches.

Artificial Sky & Thermal Labs
Bartlett students also enjoy access to advanced equipment in thermal monitoring and lighting simulation, facilities that are run by the Faculty's School of Graduate Studies.

Over the summer of 2013, The Bartlett will be recruiting for a new Technical Director of B>MADE who will lead these unrivalled facilities into a new era of interdisciplinary research and production.

Image: Tom Svilans, MArch Architecture, Unit 23

Bartlett Summer Show 2012, MArch Architecture, Unit 20

Bartlett Summer Show 2012, BSc Architecture, Unit 4

Staff

Professor Frédéric Migayrou
Bartlett Professor of
Architecture, Chair
B>PRO Director

Dr Marcos Cruz
Reader in Architecture
Director of School

Professors

Professor Peter Bishop
Professor of Urban Design

Professor Iain Borden
Professor of Architecture &
Urban Culture
Vice Dean of Communications
Director of History & Theory

Professor Adrian Forty
Professor of Architectural
History
MA Architectural History
Programme Director

Professor Colin Fournier
Professor of Urban Design

Professor Murray Fraser
Professor of Architecture &
Global Culture
Vice Dean of Research

Professor Stephen Gage
Professor of Innovative
Technology

Professor Christine Hawley
Professor of Architectural
Studies
Director of Design

Professor Jonathan Hill
Professor of Architecture &
Visual Theory
MPhil/PhD by Design
Programme Director

Professor CJ Lim
Professor of Architecture &
Cultural Design
Vice Dean of International
Affairs

Professor Jane Rendell
Professor of Architecture & Art
Vice Dean of Research

Professor Bob Sheil
Professor of Architecture and
Design through Production
Director of Technology and
Computing

Academic Staff

Laura Allen
Senior Lecturer
BSc Architecture Programme
Director

Alisa Andrasek
Lecturer in Advanced
Architectural Computation
MArch GAD Programme
Leader

Julia Backhaus
MArch Architecture
Programme Director

Dr Jan Birksted
Principal Research Associate
Coordinator Year 3 History &
Theory

Matthew Butcher
Lecturer in Architecture and
Performance
Coordinator of Pedagogic
Affairs

Dr Ben Campkin
Lecturer in History & Theory
Director of Urban Lab

Dr Marjan Colletti
Senior Lecturer
Acting MArch Architecture
Programme Director

Ruairi Glynn
Lecturer in Interactive
Architecture

Dr Penelope Haralambidou
Lecturer in Architecture
Coordinator of MPhil / PhD by
Design

Dirk Krolikowski
Lecturer in Innovative
Technology & Design Practice
Associate Coordinator of Year
4 Design Realisation

Dr Adrian Lahoud
Reader in Urban Design
MArch UD Programme Leader

Dr Yeoryia Manolopoulou
Senior Lecturer
Director of Architectural
Research

James O'Leary
Lecturer in Innovative
Technology & Design Practice
Coordinator of Year 4 Design
Realisation

Dr Barbara Penner
Senior Lecturer
BSc Architectural Studies
Programme Director
MPhil/PhD History & Theory
Programme Director

Frosso Pimenides
Senior Lecturer
BSc Architecture Year 1
Director

Andrew Porter
MArch GAD Deputy Director

Dr Peg Rawes
Senior Lecturer
Associate Director of
Architectural Research

Dr Tania Sengupta
Lecturer in Architectural
History & Theory
Coordinator of Year 2 / Year 4
History & Theory

Mark Smout
Senior Lecturer
Acting Director of Technology
and Computing

Susan Ware
Sub-Dean and Faculty Tutor
Director of Professional
Studies
Part 3 Programme Director

Patrick Weber
Senior Lecturer
BSc Architecture Year 1
Director

Research Fellows & Visiting Professors

Niall McLaughlin
Visiting Professor

Dr Hilary Powell
Research Fellow

Teaching Staff

BSc Architecture Year 1
Timothy Barwell
Margaret Bursa
Johan Hybschmann
Brian O'Reilly
Frosso Pimenides
Sara Shafiei
Matt Springett
Nikolaos Travasaros
Patrick Weber

BSc Architecture Year 2 / Year 3 (Units 0-9)
Ben Addy
Julia Backhaus
Rhys Cannon
Ming Chung
Max Dewdney
Pedro Font Alba
Murray Fraser
David Garcia
Penelope Haralambidou
Christine Hawley
Damjan Iliev
Jan Kattein
Julian Krüger
Chee-Kit Lai
Justin Lau
Ana Monrabal-Cook
Luke Pearson
Michael Tite
Kenny Tsui
Nick Tyson
Paolo Zaide

BSc Architectural Studies (Architectural & Interdisciplinary Studies)
Elizabeth Dow
Chee-Kit Lai
Barbara Penner

MArch Architecture Year 4 / Year 5 (Units 10-24)
Laura Allen
Abigail Ashton

Kasper Ax
Paul Bavister
Richard Beckett
Johan Berglund
Kyle Buchanan
Matthew Butcher
Michael Chadwick
Izaskun Chinchilla Moreno
Mollie Claypool
Marjan Colletti
Marcos Cruz
Kate Davies
Elizabeth Dow
Bernd Felsinger
Jonathan Hill
Nanette Jackowski
Carlos Jimenez Cenamor
Manuel Jimenez
Simon Kennedy
CJ Lim
Yeoryia Manolopoulou
Niall McLaughlin
Josep Mias
Philippe Morel
James O'Leary
Ricardo de Ostos
Andrew Porter
Stefan Ritter
Stefan Rutzinger
Cristina Schinegger
Bob Sheil
Mark Smout
Michiko Sumi
Emmanuel Vercruysse

MArch Urban Design
Ross Exo Adams
Yannis Aesopos
Aristide Antonas
Peter Besley
Hannah Corlett
Luca Galofaro
Beth Hughes
Platon Issaias
Sam Jacoby
DaeWha Kang
Jonathan Kendall
Graciela Moreno
Claudia Pasquero
Marco Poletto
Davide Sacconi
Camila Sotomayor

**MArch Graduate
Architectural Design**
Alisa Andrasek
Daghan Cam
Marjan Colletti
Stephen Gage
Ruairi Glynn
Xavier de Kestelier
Guan Lee
Philippe Morel
Luke Pearson
Maj Plemenitas
Jose Sanchez
Thibault Schwarz
Daniel Widrig

History & Theory
Tilo Amhoff
Nicholas Beech
Doreen Bernath

Ben Campkin
Megha Chand
Edward Denison
Oliver Domeisen
Eva Eylers
Adrian Forty
Christophe Gerard
Jon Goodbun
Anne-katrin Hultsch
Yat Ming Loo
Steve Parnell
Jacob Paskins
Barbara Penner
Peg Rawes
Jane Rendell
Tania Sengupta
Brian Stater
Rachel Stevenson
Robin Wilson

**Technology Computing
& Open Classes**
Roz Barr
Scott Batty
Rhys Cannon
Ed Clarke
Jean Garrett
Michael Hadi
James Hampton
Bill Hodgson
Steve Johnson
Tim Lucas
Luke Olsen
Jose Sanchez
ScanLAB Projects
Adam Sutcliffe
Mark Whitby
Andrew Whiting
Oliver Wilton

**Dissertation, Design
Realisation and Thesis Tutors**
Hector Altamirano
Tilo Amhoff
Francis Archer
Doreen Bernath
Andrew Best
Daniel Cash
Hal Currey
Simon Dickens
Edward Denison
Christian Derix
Justin Dirrenberger
Oliver Domeisen
Brian Eckersley
Bernd Felsinger
Stephen Foster
Murray Fraser
Daisy Froud
Stephen Gage
Pedro Gil
Ruairi Glynn
Ben Godber
Jon Goodbun
Gary Grant
Penelope Haralambidou
David Hemingway
Bill Hodgson
Tom Holberton
Anne Hultzsch
Joanna Karatzas
Sara Klomps
Guan Lee

Stephen Lorimer
Luke Lowings
Tim Lucas
John Lyall
Joseph Mackey
Eva MacNamara
Roberto Marin Sampalo
Anna Mavrogianni
Yat Ming Loo
Ed Molesley
Justin Nicholls
Domi Oliver
Rob Partridge
Jacob Paskins
Michael Pawlyn
Dean Pike
Sophia Psarra
Kim Quazi
Rokia Raslan
Peg Rawes
Stefan Ritter
Jane Rendell
Tania Sengupta
Shibboleth Shechter
Jason Slocombe
Tim Snelson
Andy Toohey
Carl Vann
Peter Vaughan
Tim Waterman
Finn Williams
Robin Wilson
Oliver Wilton
Simon Withers
Manja van der Worp
Daniel Wright

Professional Studies
Kit Allsop
Sonia Arbachi
Elena Besussi
Elizabete Cidre
Bill Hodgson
Graciela Moreno
Simon Pilling
David Rosenberg
Susan Ware
Katy Wood

Short Courses
Bill Hodgson
Carlos Jimenez Cenamor
Sabine Storp

Admissions
Abigail Ashton
Adrian Forty
Jonathan Hill
Barbara Penner
Andrew Porter
Sabine Storp

Professional Services

**Academic Services
Administration**
Rachael Burnett
Michelle Bush
Emer Girling
Tom Mole

Research
Luis Rego

Communications and Website
Laura Cherry
Jean Garrett
Michelle Lukins

Finance and HR
Sarah Clegg
Stoll Michael
Sheetal Saujani

Professional Studies
Kim Macneill
Indigo Rohrer
Naz Siddique

Facilities
John Riley
Dave Yates

B>MADE
Abi Abdolwahabi
Martin Avery
Sarat Babu
Richard Beckett
Matt Bowles
Bim Burton
Inigo Dodd
Justin Goodyer
Richard Grimes
Edgardo de Lara
Robert Randall
Matthew Shaw
Paul Smoothy
Will Trossell
Emmanuel Vercruysse
Martin Watmough

Bartlett Summer Show 2012 opening party

bartlett.ucl.ac.uk/architecture

Publisher
Bartlett School of Architecture, UCL

Editor
Marcos Cruz

Graphic Design
Patrick Morrissey, Unlimited
weareunlimited.co.uk

Editorial Coordination
Michelle Lukins, Laura Cherry

Photo credits
Virgilio Ferreira
Simon Kennedy
Paul Smoothy
Richard Stonehouse

ISBN 978-0-9572355-3-3

For more information on all the programmes and
modules at The Bartlett Faculty of the Built
Environment, UCL, visit bartlett.ucl.ac.uk

The Bartlett School of Architecture, UCL
Wates House
Gordon Street
London WC1H 0QB
T. +44 (0)20 7679 7504
F. +44 (0)20 7679 4831
architecture@ucl.ac.uk